CRUEL MODERNITY

CRUEL MODERNITY | Jean Franco

DUKE UNIVERSITY PRESS | DURHAM AND LONDON | 2013

Printed in the United States of America on acid-free paper ∞
Typeset in Arno by Copperline Book Services, Inc.

Library of Congress Cataloging-in-Publication Data
Franco, Jean.
Cruel modernity / Jean Franco.
pages   cm
Includes bibliographical references and index.
ISBN 978-0-8223-5442-0 (cloth : alk. paper)
ISBN 978-0-8223-5456-7 (pbk. : alk. paper)
1. Latin America—Politics and government—20th century.
2. Latin America—Politics and government—21st century.
3. State-sponsored terrorism—Latin America—History—
20th century. 4. State-sponsored terrorism—Latin America—
History—21st century. I. Title.
F1414. F 823   2013
980.03—dc23   2013003141

WITHDRAWN

CONTENTS

ACKNOWLEDGMENTS

If anything tests your ideas, it is teaching, which affords you the sounding board of colleagues and students. In retirement you have no such sounding board, and it was for this reason that I floated the idea for *Cruel Modernity* to a group of colleagues and friends at New York University, among them Sybille Fischer, Ana Dopico, Mary Louise Pratt, and Gabriela Nouzeilles, to all of whom I owe a debt of thanks. I thank Patrick Deere for his technical help that was so necessary given my deplorable Luddite approach to machines. I thank Ruth Formanek for her generous comments on photography, Diamela Eltit and Catalina Parra for their valuable suggestions on Chile, and Marta Lamas for supplying me with information on feminicide in Mexico. The book owes much to the work of Ileana Rodríguez and María Saldaña and to the support of Ed Cohen, who helped preserve my sanity. Thanks also to Christi Stanforth, the production editor, and to April Leidig, the designer and typesetter.

I owe a special debt of gratitude to Cristina Camille Pérez Jiménez, who helped prepare the manuscript for publication, and to the Mellon Foundation for financial support toward the manuscript's completion.

INTRODUCTION

Cruelty, a word that suggests a deliberate intention to hurt and damage another, is not only practiced by governments, including democracies, that employ torture and atrocity for many different reasons — from the extraction of information, to the suppression of dissident and ethnically different groups — and by criminal groups, especially drug gangs that use mutilated bodies as warnings. It is now deeply embedded in fantasy life: in cartoon violence, in video games, in literature and visual art, in mass media versions of the Holocaust and the "dirty wars." Consider a film like Quentin Tarantino's *Inglourious Basterds*, in which extreme cruelty is played for laughs as Jewish commandos in Nazi Germany rival the ss in horrendous acts and scalp their prisoners. Tarantino boasted that "taboos are meant to be broken," but when the taboo against harming another is broken, there can be no limits, no social pact. Jonathan Littell's novel *The Kindly Ones* devotes several hundred pages to acts of cruelty as the protagonist, a Nazi officer, welcomes the reader as his brother, as someone who in the same circumstances would behave just as he did. Postapocalyptic devastation in countless films, in comics and in novels takes us back to primitive states where violence was the necessary tool of survival. Notorious crimes are rapidly fictionalized or adapted to the cinema. The young women murdered in Ciudad Juárez were scarcely cold in their graves before a feature film, *Border Town*, was released, with its sickening vulgarization of the murders. Holocaust films such as *The Boy in the Striped Pajamas*, *The Pianist*, and *The Reader* bring together enemies — the Nazi and the Jew, the German officer who loves music and the Jewish musician, a former camp policewoman and an adolescent boy — in a manufactured reconciliation. Neither cruelty nor the exploitation of cruelty is new, but the lifting of the taboo, the acceptance and justification of cruelty and the rationale for cruel acts, have become a feature of modernity.

Although *Cruel Modernity* focuses on Latin America, I do not intend to suggest that cruelty is uniquely exercised there; rather, I examine under what conditions it became the instrument of armies, governments, and rogue groups and how such conditions might be different in these cases than in the often-discussed European cases. Why, in Latin America, did the pressures of modernization and the lure of modernity lead states to kill? The anxiety over modernity defined and represented by North America and Europe all too often set governments on the fast track that bypassed the arduous paths of democratic decision making while marginalizing indigenous and black peoples. States of exception and states of siege not only justified the suppression of groups deemed subversive or alien to modernity but also created an environment in which cruelty was enabled in the name of state security. Although democratization has recently tempered some formerly authoritarian states, the flourishing drug trade has created zones where all manner of cruelty can be exercised with impunity. Writing of the murder of hundreds of women in Ciudad Juárez, Rita Laura Segato argues that here, as with the Holocaust, "the historical conditions that transform us into monsters or accomplices of monsters lie in wait for us all [nos acechan a todos]."[1] To this must be added another factor in Latin America, where the "war on communism" brought US advisers who remained aloof from the atrocities on the ground yet provided the justification, the weapons, and the training.

It took the atrocious death of millions during the First World War and the Holocaust to raise the problem of evil in relation to particular events. In 1915, confronting the fact that the Great War was as bloody as and more destructive than previous wars because weaponry had become more sophisticated, Sigmund Freud wondered how it came about that "the world-dominating nations of the white race, to which the leadership of the human race has fallen and which we knew to have the interests of the world at heart," could find themselves involved in such devastation.[2] The "civilized cosmopolitan" finds himself in disarray, for the war seems to have reversed human development. "It is just as though, since we take a large number, even millions of people, all the moral acquisitions of individuals are obliterated, and only the most primitive, the oldest and most brutal psychical attitudes remain" (182).

In 1932, in a letter to Einstein, Freud acknowledges that his work, like every science, is a kind of mythology and argues that "there is no point in wishing to wipe away mankind's aggressive tendencies," although they can be diverted.[3] Although they were written at very different times, these essays clearly document his shaken belief in a civilized Europe in which people form mutually beneficial communities. Between the two essays on war, Freud wrote *Civilization and Its Discontents*, in which he was forced to recognize aggression as "an original, self-subsisting instinctual disposition in man" that "constitutes the greatest impediment to civilization."[4] He acknowledged that for a long time he had been reluctant to engage with this nonerotic aggression (79). Whereas the work of Eros binds humanity into a community, aggression threatens this bond, but in the best of cases it is checked by the superego, which watches over the individual "like a garrison in a conquered city" (84). Throughout his writing, Freud insists on community as an achievement and guilt as its instrument. The murder of the father in *Totem and Taboo* consolidates through their common guilt the band of brothers and, at the same time, founds the community on the basis of prohibition. But what happens when conscience does not repudiate cruelty, when the superego fails to kick in, and when the band of brothers feels no guilt but rather celebrates their bonding through some infamous act of sacrifice? After the Pinochet coup in Chile in 1973, the military and the police immediately set on unarmed men and women and executed hundreds of them, consolidating their own loyalty to each other and to the new regime.

For Derrida, "it is the obscure word *cruelty* that concentrates all the equivocations. What does 'cruel' mean? Do we have, did Freud have, a rigorous concept of the cruelty that, like Nietzsche, he spoke of so much (as regards the death drive, the aggression drive, sadism, etc.)? Where does cruelty begin and end? Can an ethics, a legal code, a politics put an end to it?"[5] Such questions have to be asked, but all too often the European perspective narrows the enquiry by focusing on one event, the Holocaust, as the *nec plus ultra*. Hannah Arendt described the Holocaust as a manifestation of radical evil that could no longer be understood and explained by "the evil motives of self-interest, greed, covetousness, resentment, lust for power and cowardice and which therefore anger could not revenge, love could not endure, friendship could not forgive."[6] Because the Holocaust is generally depicted as unique in its horror, other environments in which cruelty was practiced have received less attention. The concentration camp horrified because it was the place where extreme cruelty was enacted, where humans were reduced to the living dead in one of the most advanced industrial nations of the world. Because Germany was technologically advanced, the breakdown of the link between civilization and progress was dramatically thrust before a global public when the crude barbarism of the camps was exposed to the world at the end of the Second World War. People were then forced to ask "how crimes of such atrocity can be committed against human beings"—a question that Giorgio Agamben dismisses as hypocritical, arguing that "it would be more honest and, above all, more useful to investigate carefully the juridical procedures and deployments of power by which human beings could be so completely deprived of their rights and prerogatives that no act committed against them could appear any longer as a crime."[7]

Both Arendt and Agamben are eager to claim not only the uniqueness of the concentration camp but also the fact that it exemplified universal developments. Arendt, for example, claims that the camp's destruction of the individual reflected "the experience of the masses of their superfluity on an overcrowded earth" (457). Agamben greatly amplifies this global claim. Drawing on Foucault's term "biopolitics" (the management of populations and the control of their bodies through the diffuse micromanagement or governability), he argues that the camp is the very space where politics becomes biopolitics, that is, where life itself is at the center of state politics. Thus "the birth of the camp in our time appears as an event that decisively signals the political space of modernity itself" (147). However, he overlooks the fact that the "political space of modernity" can take on many different forms. In his influential essay "Necropolitics," Achille Mbembe asserts that "any account of the rise of modern terror needs to address slavery, which could be considered one of the first instances of biopolitical experimentation."[8] He then goes on to argue that, with the apartheid state, there comes into being a peculiar terror formation, which combines "the disciplinary, the biopolitical and the necropolitical."[9] Mbembe's essay makes it clear that terror formations take on distinctive characteristics according to their regional histories and forms of oppression.

To consider the exercise of cruelty in Latin America moves the debate into a different and complex terrain that links conquest to feminicide, the war on communism to genocide and neoliberalism to casual violence without limits. What makes the Latin American case unique is, as Enrique Dussel argues, that the Spanish conquest of the Americas was an event that inaugurated modernity, giving Europe the advantage over the Muslim, Indian, and Chinese worlds.[10] "For modernity, the barbarian is at *fault* for opposing the civilizing process, and modernity, ostensibly innocent, seems to be emancipating the *fault* of its own victims" (137). This is what Dussel describes as modernization's "ambiguous course by touting a rationality opposed to *primitive*, mythic explanations even as it concocts a myth to conceal its own sacrificial violence towards the other."[11]

Dussel's second paradigm is the rationalization inaugurated in seventeenth-century Europe, which he sees as a way of managing a world system by simplifying its complexity. I would emphasize, however, that this does not mean that the two modernities take place in strict sequence. On the contrary, the mentality and practice of conquest extend well into the twentieth century. Up to the near present, many areas of Latin America have remained outside legal restraints on the ill treatment of the original peoples and the descendants of slaves. In remote areas like the Argentine desert in the nineteenth century and the rubber plantations in the Amazon in the early twentieth, where the robber baron Arana referred to the treatment of the slave labor as *conquestación*, there was no international outcry at the ill treatment of native peoples.[12]

As if the conquest were still going on, the special forces of the

Guatemalan army appropriated the name *kaibiles* from an Indian chief who fought against the conqueror Pedro de Alvarado, thus taking on the courage of the indigenous peoples while committing the atrocities attributed to the conquerors. Atrocity has changed very little since the sixteenth century. Las Casas's description of Indians being thrown into the holes they had dug—"And thus children and old men and even pregnant women and women but lately in childbed were thrown in and perished"[13]— is eerily similar to accounts of the massacres documented in the Guatemalan report of the Commission on Truth and Reconciliation, *Memoria del silencio.* In the prologue to that report, members expressed the "sadness and pain" of listening to the evidence of acts of extreme barbarism.[14]

Dussel's second paradigm of modernity, the rationalization and simplification of global economic relations, was pursued as a goal for Latin America in the twentieth century through a variety of projects, the most important of which was developmentalism.[15] Under the hegemony of the United States, the goal of developmentalism was to remove opposition to the world system. When challenged by the insurgency and guerrilla movements of the 1960s and 1970s, the military, already powerful, took charge of what it termed "the war against communism" and resorted to extreme terror and blanket repression not only of militants but also of their supposed supporters. Although the repressive measures made a pretense of being sophisticated, the electric prod and electrically charged wires were the only modern instruments. Simulated executions and burials, repeated beatings, hanging so that the feet barely touched the floor, the "submarine," are all age-old practices. Jacobo Timerman, an early victim of the Argentine military, saw through the theater, pointing out that the torturers were "trying to create another, a more sophisticated image of the torture sites, as if thereby endowing their activity with a more elevated status. The military encourage the fantasy; the notion of important sites, methods, original techniques, novel equipment, allows them to present a touch of distinction and legitimacy to the world."[16] The modernization of torture he found ludicrous: "that conversion of dirty, dark, gloomy places into a world of spontaneous innovation and institutional 'beauty' is one of the most arousing pleasures for the torturers. It is as if they felt themselves master of the force required to change reality. And it places them again in a world of omnipotence. That omnipotence in turn they feel, assures them of impunity — a sense of immunity to pain, guilt and emotional imbalance."[17]

But even though acts of cruelty have changed little, their justification has. My book begins with a most egregious event — the massacre of black settlers on the border of the Dominican Republic on the orders of General Trujillo in an attempt to create an absolute division between the black population of Haiti and the "white" population of the Dominican Republic. The chapter introduces many of this book's recurrent themes — the dehumanization of the victims, the attempted suppression of their memory, and the legacy of inexplicable loss belatedly registered in literary texts.

Alien to Modernity

In Guatemala and Peru, the major casualties in the civil wars of the 1980s were the indigenous, who were deemed "alien to modernity." Foucault had claimed, in defining biopower, that "racism develops primo with colonization, that is to say with colonizing genocide. When it is necessary to kill people, kill populations, kill civilizations, how can one debate on the basis of biopower? Through the themes of evolutionism, through racism."[18] But in Latin America racism preceded evolutionism. It was instilled with the Conquest, which left an inheritance of guilt and above all the long-standing fear that the old gods would return. And indeed they did return, in Bolivia during the *katarista* rebellion; in the Caste Wars in Yucatán during the nineteenth century; and in the hundred or so Indian uprisings in Peru, the largest of which was led by José Gabriel Condorcanqui, who took the name of Túpac Amaru II.[19] In the frontier lands, people lived in fear of an Indian raid. The well-known opening paragraphs of Domingo Sarmiento's *Facundo: Civilización y barbarie* (*Facundo: Civilization and Barbarism*) describes travelers in the Argentine pampa fearfully listening to the wind in the grass and peering into the darkness, "seeking the sinister shapes of the savage horde that may, from one minute to the next, surprise them."[20] Wars of extermination such as the Argentine "war of the desert" and the drive against the Mapuche of Chile were couched in terms of conquest,[21] as was the exploitation of the indigenous during the rubber boom in Colombia at the end of the nineteenth century.[22]

For the conquerors, the practice of human sacrifice had been the barrier that divided civilization from barbarism, modernity from antiquity; their accounts of the cruel actions of the indigenous created a recurrent fear that barbarism lurked on the dark side and could resurface as a threat to modern man. In "Huitzilopochtli," a story by Rubén Darío, a North American becomes a sacrificial victim to the Huitzilipochtli cult during the chaos of the revolutionary war, leading one of the revolutionary officers to comment, "There is an Aztec in the heart of every Mexican."[23] This fear surfaces in stories by Darío, Carlos Fuentes, Julio Cortázar, Gustavo Saenz, and Carmen Boullosa. It reaches its most extreme in Octavio Paz's essay *Postdata*, written after the massacre of demonstrators in Tlatelolco in 1968, which was intended to cleanse Mexico of disorder on the eve of the 1968 Olympic Games; Paz attributed this atrocity to the oppressive shadow of the Aztec pyramid.[24]

What the "heart of darkness" fears reveal, however, is not only fear of regression to a prior state but also an anxiety over modernity and the fear that the indigenous — especially in countries such as Peru, Guatemala, and Mexico, where they constituted a substantial percentage of the nation — would put a brake on modernization. Labels including "underdeveloped," "marginal," "peripheral," and "third world" placed Latin America on a lower rung than the developed world that was the advance column of technological sophistication associated with the modern. Becoming modern meant overcoming underdevelopment by loosening the drag of those sectors of the population that were stigmatized as "downstream," "unproductive," "traditional," or, to borrow a term coined by Noam Chomsky, "unpeople."[25] That is why the urgency of modernization transposed racism into a different key and turned the indigenous from an exploited labor force into a negative and undesirable mass. The doctrine of developmentalism widely disseminated after the Second World War emphasized the independent self-determined individual.[26] By contrast, the basis of indigenous life was the community, which for the modernizing intellectual was an anachronism. During the civil wars of the 1980s, the Guatemalan military targeted the indigenous, whose extermination or forced assimilation was deemed essential to the thorough overhaul of the state in the name of modernization.[27]

Despite indigenous activism in numerous organizations, the military considered native groups primarily as obstacles that had to be removed or thoroughly altered. In the words of Greg Grandin, the Guatemalan army "produced an analysis that understood terror not as a result of state decomposition, a failure in the institutions and morals that guarantee rights and afford protection, and rather as a component of state formation, as the foundation of the military's plan of national constitutional rule."[28] In Peru, sophisticated thinkers, not to mention left-wing revolutionaries, "believed that the Andean world was radically Other."[29] This belief sustained a national imaginary and a practice based on the segregation of the Andean masses. Thus projects of modernization were built on the colonial structure of separation.[30]

Not only culture but skin color was a problem as long as civilization was identified with whiteness. In 1938, General Trujillo of the Dominican Republic undertook an ethnic cleansing of black Haitians who had settled along the Rio Masacre, the river that marked the border between the two countries, in an attempt to exploit nationalist sentiment and define the Dominican population as whiter and more civilized. Referred to, in diplomatic correspondence, as an "insignificant incident," the massacre received the ideological support of a phalanx of ideologues who diverted the blame from the Dominican army to the supposedly criminal Haitians who were said to have invaded Dominican territory.[31] Trujillo wanted to consolidate what had been a porous border and make it an absolute barrier between the two nations, and he did this by creating the myth of the white Dominican, spiritually and physically different from the black Haitian. What he also created was a melancholy aftermath reflected in the novels that I discuss in the opening chapter. Cruelty leaves long-lasting memory traces — hence the recurrent theme of buried books, faded photographs, fragmented testimonies, exhumed bodies, harvests of bones.[32]

Reason of State

In many Latin American nations, "there was an iron-clad civility for the privileged few, and violence against the underprivileged masses was a routine affair."[33] Striking workers, rebellious students, and oppressed peasants all became targets of the military, which, with its strong sense of corporate identity and privilege, was responsible for installing authoritarian governments and protecting them against the threat of strikes and protests.

The "method" for exterminating opposition under dictatorships was described by the Cuban writer Alejo Carpentier in his novel *El recurso del método* (*The Recourse of the Method*). This was the infallible "method" by which governments got rid not only of blacks and indigenous peoples but of striking workers, leftists, and demonstrating students whose demands were seen as destabilizing factors. The title is a sly allusion to Descartes's *Discourse on Method*. The protagonist is a cultivated dictator, fond of luxury and educated in the classics. Faced with an uprising, his German colonel, Hoffman, conducts a scorched earth campaign and justifies it by quoting Helmuth Molke, the general who led the German invasion of Belgium and France during the First World War, to the effect that "in war it is best to finish it quickly. To finish it quickly all methods are good including the most blameworthy." The president (always referred to as the *primer magisterio*, as if he were in charge of the law) argues that in countries such as his, they must still fight much as Julius Caesar had done, "what for Caesar were vénetas, marcomanes, hérulos, triboques . . . ; for us are guahibos, guachinangos, bochos and mandingas" (i.e., blacks, escaped slaves, and the indigenous) (133; my translation). In other words the civilized Roman confronting barbarians becomes the classical model for the dictator confronting barbarous blacks and the indigenous. The slaughter of the "mandingos," however, is only the beginning. In the city of New Córdoba, students and workers revolt and barricade themselves in the cathedral, which is destroyed by Hoffman's Krupp gun. The survivors are massacred, the women raped. When news of the atrocities reaches Europe, the *primer magisterio* is given the soubriquet "Butcher of New Córdoba." Shunned by most people, he is welcomed in Paris by the Illustrious Academic, who asks, "Whoever had been able to contain the fury, the excesses, the cruelties — lamentable but always repeated throughout History — of an unleashed army, drunk with triumph? And the more so when it was a matter of putting down a rebellion of Indians and blacks" (171; my translation). The cruelties are the inevitable outcome of victory, and the dead are, in any case, the outcasts of civilization. Carpentier had plenty of experience of dictators, having been imprisoned during the Machado regime in Cuba. But rather than speaking from a pulpit to denounce atrocity, he opts for the grotesque: "The last resistance fighters — some thirty-four of them — were taken to the municipal slaughterhouse, where, among cattle skins, innards, guts, and animal bile, over pools of coagulated blood, they were hung from hooks and gaffs by the armpits, by the legs, the ribs or the chin, after kicking and beating them to a pulp." The resistance fighters have no names; they are simply dead animals, certainly not citizens of the state, making it impossible for the reader to experience the event as anything other than a grotesque example of the dictator's excesses. Carpentier's novel belongs to a subgenre of dictatorship novels that portray dictators as grotesque, bordering, in some cases, on the comical. Valle Inclán's *Tirano Banderas*, Miguel Angel Asturias's *El señor presidente*, García Márquez's *El otoño del patriarca*, and Roa Bastos's *Yo el supremo* are outstanding examples of the genre. Their all-powerful protagonists exemplify the absolutist state and need no alibi for eliminating dissent and especially movements of workers and peasants. Scores of such massacres had scarred the historical record of Latin America, from the suppression of the petroleum strikers in Comodoro Rivadavia, Argentina, in 1932, to the slaughter of striking Bolivian miners in 1942. The *semana trágica* in Buenos Aires at the beginning of 1919 occurred when a workers' strike for shorter hours brought out the army. But in the 1970s, these local events were superseded by the continental war on communism, vigorously preached by the United States, which justified a policy of exterminating not only guerrillas and insurgents but also their alleged support networks that involved thousands of people. In Colombia and Guatemala, in Peru and El Salvador and in the aftermath of the Pinochet coup in Chile, armies engaged in killing sprees. The most notorious of these were the incidents at Dos Erres in Guatemala, El Mozote in El Salvador, and the Death Caravan in Chile, orgies of collective violence that consolidated the executioners as bands of brothers.[34]

Massacres represent the "degradation of war." As the National Committee for Reparation and Reconciliation of Colombia commented, "The massacre has a triple function — preventive, punitive, and symbolic. It is symbolic in that it disrupts all religious and ethical taboos. It represents the degradation of warfare."[35] In Colombia, whole communities stigmatized as subversives were wiped from the map by the paramilitary forces, which did not consider them members of the national community. Such was the fate of El Salado (in the Cauca Valley) and Trujillo between 1988 and 1994, where large numbers of citizens were tortured and killed.[36] Torture, in this case, was not primarily for extracting information, since the whole population had already been labeled "subversive"; rather, it was a demonstration of extreme cruelty that included quartering bodies with an electric saw so that victims witnessed their own dismemberment. The progressive priest Tiberio Fernández had his hands amputated, then his feet, and finally his captors beheaded him.[37]

How were men (and some women) persuaded to commit acts that were not killings at a distance like bombings but involved an intimate connection with the victim's body, a willingness to cut, rape, and mutilate? For such actions to become an accepted practice, there had to be training, and the one organization with this capacity was the army. In most societies, soldiers are trained not to kill women and children, but once these are counted as the enemy, they too become targets. The hierarchical military structure makes it possible for higher officials to act as caretakers of the state while remaining distant from the dirty work of extermination.[38] The role of the United States as facilitator and distant adviser was crucial during the dirty wars in the Southern Cone. The great standard-bearer of democracy secretly endorsed not only the torture and killing of the avowed enemy but also that of their social network, and there is a certain irony in the contrast between the public face of the United States and its underhanded permissiveness when it came to the antics of its protégés.[39] The US-trained Atlacatl battalion responsible for the Mozote massacre in El Salvador in 1981 invented its own style. Its members wore the figure of an Indian on their uniform and were named Atlacatl after an Indian warrior who resisted the conquerors; they also invoked the name of General Martínez, who had ordered the massacre of Indians and communists in 1932. The conviction that communism was a cancer that had to be cut out, a conviction instilled by their US allies in the war on communism, was all the justification they needed. Their aim, like that of other counterinsurgency operations that had received training in the United States, was to "drain the sea," that is, to wipe out not only the guerrillas themselves but their support network as well. "And so if you are a guerrilla they don't just kill you: they kill your cousin, you know, everybody in the family, to make sure that the cancer is cut out."[40] This was the lesson they learned too well. General Monterrosa, the commander of the battalion, created a mystique around his troops. "They shot animals and smeared the blood all over their faces, they slit open the animals' bellies and drank the blood." They celebrated graduation by collecting dead animals and boiling them "into a blood soup, and chugged it down. Then they stood at rigid attention and sang, full throated, the unit's theme song, 'Somos Guerreros,' which boasted that they were going forth 'to kill / A mountain of terrorists.'"[41] Wolfgang Sofsky writes that rituals facilitate transgression and that ritual violence and sacrifice and murder "as communal acts establish bonds of loyalty."[42] Certainly, the solidarity of the "band of brothers" was an important aspect of the scenes of cruelty not only in Guatemala but also in Peru, in the Southern Cone, and in the underground operations of those who assassinated young women in Ciudad Juárez.

Whereas atrocities are committed by the horde, torture is often a more solitary activity except when performed in public to terrorize a population. But though the band of brothers is a support network, and though the torturer is protected by an institution (including the non-state organizations of drug traffickers), loyalties forged through criminal actions are fragile. The Salvadorian Robocop, the protagonist of *El arma en el hombre* (*The Arm in the Man*), a novel by Horacio Castellano Moyá, has no skill except killing, and when peace is declared, he discovers that the old loyalties no longer protect him. None of the organizations he worked for turn out to be reliable support networks until he finally finds his niche in the US war on drugs.

Primo Levi labeled the cruelties that were inflicted on those who would die in any case "useless violence." The Nazi years "were characterized by widespread useless violence, as an end in itself . . . occasionally having a purpose, yet always redundant, always disproportionate to the purpose itself."[43] As the Norwegian mass killer Anders Breivik declared during his trial, dehumanizing the victim is essential; or, as Levi expressed it, "Before dying the victim must be degraded so that the murderer will be less burdened by guilt. This is an explanation not devoid of logic but it shouts to heaven: it is the sole usefulness of useless violence."[44] The Chilean Commission of Truth and Reconciliation expressed astonishment that those who were to be executed were first horribly tortured: "The Commission feels that it must make it clear that in many instances the killing was carried out with such forms of torture and viciousness when the only objective seems to have been to intensify the suffering of the victim to an unspeakable degree." They cite the case of Eugenio Ruiz Tagle, killed in October 1973. His mother saw the body and described its terrible state: "An eye was missing, the nose had been ripped off, the one ear visible was pulled away at the bottom. There was a deep burn mark as though done by a soldering iron on his neck and face, his mouth was all swollen up, there were lots of cuts and cigarette burns and judging from the angle of his head, the neck was broken; there were lots of cuts and bleeding."[45] Debasement that included curses, beatings, and all kinds of humiliation was practiced on both sexes, but in the case of women it was taken to extremes, as the victims were not only submitted to rape and even worse but were also insulted as whores. Moreover, rape was seldom the sexual act *tout court* but often involved the insertion of arms or sticks into the vagina. Referring to El Salvador, Aldo Lauria-Santiago writes, "The attack on sexual organs, even after the victim's death, and decapitation — apparently practiced in a slaughterhouse with specialized equipment — were methods of torture that established their own goals and justification and provided the security agencies and rightist groups with iconic power far beyond the tactical elimination of people perceived as activists or revolutionaries."[46]

It was not only the living whose bodies were violated. The extreme desecration of cadavers is a practice that might seem completely alien in societies where the dead were honored with wakes, where the *cuerpo presente* (viewing of the body) and the funeral ceremony and the care of the grave were significant rituals of mourning. But in atrocities, in disappearances, in revenge killings, desecration was, and still is, a regular practice and a warning to others. Cadavers became objects for transmitting messages to the civilian population or to the enemy. It was a practice that became notorious during La Violencia in Colombia, where different cuts were used to send messages: "In the 'necktie cut,' the victim's tongue was pulled down through an opening in the throat: in the 'florist's cut,' severed limbs were inserted in the neck after decapitation; in the 'monkey's cut,' the victim's head was placed on his or her chest."[47] From civil war to the Medellín drug gangs, such practices passed with the drug traffic into Mexico, where cruelty is at its most extreme and where the expressive use of the cadaver has become common practice, a form of macabre theater addressed not only to rivals but also to the public.

Extreme Masculinity

What massacres, rape, and desecration suggest is a meltdown of the fundamental core that makes humans recognize their own vulnerability and hence acknowledge that of the other. I term this phenomenon "extreme masculinity," for I do not believe that *all* men are necessarily prone to violence or that women do not torture. Further, as I show in the chapter on revolutionary violence (chapter 5), women who belong to armies or insurgent groups do fight and execute enemies. But in most parts of the world, women are not regarded as the equals of men. Even when there is legal equality, popular culture reinforces their subjection. One has only to read the litany of sexist jokes catalogued in Roberto Bolaño's novel *2666* (discussed in chapter 9) to understand the casual but constant reinforcement of misogyny. The subjectification of the male within the traditional family confirms his status as the superior sex, and although it does not follow that he is therefore prone to cruelty, there is still, in some quarters, an idealization of the dominating and ruthless male figure. This tendency is further encouraged by popular literature. The best-selling books by John Eldredge have been used as training manuals for the drug cartel known as La Familia, in Michoacán, Mexico. His idealization of male development from boy to cowboy and his endorsement of the support offered by a band of brothers might sound perfectly innocuous, yet the cartel that adopted his code was deadly.[48]

The implacable, all-powerful male requires subjugated victims. In the genocidal wars in Guatemala and Peru, rape, almost always committed against women, was a crucial and symbolic weapon. It was not simply a sexual act committed by overexcited warriors but also a declaration of superiority and a form of torture that often ended in death.[49] Gang rapes consolidated the rapists as a group who mingled their seed in an abject female body. Raped corpses had stakes thrust into the vagina symbolizing the will to prevent a population's reproduction through complete sterilization. Rapes were often accompanied by the slaughter of children and, since the seed had to be eradicated, the extraction of the fetus from the mother. Even when the woman was left alive, the birth of the child of rape was intended to shame her and, among the indigenous, to separate her from the community.[50]

I stress that rape is a form of torture if torture is defined as the infliction of extreme pain. In the Western tradition, the purpose of torture was to exact truth, but in contemporary times, this is not always the case.[51] While it is true that during the military regimes, torture did in fact yield important information and often led to the discovery and death of opponents, it was also applied when there was little or no information to be obtained. In her influential book *The Body in Pain*, Elaine Scarry writes that during torture, the body of the tortured prisoner is very much present, all other sensations having been subjugated by pain, while the torturer's body is correspondently "absent"; the tortured is reduced to speechless agony, while torturer's body is aloof from the experience.[52] But when rape is recognized as a form of torture, the scene changes and other factors come into play, particularly the torturer's pleasure in this display of power and subjugation; and when rape is authorized by conquest, there are no limits. Contemporary examples abound. In the Congo, rape victims are said to total millions.[53] How much of a surprise is it to learn that a female journalist covering the recent Egyptian uprising against Mubarak was gang-raped or that female Peace Corps volunteers sent to remote areas were raped? The drama of masculinity is performed on the body of the helpless woman. Women gang-raped in Peru and Guatemala during the civil wars were a "gift" to the ranks for doing a good job, underscoring the women's less-than-human status. In the introduction to the edited volume *When States Kill*, Cecilia Menjívar and Nelson Rodríguez use the term "violence workers" and point out that torturers undergo training and attend seminars.[54] But this terminology does not recognize the sexual and erotic elements in rape, or the fact that raped women have accounted for a substantial number of the victims in civil wars. War permits, justifies, and rewards the predatory male, who can even take pleasure in the gang rape of the corpse or the virtual corpse.

Ileana Rodríguez, writing of the murder of women in Ciudad Juárez, Mexico, compared the atrocities committed against women to snuff films.[55] She argues that "sexual crimes are a social warning to everyone, an act of power, and discipline, a sign of masculine, brutal, natural, social and political power, and an invasion of the public space — when not a complete takeover."[56] But while this public display applies to contemporary feminicides, it does not apply to mass rape during civil war, when, far from reflecting a crisis of authority, it represents an extreme assertion of authority, sanctioned by officers in the field and in detention centers operated by the secret services. In these cases, the state shelters and encourages perversion, a situation brilliantly fictionalized by Bolaño in his novel *Distant Star*, which I discuss in chapter 4. Although drugs and liquor help to eliminate taboos on killing and torture, the group's staging of collective fantasy also plays a significant role. The rape of women during the Peruvian and Guatemalan civil wars and the assassination of female workers in Ciudad Juárez (discussed in chapter 9) are, as one critic maintains, not individual but "corporate acts." This important insight dramatizes a collective shared fantasy of male power and female subjection.[57]

Torturers, unlike many of their victims, live to tell the tale, but their need to tell the story usually springs not from remorse but from resentment when they are named and accused while superior officers go scot free. Chapter 4 considers the torturers' stories as told in interviews, which they are all too eager to give.[58] These are men like Adolfo Scilingo in Argentina and Oswaldo Romo in Chile, who found themselves accused, put on trial, and given prison sentences. The Peruvian mass killer, Jesús Sosa, an expert executioner who shot many prisoners, was ready to obey the most bizarre orders before he was caught out for his participation in a notorious incident — the massacre of students from La Cantuta Agricultural College. When the clandestine cemetery in which the students had been buried was discovered and the press began to piece the story together, he and a fellow executioner displayed no remorse for the deaths but debated over the question of whether a civilian court was a better bet for them than a military court.[59] In this chapter I confront the major question of how men and women come to perform acts of extreme cruelty and their apprenticeship in the degradation of humanity. The Brazilian film *Elite Squad*, which traced the development of a mild-mannered law student into a fierce killer in the favela war against drugs, offers a triumphant account of this process and has become one of the most popular films in Brazil. Its popularity raises the question of how people in general have come to uncritically accept such a high degree of violence from the forces of law.

In their memoirs and confessions, of which there are many, torturers tend to defend themselves by saying they were just doing a job or obeying their superiors. This tendency explains why Hannah Arendt's phrase "the banality of evil," which she herself acknowledged was not the best possible description of Eichmann's crimes, has been echoed by several critics in their discussion of Latin American torturers. But this is to confuse belated self-justification with the event itself. I concur with the Argentine philosopher León Rozitchner, who states categorically "that crime and murder, whether individual or collective, by the state or by society, although they may be "normalized" and bureaucratic, are not and can never be banal. . . . The evil that leads one to delight in the murder and torture of another human being can never be, in our view, an indifferent experience for the perpetrator."[60]

The interviews and confessions of torturers are proofs, if proofs are needed, that testimony is anything but transparent. The testimonies of women who, after torture, went to work for the secret services in Chile and Argentina are even more difficult to assess because their stories directly challenge the reader with the question "What would you have done?" It is a trick question, one that has been dramatized and narrated in hundreds of plays and books. In chapter 7, I discuss the Chilean Luz Arce as the contemporary "ancient mariner" who is compelled to tell her story over and over as she challenges those who have never had to choose between betrayal and death. But unlike many others who gave up information during torture, Arce was able to convert her story into a national allegory of reconciliation, deflecting attention from other issues, notably her work for the secret service, which continued after the end of the Pinochet regime and her liaison with the second in command at the Villa Grimaldi prison. In Argentina, where the survivors of the camps were labeled traitors while those who died were regarded as heroes and heroines, it took years for former prisoners whom the military had recuperated to tell their side of the story — a story that confirmed the effectiveness of torture not only in producing information but also in changing the very personality of the former prisoners.[61]

Terror was of course not the exclusive strategy of the right but was also deployed by some guerrilla groups, sometimes against their own members. In chapter 5, I discuss the notion of sacrifice that was embraced by both the Guevarist guerrillas and the Shining Path of Peru.[62] The macho subject surfaces almost as parody in the episodes that occurred in Argentina and El Salvador when minuscule guerrilla groups turned on their own recruits and killed them for their incompetence or disobedience. But the most egregious example of guerrilla sacrifice is undoubtedly that demanded by the leadership of the Shining Path of Peru, whose hierarchy of command exacted extreme sacrifices from the lowest ranks. Those who accepted the challenge of crossing the river of blood also accepted that killing others was part of that sacrifice. What makes the Shining Path experience so strikingly different, however, is that women formed a substantial percentage of the warriors and were as capable of killing as the men. In an earlier version of this introduction, I had attributed cruel practices to "rogue males," but on reflection, I found the term misleading. "Rogue" suggests aberration from a norm, but the "normative" is not a stable or universal category because we are dealing with the complex question of subjectification. One of the few studies to understand this is Klaus Theweleit's encyclopedic and immensely interesting *Male Fantasies.* Theweleit rejects Freudian categories in favor of Deleuze and Guattari's account of subjectification as desiring production and introduces the term "anti-production" for those whose "mode of production is the transformation of life into death, and dismantling of life."[63] But we still need to understand by what means killers dehumanize their victims and make them beings for death. What the Shining Path example shows is the power of indoctrination through the repetition of slogans to confirm the collective will and give the participants a sense of power beyond the individual, since collectively they have become the ineluctable forces of history. This is not only a male fantasy. Women too experienced this power and were intoxicated.

Questionable Truths

Some events are difficult or impossible to narrate because there are no precedents, no frameworks. The halting stories of the living dead who fortuitously had survived massacres hover in stark contrast to Luz

Arce's fluent "verbalization," examined in chapter 7. Those who faced the firing squad or survived an army massacre were rarely able to tell the tale. Except for the communist Miguel Mármol, who survived General Martínez's mass execution in El Salvador in 1931 and who was able, many years after the event, to narrate it as a story of communist heroism, the survivors whose stories I discuss in chapter 6 have no narrative framework for their experience. Like La Llorona, a character from Central American folklore, Rufina Amaya, one of the few survivors of the El Mozote massacre in El Salvador, perpetually hears her dead children crying out for her. The survivors of Chile's "caravan of death," during which Pinochet's army rounded up and killed farmers and laborers, for the most part, live in a perpetual state of shock, unable to remake their lives after resurrection, unable to find an explanation or fit their experience into a heroic narrative. Some social scientists and human rights specialists rightly criticize the blanket representation of the tortured, the executed, and the disappeared as victims, a term that places party members, militants, and those active in civil rights organizations under the same rubric without distinction. But in massacres, there are no distinctions; the aim is to banish the memory of the victims from the earth.

The massive repression under the military regimes of the Southern Cone was indeed motivated by this strategy of extermination that would remove all traces of the militants' ideals, motives, and passions from the national memory. But the mass killings of opponents had to be done in secrecy in order to hide the extent of the atrocities from the world. Although bodies were disappeared, buried in the desert, thrown into pits or into the sea, their memory, guarded by family members, lived on. The military could not hide the fact that thousands of people whose existence was recorded in photographs were unaccounted for. These were the ghosts that could not be laid to rest.[64] In the absence of any possible narrative, the photograph of the disappeared person became an icon, the accusatory evidence of a life whose existence had been denied. Families used the photographs of sons and daughters to undo the official story and to demand counterfactually that they be returned with life. Years after their disappearance, their photographs have grown faded, underscoring the years of impunity and challenging the amnesia decreed by the governments not only of the Southern Cone but also of Colombia,

Guatemala, Peru, and Mexico. In chapter 8, I discuss the role of photography and film in memorialization of the disappeared and the long-term effects of disappearance not only on parents but also on the next generations. Disappearance has generated a vast archaeological search, a whole science of recovery, an archive of films, installations, writing, the aide-mémoire of what was scheduled to leave no trace.

The Truth Commissions set up in the aftermath of atrocity called for reconciliation that more often than not was a purely rhetorical gesture, leaving many countries (Chile, Peru, Argentina, Uruguay, Colombia, Brazil) divided about the past. The huge literature on memory testifies to the extent of loss even as these countries settle into what is termed "redemocratization," which leaves unjust social structures intact. What has been my focus, however, is not memory, however important to the wounded peoples, but the magnitude and the incalculability of loss, for which my own country must take some share of the blame for supplying, training, and encouraging the executioners.

In the final chapter, I come to the more recent war, described in the United States as the war on drugs as if it is a war that can be waged only south of the border. In Mexico, Colombia, and Central America and in some areas of the Southern Cone (for instance, the border between Paraguay, Brazil, and Argentina), young men are drawn into the drug gangs whose violence exceeds that of the military governments. Mexico, a country that avoided the extreme consequences of the war on communism has become the showcase of contemporary atrocity. In the 1990s, the murder of several hundred women in Ciudad Juárez first drew attention to "expressive crimes." These crimes publicized the killers' power and impunity, and the victims' mutilated bodies dramatized the killers' deep-rooted misogyny.[65] Expressive crimes are those in which bodies illustrate the logic of the killers. In the case of the murdered women in Ciudad Juárez, it is clear that, as female workers in Mexican assembly plants, they disrupted what had been a sexual division of labor. The mutilated and beheaded male bodies, on the other hand, are revenge killings that speak of treachery and betrayal. Thus both the murder of women and the beheading of males intentionally publicize the persistence of archaic codes.[66] Such crimes effectively foment the culture of fear that dominates many areas of Latin America and has created mini-totalitarianisms on the frontier between Mexico and the United States, in the favelas of Brazil and the slums of El Salvador. By mini-totalitarianism, I mean control of the population's everyday life through fear. In some parts of northern Mexico, children stay out of schools after threatening messages appear on walls, people do not go out after dark, those with relatives north of the border simply leave. The daily death toll in northern Mexico resembles a list of wartime casualties; 2010 was a record year, with 3,080 deaths — that is, one-fourth of the total deaths in the entire nation.[67] Kidnapping and extortion are so routine that they seldom merit a line in the newspapers. The ante has been raised for the foot soldiers, among them youths in their teens, who are required not only to kill and torture but also to be indifferent to their own deaths. Drug cartels publicize their supremacy with expressive crimes and the public display of threatening *mantas* (sheets used as posters) that are displayed on bridges over highways. The internecine wars between the cartels and the army that was sent in by President Calderón have turned many parts of Mexico into a battleground where killing is not only routine but also sanctified by prayers to the Santa Muerte (Saint Death) among the Zetas or, in the case of La Familia, by appeals to divine justice. In the midst of this drug war, crimes against women go on with *levantones* or temporary kidnappings, especially in the "black triangle" (El Salvador, Guatemala, and Honduras), where the attacks have reached an unprecedented level. For many, this violence marks the end of "civil" society and the start of a dark time in which humanity reaps the reward of its fecklessness, giving rise to the apocalyptic forebodings that I examine in the essays of Sergio González Rodríguez and Rita Segato. Carlos Monsiváis's last collection of Mexican chronicles, *Apocalipstick*, depicts contemporary Mexico as an overcrowded disaster that hides behind the cosmetic gloss "suitable for the farewell kiss." My final chapter, "Apocalypse Now," emphasizes that cruel practices leave long-term damage and lurking fears that are shaping our present and our future. If *Cruel Modernity* lingers on this dark side, it is because I believe that unless there is a better understanding of the social vacuum that allows cruel acts, political solutions and ethical principles will remain in the realm of the abstract.

ONE | The "Insignificant Incident" and Its Aftermath

Between 2 and 8 October 1937, an estimated twenty thousand Haitians living on the Dominican side of the border were massacred, many of them with machetes. The six-day massacre, known as El Masacre, was ordered by President Trujillo.

The conflictive histories of Haiti and the Dominican Republic date back to the division of the island of Hispaniola into two colonies, one French and the other Spanish. The French had arrived in the seventeenth century as buccaneers who took over the island of Tortuga off the coast of Hispaniola; the Spanish garrisons were unable to protect their territory from the pirates who paved the way for the takeover of part of Hispaniola by the French West India Company, and there developed a flourishing trade in sugar, indigo, and coffee based on the slave labor of Africans who came from different tribes, spoke different languages, and soon formed the majority of the population of the French colony.

Achille Mbembe coined the word "necropolis" to describe plantations in Africa where a permanent state of emergency prevailed. The population was degraded, for "the slave condition resulted from a triple loss: loss of the "home," loss of rights over his or her body, and loss of political status. This triple loss is identical with absolute domination, alienation, and social death (expulsion from humanity altogether).[1] The slaves in the French colony suffered this triple loss, and the *code noir* issued by Louis XIV in 1685, which was intended to protect the slaves from excessive abuse and to decree paternalistic care for them in sickness or old age, clearly treated them as commodities. The masters were allowed to chain their slaves, but though they could punish them by beating them with rods or straps, they were forbidden to torture them or mutilate their limbs. Freed slaves were given the same rights, privileges, and immunities enjoyed by freeborn persons: "We desire that they are deserving of this acquired freedom, and that this freedom gives them, as much for their person as for their property, the same happiness that natural liberty has on our other subjects." The distinction in this sentence between "natural freedom" and freedom bestowed is a subtle one, for it suggests that the Africans were slaves by nature and yet could earn their freedom.[2]

Royal decrees were all very well, but in Saint Domingue as in the Spanish colonies the rule was "Obedezco pero no cumplo" (I obey but do not comply). Slave owners not only tortured slaves but did so in particularly cruel ways. The historian P. de Vassière listed, among the cruelties inflicted, the placing of irons on hands and feet, the application of salt, pepper, cinders, and hot ashes to wounds, and mutilation. Women were forced to wear the iron collar.[3] Who, then, were the savages? The colonial powers divided the island, as they did so many other areas of the world, with little thought for the consequences, which in the case of Hispaniola would be devastating.

In the French-controlled section of the island, the lucrative trade with France in coffee and sugar brought so many slaves that they soon outnumbered the white population, and because of death and desertion, new bodies were constantly needed. Thus many of the slaves were African born, speaking their different languages and bringing their customs to the new land. There was also a class of *gens de couleur*, the mulattoes who would have such a decisive impact on the political future of the island. The presence of a majority African-born population became a dangerous situation: the discontent of a growing mulatto population exploded into revolt when news of the French Revolution reached the island. In France, the legacy of the Enlightenment and the Declaration of Rights had produced a clash of values between the universality of rights and the colonial exception. The debates in the Assembly were as significant for the slaves as those that occurred in Spain after the conquest when the question of the souls of the conquered was debated, though the terrain had shifted from souls to citizens' rights.[4] The *gens de couleur* had immediately lodged their claim to be French citizens, the slaves were quick to follow, and the black population of Saint Domingue under the leadership of Toussaint L'Ouverture seized the day. His army repelled a British invasion, and by 1801 he was in control of the island, including Spanish Santo Domingo. Napoleon, planning to restore slavery, sent an army to invade the island and eventually deceived Toussaint into surrender. The French atrocities (including an early form of the gas chamber) spurred the rebels under the command of Jean-Jacques Dessalines to repay "these cannibals, war for war, crime for crime, outrage for outrage." Dessalines not only defeated the French but also, in the Constitution of 1804, declared all citizens of the free nation of Haiti to be black. White men were not allowed to hold property or domain on Haitian soil.[5] As Sybille Fischer argues, the various Haitian constitutions "infuse distinctions of skin colour with political meaning." What is important about these constitutions, Fischer argues, is the political and social desires they emulate: "They are expressions of aspirations and desires that went beyond any given political and social reality."[6]

While Haiti was founded on a revolutionary ideal of emancipation, the history of the Hispanic part of the island took a different turn. It was nominally a Spanish colony before the Spaniards abandoned it in 1821, handing it over to Haitian ruler Jean Pierre Boyer, who instituted a program of agrarian and legal system reform. The Hispanic territory did not gain independence until 1844. Thereafter it staved off five invasions from its neighbor and was briefly reannexed to Spain. It was occupied by US marines in 1916, a year after the marines had invaded Haiti. Though it met with opposition, the US occupation of the Dominican Republic ultimately shaped the future of the island. The US-controlled sugar industry brought in Haitians as laborers and restructured the army that eventually became a power base for General Trujillo.

The area along the border with Haiti was cattle country, remote from the capital, a multicultural free zone in which Dominicans shopped at

Haitian markets and Haitians settled on the Dominican side of the border to work on the cattle ranches or as artisans and where people spoke patois and Spanish. It was easy to cross without papers or identification. But General Trujillo, who took power in 1930, converted the Dominican Republic into a totalitarian state with an efficient secret police, a huge national guard, and a system of citizen identification that required people to carry good conduct passes. The horrors of his regime have been amply documented by historians as well as the novelists Mario Vargas Llosa, Junot Díaz, and Julia Alvarez, all of whom re-create the fear and the monstrosity primarily through the fate of attractive women who fell prey to the leader, his sons, or his henchmen.[7]

Junot Díaz writes,

> Almost as soon as he grabbed the presidency, the Failed Cattle Thief sealed the country away from the rest of the world — a forced isolation that we'll call the Plátano Curtain. As for the country's historically fluid border with Haiti . . . the Failed Cattle Thief became Dr. Gull in *From Hell*, adopting the creed of the Dionysian Architects, he aspired to become an architect of history, and through a horrifying ritual of silence and blood, machete and perejil, darkness and denial, inflicted a true border on the countries, a border that exists beyond maps, that is carved directly into the histories and imaginaries of a people.[8]

The massacre of 1937 hardly seems material for a novel. It is difficult to extract pathos from mass murder. There are no intellectual heroes or defiant and ultimately martyred women, only an anonymous mass. In *The Brief Life of Oscar Wao*, the story is told in footnotes. Vargas Llosa slips a brief mention of the massacre into his novel *La fiesta del chivo* (*The Feast of the Goat*), but as an incident that the dictator regretted rather than one he must have regarded as nation-building.

In the diplomatic correspondence, the massacre is referred to as *el insignificante incidente* (a minor incident) provoked by unruly criminal elements crossing the border from Haiti. But the massacre was foretold by Trujillo himself when, visiting the region in October 1937, he abruptly announced that "to Dominicans who were complaining of the depredations by Haitians living among them, thefts of cattle provision, fruit etc. and were thus prevented from enjoying in peace the fruits of their labour, I have responded, 'I will fix this.'" He also reported that there were already three hundred dead in Bánica and that "the remedy will continue."[9]

A state of emergency was declared, and even as Trujillo uttered his threat, the massacre was already in progress, committed, for the most part, by army recruits wielding machetes rather than guns, perhaps because bullets implicated the army while machetes were the silent arms of a farming community. The machete lent credence to the official story of spontaneous vengeance executed by outraged Dominicans, who could then be represented as defending their property. The Haitian victims were identified by their accents. When pronouncing words such as *perejil* (parsley), the giveaway was the glottal pronunciation of the *r*, as in French. According to one historian, this distinction was intended to impute to their victims "radical cultural difference that served to rationalize and ethnicize images of the nation. Thus the violence in the Haitian massacre and the discourse within which it took place were themselves performances that helped constitute notions of inherent and transhistoric difference between Haitians and Dominicans."[10]

Though the news in the Dominican Republic was carefully controlled, it was difficult to suppress the magnitude of the killings despite the smokescreen of denial. Haitians fleeing back across the border told their stories, arousing protests in Haiti among both the masses and the elite. But the Haitian government under President Vincent was cautious, fearful of internal disorder, and asked for the mediation of Mexico, the United States, and Cuba. In the diplomatic exchange, the Haitian president speaks of *hechos sanguinarios* (bloody events) but appears most perturbed over the agitation of his own people, which threatened the stability of his government. His fear was somewhat justified. The Dominican trade representative in Port-au-Prince, Adriano Mejía, complained that he could not leave his house "for fear of exposing himself to questions and ironic commentaries."[11] The killings were bloody indeed, according to the accounts of eyewitnesses and participants, some of whom were convicts who had been recruited from prison to participate in the massacre. One of the men interviewed had been recruited at the age of thirteen to kill Haitians and was afterward imprisoned as Trujillo attempted to find culprits for what was supposedly a spontaneous event: "I remember that it was an indiscriminate thing and there was no mercy for anyone. We killed young and old, the aged, women. After they were dead, we cut off their fingers and if they wore gold rings or jewellery we took it; if they had cows we took them and if they had hens we took them."[12]

According to US Military Intelligence, "the soldiers who carried out the work are said in many instances to have been sickened by their bloody task. A few are reported to have been summarily executed for refusing to carry out their orders, while many overcame their repugnance to the task by fortifying themselves with rum."[13] The Dominican government, meanwhile, made every attempt to hide the atrocity, using diplomatic language that described the Haitians as hungry marauders who had illegally encroached on Dominican land. Official newspapers referring to the "insignificant incident" insisted that the Haitians had provoked the attacks. But the foreign press could not be muzzled, and after at first dismissing the incident, the Dominican government and its supporters, in an attempt to stave off the mediation of Cuba, Mexico, and the United States that Haiti had requested, played the race card. Thus when the National Black Caucus met in New York to investigate the slaughter of black Haitians, the Dominican ambassador (*plenipentencionario*) commented cynically that "many of our friends in this country consider that the intervention of the coloured race of America can be favourable to our cause; since there exists such a marked racial divide, any hostile activity of the black organizations could allow us to gain the sympathy of the other race."[14] The apologists for the Dominican government insisted that the frontier was not simply an arbitrary line. It separated "that Spanish, Christian and Catholic nation that we Dominicans are, that arose pure and homogeneous in the geographical unity of the island that would have been preserved today if, from the end of the seventeenth century, there had not been the splicing onto the pristine trunk into which it injected its sap with profound and fatally different agents from those on which Hispaniola initially grew."[15] Not only were the two countries said to be culturally and ethnically different, but the Haitians who had invaded were said to be undernourished and sick; worse yet, they brought with them voudou, whose worshipper "is the most dangerous type of paranoid."[16] Manuel Arturo Peña Batlle, who pronounced this apologia for the Trujillo policy, was sophisticed enough to have read the work of the Haitian intellectual Jean Price-Mars and to quote him as a source that demonstrated the Africanization of Haiti.

The "new nationalist posture" of Trujillo involved the reconstruction of the nation behind an impermeable border. On the international scene, however, it was important not to admit that the slaughter of Haitians was part of this policy. An army of Dominican intellectuals was ready to support the view that what had happened on the frontier was a minor skirmish. Among them was Max Henríquez Ureña, a member of one of the foremost intellectual families of the nation and the author of a book on modernism. Sent to Mexico to meet President Cárdenas and US representatives, he was pleased to record that there seemed to be no interest in the little incident among the general public of that country and that the Mexican government "seems to prefer to leave things as they are."[17] He either did not know or chose to ignore the full scope of the massacre, which he would explain by faithfully repeating the official story that it had been the spontaneous reaction of Dominicans because of the "violation of the immigration laws by hordes of hungry Haitians who rob animals and destroy agricultural land, groups of Haitians against public order etc."[18] Either Ureña was in the dark or, more likely, he was unwilling to explore the murky depths of official discourse. A more elaborate historical narrative was supplied by Julio Ortega Frier, interim secretary of foreign relations, who in a 1938 letter attributed the Haitian border incursions to the buccaneer origins of Haiti. The descendant of the buccaneer was "el marotero, merodeador haitiano de nuestra región fronteriza" (the *marotero*, the Haitian marauder of our frontier region).[19] The "vegetative growth" of the Haitian population, which had regressed rather than progressed, was responsible for the lawlessness of the frontier. Ortega Frier was adept at quoting from sources that denigrated the Haitians. With some satisfaction he quoted *Cartas de St. Thomas* by a certain "Fermín," who reports that Haitians are thoroughly corrupt:

> Mientras que la masa del pueblo se desliza por la pendiente de todas las degeneraciones humanas, su miseria, su ignorancia y su inmoralidad se extienden como una ola de maldiciones que contamina a los mas

altivos de la aristocracia, cuya mayor parte pierde gradualmente, sino la
inteligencia, por lo menos la integridad moral, mientras que casi todos se
ven envueltos por la miseria general, que los abate y los hace indigno de
figurar como clase dirigente.

(While the mass of the people slide down the slope of all human forms
of degeneration, their poverty, their ignorance and their immorality extends like a wave of curses that contaminates the highest members of the
aristocracy the majority of whom gradually loose if not their intelligence,
at least their moral integrity, while almost all of them are steeped in the
general poverty that reduces them and makes them unworthy of being
a ruling class.)[20]

Seeking to repatriate such immigrants, the Dominican government
had set up concentration camps for Haitians waiting deportation. Sum-
ming up the argument in 1941, when the problem had been settled by
a payment from the Trujillo government and when an amenable Elie
Lescot had become president of Haiti, Ortega Frier came to the dire
conclusion that another clash between these unleashed hordes and the
Dominican farmers and ranchers could not be avoided without the ex-
tirpation of the *marota*. What is implied here was truly sinister, for fear
of the *marota* was a pretext intended to conceal the real aim of keeping
the Dominican Republic as white as possible. The intellectuals backed
up the Trujillo position by citing experts. Manuel Arturo Peña Batlle, for
example, mentions a Brookings Institute report warning of the possible
"blackening" of the "white" Dominican population and suggesting that
there was a racial Gresham's law according to which those at the bottom
of the economic scale were likely to absorb those who were whiter. It
was a report that no doubt reflected some US fears. The paradox was
that during the massacre, skin color could not determine the difference
between Dominicans and Haitians, hence their reliance on the pronunciation of *perejil*.

Trujillo's diplomatic blitz was more effective than the protests from
Haiti. In letters to President Roosevelt and President Cárdenas of Mexico, he denied having knowledge of any problem, while his right-hand
man and the future president, Joaquín Balaguer, rallied the intellectuals
in support of his "splendid work." In a letter to them, Balaguer stated

that the enemies of the Dominican government had tried to depict the events of 1937 as an iniquitous massacre of hapless Haitian masses, whereas it was "the explosion in our peasantry of a sentiment of defence and protest against four centuries of depredations in the northern provinces of the country by great gangs of Haitian marauders."[21] The final sentence of the letter is a masterpiece of cynical reason. After a century of independence, he argues, the Dominican Republic "cannot afford the luxury of sterile discussion in the ineffable manner of the courtesans of the *Decameron*, who entertain themselves telling amusing stories while the plague takes over Florence." Richard Lee Turits argues that "it seems doubtful whether the massacre would have occurred had intellectuals like Balaguer not provided the powerful anti-Haitian ideologies which served to legitimate the slaughter."[22] Turits concludes that "the Trujillo regime's anti-Haitian discourse was the product of rather than the precursor to state terror" and that the violence was "a catalyst" to further Trujillo's modernization of the nation and his fortification of the border, "not simply a consequence of racism and identity formation."[23] This conclusion is important, stressing as it does that the racism was actively invented so that the massacre could take place. And since there was a huge influx of Haitians attempting to escape poverty by crossing the river, fears were not difficult to arouse in the general population, especially as the Haitians were portrayed as badly dressed, sick, immoral, and prolific. Worse, the practitioners of voudou were said to be "paranoids of the most dangerous type."[24] Just as significant is the way that language worked to minimize the incident for the world beyond the island. Atrocities disappeared under the bland serenity of diplomatic exchange. The climate of fear created by the Trujillo regime and continued under Balaguer after Trujillo's assassination eliminated "the insignificant incident" from official memory in the Dominican Republic. The death toll along the now "dominicanized" frontier could simply be forgotten.

Though the indemnity offered and accepted by the Haitian government was supposed to signal the end of the affair, the ghosts would make their comeback. In 1974, a novel titled *El masacre se pasa a pie* (*The Massacre Walks By*) written by a judge, Freddy Prestol Castillo, in an antiquated style full of exclamations and abrupt interventions by the narrator, was published in an edition of two thousand copies. José Israel Cuello, who documented the events of 1938, dismissed the novel as "a crude exposition of the tragedy."[25] A native of San Pedro Macorís, Prestol had been sent to Dajabón, a remote frontier area that was utterly strange to him, to serve as an attorney general. Here he confronted the horror of a massacre about which he was unable to speak openly. The novel, written by candlelight during the small hours, would have earned him a death sentence had it been discovered. In fact the story of the survival of the manuscript is a story within a story and an oblique comment on print culture's powers of survival. The novel relates how the narrator's fiancée, a schoolteacher, takes the manuscript to his mother, who has it buried in the patio. Yet in the foreword to the novel Prestol tells a slightly more complex story. He had given his one copy to a doctor friend for him to read, and it was lying open on the doctor's desk when the secret service came to arrest him. The illiteracy of the police spared the manuscript from destruction, but the doctor was arrested and committed suicide. A priest rescued the manuscript from the doctor's study, and thereafter it found its way to the writer's mother, who buried it in the patio, where it was forgotten even by the writer. Years later it was disinterred, with "torn pages, almost illegible, parts gnawed by insects, parts converted into manure." The manuscript is described as a decaying, buried corpse whose defects are attributed to its long burial. It is also a dead child, his "monstrous, deformed son." "I took the corpse into my hands. With the solicitude of a father, I have tried to give him life." This extraordinary passage performs the miracle of resurrection while underscoring the peculiar nature of a written text that, unlike memory and oral tradition, is preserved as written. Oral culture, on the other hand, is an event that moves on and is modified with the passage of time and in this case, had been suppressed by fear. Though writing can be hidden and resurrected, it returns in an altered state. In an uncanny repetition of the Dominican buried book, the Argentine postdictatorship would yield up "seditious" books buried by their Argentine owners during the military regime.

The events and conversations of the novel are reimagined by a first-person narrator who slips in and out of the text as the young public prosecutor. He moves like a phantom, reporting conversations he could not possibly have overheard. Riding his donkey across the countryside along a "peaceful" frontier, he ponders the meaning of justice and diplomacy as if detached from the events that will later overwhelm him. If there is a plot to the story, it concerns the narrator's escape from Dajabón and (temporarily) from the clutches of Trujillo's police.

The narrative begins and ends as autobiography. Son of a wealthy landowner who loses everything, the author describes himself as a victim of the worldwide depression and son of a ruined father. Following his legal studies, his father's death leaves him penniless and unable to pay for his license, and he is forced to solicit patronage from a man of influence. This is how he comes to be appointed (or relegated) to Dajabón, a remote town whose name has African resonances and that is near the frontier line established by the Treaty of Aranjuez in 1777. He finds Dajabón an eerily silent place depopulated because of El Corte, that is, the cutting down of the Haitian settlers. *Corte* is a word used for felling trees or sugar cane but also for felling those who could not pronounce the Spanish *r*, which in Trujillo's view separated the true Dominican from the marauding Haitian. What makes up the bulk of the text is not a narrative in the usual sense but a litany of the resurrected voices of the dead and those of the killers woven into the author's interpellations. Prestol transcribes the speech of the victims and the murderers sometimes as a mixture of French and creole, and sometimes in creole, that is, in a language that differs markedly from the rules of standard speech and pronunciation. There is an irony in the fact that speaking in dialect the killers themselves cannot pronounce the letter *r*: they say *óidenes* for *órdenes*, *seivicio* for *servicio*.

Trujillo had wanted to make a clear separation between the Dominican and the Haitian, a division of race, language, and character, although there was no basis for a clear distinction. The frontier was a zone of cross-border commerce, of intermarriage, of bilingualism, a zone where Haitians came to work, to plant, and look after the cattle. It was a place where the national imaginary had not yet taken over, where national government was remote until the Corte divided the community into murderers and victims. Composed as a series of vignettes that depict repentant killers, drunken officers, Dominican ranchers left without any labor force, and ex-prisoners maddened by the killing, the novel again and again repeats the refrain "And this is the Corte." The "cut" means not only the act of killing but also the cutting of a line between Dominican and Haitian.

For Captain Venterrón and Sergeant Tarragona, the drunken officers who organize the massacre, rum serves as a kind of anesthetic that does not quite deaden their self-disgust. The effect of killing is devastating for both the killers and the destitute locals who have been rounded up and made to kill on orders of the Supreme Commander, the mysterious being who guides their destinies and whom they serve as mere instruments. They join in the killing out of hunger or because it offers them an escape from a prison sentence, though they do not know whether the Supreme Commander is simply an insatiable monster or does not even exist. Those who complain are shot, a fate that is considered better than that of Haitians, who are cut down with machetes. In the novel, these latter are often presented only as pleading voices, but some are named, like the trusted hotel maid, Moraime Luis, who is raped and killed as she tries to cross the Masacre River, which separated the frontier. A few escape to Haiti because they are relatives of the killers or thanks to the protection of the schoolteacher, the narrator's fiancée, who loses her job for rejecting the captain's advances. Prestol does not represent all Haitians as innocents or all Dominicans as evil. The Haitians steal cattle; Dominicans sometimes save Haitians. There are hardworking peons as well as cattle rustlers among the dead. But El Corte depopulates the area, leaving only cadavers that are eaten by dogs and pigs before being burned. To encourage new (supposedly white) settlers from the city, the government offers them land even though they have no farming skills and no intention of learning them; instead the land is colonized by brothel owners and a crime wave erupts until the unruly settlers are once again returned to the city.

The final act of the tragedy is marked by the arrival of judges, whose task is to fabricate the official story — that the killing was the work of local agents infuriated by the thieving Haitians: "Thus the lie in the annals of our jurisprudence went on growing. Thus they fabricated a comic and cruel plan to satisfy diplomatic and negotiable Haiti, the Haiti of the mulattos brought up in Paris who will then exchange the blood of their brothers for the coins offered to them by the strong man who rules my country" (152). Here Prestol refers to the indemnity offered by Trujillo to the mulatto president of Haiti, who was fearful of his own black population. Yet when one of the judges tries to hang himself, it is clear that they too are victims in whom some vestige of shame persists, just as the writer is a victim, just as the conscripted killers are victims. Prestol describes the judges as pigs but immediately reflects that he too will be a pig if he remains silent: "These judges like myself were thrown into this land of poverty." When they are photographed alongside the criminals, it seems like a cruel joke, the sign of "our national poverty [*miseria*]." What Prestol suggests is that in a totalitarian regime held together by fear, those who execute the repression as well as those who remain silent become both culprits and victims. Everyone is trapped in the murderous system; only the narrator's fiancée manages to escape to Venezuela. The indecisive narrator, unable to flee the country when he has the chance, is imprisoned and given a five-year sentence for abandoning his post on the frontier. The written testimony buried in the earth — not memory — is the insurance against forgetting.

Prestol's novel contains elements of denunciation, sentimentalism, and existential fiction. One of the most striking chapters details the nightmarish haunting of the narrator by phantoms of the past who are engaged in a never-ending cycle of atrocity and revenge. Thus Toussaint L'Ouverture turns on the white inhabitants of the island to avenge the ill treatment of the blacks. The contempt of the Spaniards provokes the vengeance of the slaves, who respect neither women, priests, nor children. In the narrator's nightmares, Dessalines promises that no whites will be left in the country and that Haiti will be for blacks alone. How can there be an end to the cycle when the present is written in characters of blood, when the history lessons learned in childhood perpetuate the cycle? What dominates historical memory is the pattern of atrocity and vengeance, not the history of emancipation from colonial servitude. Yet the inhabitants of the frontier had once spoken and understood each other's language, had inhabited the same territory and even intermarried before the Corte cut through similarities and mutual dependence and re-created the Dominican and Haitian nations on spurious racial lines.

The novel raises several questions: For example, what meaningful action other than suicide could have been taken in the totalitarian state?

And must nations be constituted on the basis of enmity? Fear in this society is experienced consciously; it separates individuals, entrapping each person in a lonely, friendless isolation. This is the price a whole population paid for its constitution as a modern nation. Not only has modernity been paid for in blood, but the record is now buried (just as the narrator is buried in prison), and what eventually emerges is unavoidably damaged. As Walter Benjamin puts it, "Whoever has emerged victorious participates to this day in the triumphal procession in which the present rulers step over those who are lying prostrate."[26] This is perhaps, the most important insight of the book: that a historical narrative is not a seamless curve toward the present but the broken remains that are buried and waiting for their resurrection.

While Prestol's novel views the massacre from the point of view of a fearful and outraged outsider, Edwidge Danticat's *The Farming of Bones*, a melancholy wake in the face of irretrievable loss, raises the question "What remains?" Can there be remainders from catastrophic losses, as Prestol's buried manuscript claims? The epigraph of Danticat's novel refers to a biblical disaster described in the book of Judges. The Ephraimites, when attempting to cross the Jordan, were asked to pronounce "shibboleth"; those who could not pronounce the word correctly were seized and killed. The word "shibboleth," meaning "stream," entered the universal language to represent a password that divided the permitted from those who could not pass. On the Dominican border, language — not skin color — becomes the test of national purity. The language of the Haitians is a mixture of Kreyól and Spanish, "the tangled language of those who always stuttered as they spoke, caught as they were on the narrow ridge between two nearly native tongues." (69) The French *r* and the Spanish *r* lie on different sides of the ridge, so that the pronunciation of words like *perejil* (parsley) and *claro* (clear) divides one group from another, a distinction that would prove fatal to the Haitians. Parsley, a harmless and useful domestic plant, becomes the shibboleth. Early in the novel, the Haitian laborer Kongo, whose only son has been killed by a speeding car, cleanses his body with parsley. Amabelle Desir, the melancholy protagonist, comments,

> We used pèsi, perejil, parsley, the damp summer morningness of it, the
> mingled sprigs, bristly and coarse, gentle and docile, all at once, tasteless

and bitter when chewed, a sweetened wind inside the mouth, the leaves a
different taste than the stalk, all this we savoured for our food, our teas,
our baths, to cleanse our insides as well as our outsides of old aches and
griefs, to shed a passing year's dust as a new one dawned, to wash a new
infant's hair for the first time and — along with boiled orange leaves —
a corpse's remains one last time. (62)

For her, parsley is a sensual experience, an experience of taste and of
touch. Later she would speculate that perhaps the general was using it
to cleanse his country (203).

Amabelle is an orphan whose parents were drowned crossing the Masacre River as they returned from buying pots on the Dominican side.
Her father leaves her on the riverbank while he carries the mother across
the river, but the river is flooded, and she watches helplessly as they both
drown. This catastrophic but accidental loss shapes her life. She is found
sitting near the river by Valencia and her father, Papi, a Spanish immigrant, "sitting on a big rock, watching the water as if you were waiting for
an apparition" (91). Adopted as a maid by Valencia, who marries a Dominican army officer, Don Pico Duarte, Amabelle has a loving relationship with her mistress and her father, although she cannot transgress the
boundaries imposed by her subordinate status: "Working for others,"
she reflects, "you learn to be present and invisible at the same time" (35).

Amabelle has inherited healing and midwifery skills from her parents. The novel begins with her helping Valencia to give premature
birth to twins, a boy and a girl. Only the latter survives, much to the
disappointment of the father. But while indispensable to the household,
Amabelle is never anything other than a dependent, a presence visible
only when needed. She takes solace from her lover, Sebastian, a Haitian
cane-cutter whose body bears the marks of the brutal labor. Amabelle's
description, "travay tè pou zo" (work for bone), is one of the meanings of
"the farming of bones." Literally the phrase means "work to the bone";
it signifies the harsh exploitation of cane-cutters, whose bodies visibly
display the scars of their work, but also alludes to the cutting down of
bodies during the massacre.

Even before the disaster of the Corte (*kouto kouto* in patois), Danticat
had assembled a group of melancholy characters. Valencia's Spanish
father is an exile from his country and is bound to the radio, which

brings him news of the Spanish Civil War; the servant, Juana, raised in a convent school, abandoned her religious calling but could not have children; the Haitian priest, Father Romain, whose "creed was one of memory, how remembering — though sometimes painful — can make you strong" (73), was similarly an exile. Sebastian's father had died in a hurricane. His friend Yves's father had been killed fighting against the US occupation.

Amabelle is haunted by loss not only of her parents but also of a homeland dominated, in her imagination, by the great citadel of King Henri that towered over her childhood home, a witness to lost glory. Loss is the leitmotif of the novel. Even Señora Valencia's husband, Señor Pico, a staunch Trujillo supporter, who seems outside this melancholy circle, mourns when his newborn son Rafael (named after Trujillo) dies. In his hurry to see the new twins and especially the boy, he had driven through a group of workers, knocking one of them, Joel, the only son of Kongo into a ravine. The manner of Joel's death breeds a mute resentment among the Haitians, while the death of his son leaves Señor Pico bereft and angry, more dedicated than ever to Trujillo's grand design and the "special operation" whose goal he does not divulge. Yet rumors have begun to circulate of "Haitians being killed in the night because they could not manage to trill their r and utter a throaty J to ask for parsley, to say perejil." Though Amabelle is reluctant to believe that anything will happen to her or to the cane-cutters, Sebastian persuades her to cross the border with him. But before she has time to leave, she becomes a helpless witness to atrocity, seeing Señor Pico loading workers armed with machetes onto trucks and observing what happens to those who resist. When she arrives late at the church where she was to have met Sebastian, she learns that the Haitian doctor and priest have been taken away, along with Sebastian and his sister. With Sebastian's comrade, Yves, she sets out on the dangerous journey to the border along with other refugees, including Odette and Wilner, the millworkers whom they have met on the way, all the time seeking news of her man as if he might miraculously have survived while hearing the tales of atrocities, of Haitians forced to jump over a cliff and of executions. She witnesses acts of brutality and comes across a house in which an entire family has been hung from the rafters. But when they reach Dajabón, she and Yves experience the full force of hostility. Taunting youths beat them and force them to swallow parsley; only the arrival of General Trujillo to attend mass distracts the attention of the mob and saves her, although she is permanently scarred by the experience. Reaching the river, they attempt to cross, but the Masacre takes its toll. Wilner is shot and Odette drowns, muttering the deadly Kreyól word *pèsi* (parsley) and leaving Amabelle to reflect on its dire effect: "Was it because it was so used, so commonplace, so abundantly at hand that everyone who desired a sprig could find one? We used parsley for our food, our teas, our baths, to cleanse our insides as well as our outsides. Perhaps the Generalissimo in some larger order was trying to do the same for his country" (203). In this way, she comes to some kind of understanding of the perverse event.

At the Haitian hospital where she recovers from the beating, she hears more tales of atrocities, more reflections on the strange fate of Haiti, once a nation of heroes like Dessalines, Toussaint, and Henri and now filled with self-hatred. For the refugees there is little help. When a riot erupts because of the government's inaction, a photograph of President Vincent that shows him wearing a medal awarded by Trujillo "as a symbol of eternal friendship between our two peoples" is burned by the angry refugees. Amabelle has made her way to Yves's family in Cap Haitien, though she will never wholly accept him as a substitute for Sebastian. From Sebastian's mother she finally learns of his death and his sister's. But knowing Sebastian is dead is no cure. She is sick, unable to accept her lover's death, just as she was unable to accept her parents'. Suffering from melancholia, she scarcely eats and only wants to sleep. When she lines up fruitlessly for government compensation, she recognizes that she is one of the living dead.

Yves, on the other hand, is burdened by the guilt of survival. He confesses that Joel, the man run down and killed by Don Pico, had saved his life by pushing him out of the way of the car. And because he had lingered, he was not at the church when Sebastian, his sister Mimi, the priest, and the doctor were captured but had watched their abduction from the road. The labor of farming is his only relief: "His silence before he fell asleep was weighed with rage and guilt. Now all he could do was plant and sow to avoid the dead season" (263). But the slaughter had affected him physically. "He detested the smell of sugar cane (except the way it disappeared in rum) and loathed the taste of parsley; he could not swim in rivers; the sound of Spanish being spoken — even by Haitians — made his eyes widen, his breath quicken, his face cloud with terror, his lips unable to part one from the other and speak" (273). And though he and Amabelle live together, they cannot bond. Each is alone in their version of grief. After learning that the doctor and the priest had been released from prison, Amabelle writes a letter to the doctor appealing for information and then sets out to visit Father Romain, only to find that he has been broken by the prison experience and that when he speaks he can only parrot the Trujillo doctrine. But unlike Amabelle, Father Romain will be cured and will start a new life not as a priest but as a family man.

Without family or love, but with her memory intact, Amabelle reflects, "It is perhaps the great discomfort of those trying to silence the world to discover that we have voices sealed inside our heads, voices that with each passing day, grow even louder than the clamour of the world outside" (266). The memory of the slaughter "is the only thing that is mine enough to pass on. All I want to do is find a place to lay down now and again, a safe nest where it will neither be scattered by the winds nor remain forever buried beneath the sod" (266). Like Prestol's manuscript, the memory is protected by a crypt as Amabelle too tries to create a safe place for it, although as a survivor who had escaped the killing, she cannot narrate the death that she has not experienced. What had Sebastian's suffering been like? There is no answer to the question. Amabelle's frustration is shared by us, the distant readers of atrocity: "What was it like?"

For twenty-four years Amabelle, maimed physically and mentally, absorbed by the past, survives by working as a seamstress. On one occasion, she follows a group of tourists around the remains of Henri Christophe's castle, hearing from the guide that "all monuments of this great size are built with human blood" and that "famous men never truly die. It is only those nameless and faceless who vanish like smoke onto the early morning air" (280). Yet Sebastian survives albeit in attenuated form, in memory. He has become a phantom that accompanies Amabelle in her living death: "His name is Sebastian and his story is like a fish with no tail, a dress with no hem, a drop with no fall, a body in the moonlight with no shadow. His absence is my shadow; his breath, my dreams."

She speaks to his ghost and asks whether he and his sister had suffered greatly, confessing that she had chosen "a living death because I am not brave." The living death is that of the melancholic. It is the living death of readers wanting to know.

In yet one more attempt to recover the past, after Trujillo's death Amabelle goes back to the Dominican Republic to look for Valencia, though what she most wants is not so much to see Valencia as to visit the waterfall where she and Sebastian had made love and where she dreams of meeting him again. Although now an old woman, she still suffers from the pain of her wounds and wants to reignite the memory of past happiness. Behind the waterfall is a place that is always light because, like her, it "holds on to some memory of the sun that it will not surrender." When she again visits the waterfall, it does not correspond to her memory, and she is not even sure that it is the waterfall behind which she and Sebastian had made love. At this point Danticat distinguishes between an encrypted memory that resists change and the disfiguring brought about by the passage of time. It is Valencia who reminds her of the healing power of water: "When we were children, you were always drawn to water, Amabelle, streams, lakes, rivers, waterfalls in all their power" (302). Water kills but also heals. It moves and rushes on like time without history. Time without history defines not only Trujillo's regime but also the lives of survivors, for whom there is no change and no record.

Amabelle now returns to the Masacre River where she sees the "Pwofese," a man maddened by the slaughter, emerging from the water. She wants him to carry her to the river, where she will seek "Sebastian's cave, my father's laughter, my mother's eternity," that is, her own private protected paradise that is beyond history. She takes off her clothes and floats in the water: "I looked to my dreams for softness, for a gentler embrace, for relief from the fear of mudslides and blood bubbling out of the riverbed, where it is said the dead add their tears to the river flow." Seeing the professor walking away enclosed in his solitude, she observes, "He, like me, was looking for the dawn" (310). But that dawn appears to be beyond the stasis of the present, and it is as yet unimaginable.

Melancholy, the impossibility of completing the work of mourning, stems from more than an individual loss. To be sure, it is Sebastian's death that brings about Amabelle's sickness, her overwhelming desire to sleep, and her refusal of Yves as a substitute, but her loss goes beyond the individual. It is the loss of all social bonds. She has neither husband, children, nor parents. Her radical solitude has come about through events beyond her control — through a history she did not make and through the dissolution of social bonds. The love of her parents and lover, with its healing power, has been violently snatched away, and although she is "looking for the dawn," this goal will remain out of reach during her individual life.

In *Mourning and Melancholia*, Freud described melancholia as a state that is characterized by self-reproach; self-torment, including the refusal to eat; sleeplessness; and an inclination toward suicide. The melancholic's inability to recognize the loss of the love object is pathological. Mourning is achieved by relinquishing the dead or absent love object. But what of situations like that of Amabelle, where the loss is not only individual, where the "farming of bones" is all that is left? In *The Ego and the Id*, Freud radically reverses the constitution of the ego, making it the repository of losses. Freudian theory focuses only on the individual and thus does not address the questions raised by Danticat's novel, in which there is no outcome to a social catastrophe that weighs on the individual but that no individual can assuage.

Given the catastrophic losses of the late twentieth and early twenty-first centuries, it is not surprising that many critics have begun to reconsider loss and mourning in different terms, and melancholy not as a state to be overcome so that the past can be forever confined to the past, but as a defiant resistance to closure.[27] The equilibrium of the ego that has successfully completed mourning and is thus presumably healed seems like a mockery when loss involves not only an individual but a group and not only present loss but the ancestral and collective losses through war and massacre. In their introduction to their book *Loss*, David Eng and David Kazanjian recast Freud's account of melancholia as a creative process, pointing out that "a better understanding of melancholic attachments to loss might depathologize those attachments, making visible not only their social bases but also their creative, unpredictable, political aspects."[28]

Such an outcome is not possible in Danticat's novel. There is no creative relief here from the collective trauma of massacre. The passing of time solves nothing in itself; it only blurs the past or reduces it to Valencia's euphemisms. It is left to the reader to wonder whether such private grief can ever be productive or whether the avenue to the social is blocked, making literature the unique place for vindication.

Danticat wrote the preface to the English translation of the novel *Le peuple des terre mêlées* (*People of Mixed Earth*) by the Haitian writer René Philoctète; the volume also has an introduction by the Haitian scholar Lyonel Trouillot. Philoctète's entire literary oeuvre was first published in Haiti at his own expense in editions of a few dozen copies that were poorly printed or even simply mimeographed on cheap paper.[29]

He "faced the worst," wrote Trouillot. "The education that moulded us, insisted, through its lousy history lessons that we were shoddy goods — because of our race, or our origins, or our poor excuse for a culture. Above all this education taught us that we couldn't be Haitian and completely modern." Clearly influenced by Alejo Carpentier, the Cuban writer who had asked in the introduction to his novel *El reino de este mundo* (*The Kingdom of This World*), "What is the history of America, if it is not a chronicle of the marvellous real [*lo real maravilloso*]?," the magic in Philoctète's novel is different from Carpentier's. It is the magic of the state in the form of a kite, the raptor that hovers over the village of Elias Piña, bringing madness and death: "All autocracy has its magic, its seduction: the troops on parade, the bright flags, the thunder of marching feet. And the people enraptured, approve, forgetting that those who tried to dispel the darkness have been swallowed up in the solitude of dungeons." The novel interweaves Trujillo's megalomaniac visions of capturing the Citadel and taking back lands held by Haiti since the Treaty of Aranjuez with the love story of the Dominican factory worker Pedro Brito and his Haitian wife, whom he does not want to send back to Haiti, despite the coming terror. Pedro seems to belong to some other literary tradition, the worker hero who has strayed from realist fiction into the surreal, who believes in peaceful coexistence and worker's rights. The love of Pedro and Adele represents the antithesis of the cruelty that the radio celebrates as it enumerates the number of heads severed in Operación Cabezas Haitianas (Operation Haitian Heads) during a broadcast that also features commercials and a commentary on a Yankee/Cubs game at Wrigley Field. Magic realism deals with atrocity by removing it from the individual to the collective. There are no subjects on the train that in Gabriel García Márquez's *One Hundred Years of Solitude* take the bodies of dead strikers to the coast. In Philoctète's novel, the magical alleviates terror as much as it represents it.

Idelber Avelar describes the present as a time of defeat and literature as an "untimely" enterprise.[30] "Untimely" is an apt description of these novels by Pressols and Danticat, which raise the questions about atrocity, loss, and mourning that recur throughout this book, questions about how, given the complete obliteration of collective memory, anything like healing or reparation can be realized. Both novels relate collective stories of loss, in which individual suffering becomes symptomatic of social trauma that extends over generations.[31] The buried book is the trope for knowledge made useless by repression and restored only in a torn and dilapidated state, while memory, in Danticat's novel, remains encrypted in the individual who has lost all social ties.

The massacre of Haitians foreshadowed things to come, for it was not a random act of repression but a cleansing operation with the aim of reinventing the nation by dividing societies into those allowed to live and those condemned to die. Trujillo's project of extermination of an enemy defined by race and color in the cause of nation formation demonstrated just how crucial it was, for nation formation, to identify an enemy.

TWO | Alien to Modernity

Foucault claimed that racism is the condition for the acceptability of putting human beings to death: "It introduces a division between peoples, between my life and the death of the other on the basis of biological difference; the death of the inferior race (the degenerate or the abnormal) is what will make life in general healthier: healthier and purer."[1] He linked racism to biopower, his term describing the regulation of and exercise of power over the life-giving bodies of the population. Racism, whose ultimate example is the Nazi death camp, is the dark side of biopower, as it justifies the eradication of any group that threatens the nation's existence. But in Peru and Guatemala, two countries with large indigenous populations, there was an undertow of fear and repulsion, for underlying the rationalization of discrimination were the habits and attitudes of conquest. The large number of indigenous dead in the civil wars of the 1970s and 1980s in Guatemala and Peru, often killed in wholesale atrocities, suggests an energy for killing beyond any tactical interest. And what was the most heinous of barbarisms? In this chapter, I examine how cannibalism that in the sixteenth century was attributed to the conquered peoples was committed not by the indigenous but by some members of the Guatemalan army, who made it part of their training and forced it on their prisoners.[2] In Peru, cannibalism surfaces not as a practice but as a myth. Attributed to the ancestors of the indigenous, it was taken as evidence of ancestral barbarism by one of Peru's most prestigious novelists, Mario Vargas Llosa, for whom it was a stain on the modern state. In both countries, cannibalism was the mark of the primitive, of that which has not been redeemed by modernity.

In the Spanish colonies, indigenous separation from the mainstream had been decreed when, in the early years of the Conquest, indigenous townships were founded that particularized Indian identity and were, according to Díaz Polanco, the most important institutions of Spanish domination.[3] The *ayllu* in the Andean regions and the pueblos in Mexico and Central America ensured the preservation of language, dress, and customs while reserving the indigenous as a workforce. The colonial divide guaranteed that the indigenous in these regions would retain traditions, customs, and languages that did not interfere with Christian belief or their use as a labor force. The Conquest constituted the indigenous as a conquered race, just as slavery constituted the image of the black as an enslaved commodity. The spiritual conquest of the New World by Catholic Spain had followed the logic of cleansing and persecution against Jews and the Muslims on religious grounds. In his debate with Bartolomé de las Casas, Ginés Sepúlveda argued not only that the indigenous were slaves by nature but also that they were contaminated with abominable lewdness: that is, they were sinners by nature.[4] Bartolomé de las Casas won the debate, but Sepúlveda's view may well have been a popular view among the descendants of the Spaniards. Nevertheless, the separation of the races clearly could not be maintained given the racial mixing, which was so complex that colonial governments required charts denoting the degree of mixture.

Over the centuries, the alibi for the subjugation of the indigenous was constantly reformulated according to the needs of the state and the definition of nationhood and in hundreds of different scenarios, from the Caste Wars of Yucatán to the desert campaign in Argentina and the seizure of Mapuche territories in Chile in the nineteenth and early twentieth centuries: the indigenous were the enemy to be subjugated. In one of the most memorable stories by José María Arguedas, a novelist and ethnographer who spent his childhood in indigenous villages, a young son of a landowning family is forced by his older brother to watch him violate an indigenous woman. As a conqueror, the brother's masculinity is confirmed in the act that is also intended to initiate the younger brother into a regime of violence.[5] Notwithstanding the persistence of such practices, there are strong reasons for viewing the atrocities of the 1980s as more than the escalation of long-standing discrimination.[6] Or, rather, long-standing discrimination became harnessed to the cause of modernization, underscoring the value of whiteness or, as Bolívar Echeverría terms it, *blanquitud*, that is, not whiteness as such but the iconic ideal of capitalism's new man.[7]

The war on communism took many different forms in Latin America and used new repressive technologies. In Greg Grandin's words, "This nationalized terror entailed the direct incorporation of independent death squads into military structures as well as an increasingly visible performance of what previously had been quotidian, private acts, such as rape, torture and murder."[8] These practices were deployed in a genocidal campaign that was designed to break down what strategists deemed the closed, castelike isolation of indigenous communities, identified as the reason for the supposed collective susceptibility of the Mayans to communism. They were thus defined as the enemy on two grounds, as guerrilla sympathizers and as enemies of the modern nation. The "war on communism" escalated into genocide as women and children were killed in the cruelest manner and entire villages destroyed. In Peru, the president of the Commission on Truth and Reconciliation, in his preface to the report, stated bluntly, "Of every four victims, three were male or female peasants whose maternal language was Quechua."[9] While denying that this was an ethnic conflict, he insisted that "these two decades of destruction and death would not have been possible without the profound contempt towards the most dispossessed population of the country, displayed equally by members of the PCP [Partido Comunista Peruano], Sendero Luminoso and agents of the State, that contempt that is woven into each moment of Peruvians' daily life."[10]

The myths and prejudices inherited from the Conquest and recast by modernization came to support the intellectual arguments that upheld the military project in Guatemala and the neoliberal project in Peru. In Guatemala, the army's policy was to discipline the indigenous who survived the massacres and refashion them as citizens of a country from which ethnic difference had been eradicated. In Peru, the transformation was to be achieved thanks to the urban melting pot. This was the "other path" advocated by Hernando de Soto and Peru's foremost writer and intellectual, Mario Vargas Llosa. Both the Guatemalan and Peruvian solutions were founded on the conviction that the indigenous as such had no place in a modern state.

Eating the Enemy

The Guatemalan Commission on Historical Clarification (CEH) was set up after protracted efforts at the end of 1996. Designated the Comisión para el Esclarecimiento Histórico de la Violaciones a los Derechos Humanos y los Hechos de Violencia Que Han Causado Sufrimientos a la Población Guatemalteca (The Commission for Historic Clarification of Violations of Human Rights and Acts of Violence That Have Caused Suffering to the Guatemalan Population), it was created by the United Nations according to the terms of the Oslo Agreement and presided over by Christian Tomuschat of Germany.[11] The commission was financially strapped and met obstructions from the armed forces, and after the presentation of the report, the then president, Álvaro Arzú Irigoyen, despite his support for peace accords, refused to express public apologies or purge the army, nor was the charge of genocide acknowledged.[12] The Office of Human Rights of the Archbishopric of Guatemala, impelled by the killings of priests and catechists, issued its own report, *Guatemala: Nunca más.*[13]

Between September and April 1997, the investigators appointed by the CEH visited two thousand communities and collected five hundred collective testimonies. Of twenty thousand people who collaborated, more than one thousand were key witnesses. But how much value should be placed on their declarations? To meet possible objections, the commission classified some of their declarations as "full conviction," that is, where the truth of the testimony was backed up either by documents or by direct witnesses; the other categories were the *presunción fundada* (well-founded hypothesis), for cases that offered no direct witnesses but provided solid foundations for the findings, and the *presunción simple*

(simple hypothesis), for cases where there were no direct witnesses but there was circumstantial evidence.[14]

The first part of the report documented the historical roots of conflict especially the long history of discrimination against the Maya, justified by the supposed cultural and biological inferiority of the indigenous. Conscious or unconscious racism, the commission argued, was an important factor in explaining the many outrageous acts (*actos desmedidos*) of violence committed in the course of Guatemala's history and during the armed struggle: "According to the racist mentality, any indigenous mobilization brings to mind the atavistic image of a rebellion. In this sense, it can be considered that racism was also present in the bloodiest moments of armed confrontation when the indigenous population were castigated as if they were an enemy to conquer."[15] The commission argued that this deep-rooted racism explained why, at some moments during the civil war, the number of Maya victims was higher and why extreme acts of cruelty took place in their communities. They commented, "There still persists in the mentality of some Guatemalans the idea that the life of the indigenous is worth less. This notion may explain why the number of Maya victims in some periods of the armed confrontation was greater and the reason for acts of extreme cruelty and crimes of *lèse humanité* committed in their communities."[16] Those acts of extreme cruelty were so savage that they could not be rationalized or explained.

As early as 1954, after the overthrow of the elected Árbenz government, a reformed and vigorous army invoked a new political order that was the product of the Guatemalan interpretation of the Doctrine of National Security of the United States, which identified communism as the first and most dangerous threat to development. The Guatemalan Military recast this policy as a Doctrine of National Stability.[17] The enemy was identified as internal, an identification that was reinforced by the activities of guerrilla groups in the 1960s and by their escalated activities in the 1970s and 1980s, and also by indigenous groups insisting on their rights. When the guerrilla group El Ejército de los Pobres (The Army of the Poor) came to villages, they found sympathizers and recruits and were able to organize meetings. But the army was not about to make distinctions between those who actively helped the guerrilla and those who sympathized. A scorched earth policy was inaugurated in areas where the guerrillas were active.[18] Under President Romeo Lucas García, who came to power in 1978, a terror was unleashed that demolished all existing social political and professional organizations.[19] After the coup that brought Efraín Rios Montt to power in 1982, a different but no less deadly kind of strategy was set in motion, designed first of all "to take the water away from the fish," that is, to deprive the insurgents of base support by occupying conflict zones and suppressing their base. In 1982, Rios Montt's spokesperson, Francisco Bianchi, said: "Clearly we would have to kill the indigenous because they are collaborating with the subversion."[20] Rios Montt, while admitting that it would be necessary to kill those who collaborated with the guerrillas, stated, "It is not the army's philosophy to kill the indigenous but to reconquer and help them."[21] The term "reconquer," with its resonances of the Spanish campaign against the Moors, clearly suggests waging a war against the indigenous, to be followed by the "conversion" of survivors into citizens of the new order. Massacres were rationalized as the prelude to the defeat of the guerrilla and the preparation for the rebirth of the nation purified of ethnic difference.

Described as "70 percent beans and 30 percent bullets," the army's program of pacification and development had the dual goal of destroying Indian communal life and rewarding survivors with tools and work in reorganized communities. The first phase of this operation, known as Operación Ceniza (Operation Ashes), led to the slaughter of about seventy-five hundred people over a period of eighteen months. In the targeted zones, the killings represented "a scientifically precise, sustained orchestration of a systematic, intentional, massive campaign of extermination" in which the army was charged with "killing and burning all living things within the 'secured area.'"[22] Villages in the red zone (the color distinguished them from the less threatening pink and green zones) were razed by the Task Forces and refugees were taken to army prisons where they were tortured and indoctrinated. The thorough reorganization of indigenous life was to be achieved through setting up model villages and Poles of Development, subjecting people to barracks-like living conditions and placing them under military surveillance.

The anthropologist Jennifer Schirmer argues that "nowhere else in

Latin America has an army managed to mobilize and divide an indigenous population against itself to such an extent — even to the point of forcing victims to become accomplices and kill one another."[23] One of the tactics was to incorporate the indigenous forcibly into civil patrols (Patrullas de Auto Defensa Civil, known as PACs), trained in the same violent tactics and interrogation techniques as the army. Some were forced to kill members of their own families. The Commission on Historic Clarification calculated that almost half of Guatemala's adult indigenous males belonged to the PACs in 1982.[24]

The ideologue and architect of the policy to restructure indigenous communities was General Gramajo, one of three officers in charge of the National Plan of Security and Development drawn up after the 1982 coup that brought Rios Montt to power. The plan was aimed at restoring some measure of constitutionality after the nation had been thoroughly pacified. There were three stages, the first of which was extermination of those in the red zones, followed by restructuring of the rest through party politics and elections. The last stage was a thirty-five-year transition by way of education, persuasion, and long-term crisis management of conflict that included selective repression and killing. Schirmer's book includes an extended interview with General Gramajo, who offers an extraordinary insight into a military policy that deployed the most savage tactics while using the language of nation building and rational development. Appointed defense minister in 1987 after helping to engineer the election of a civilian government under Vinicio Cerezo, he referred to the program for the return to constitutional rule as his "baby." Using the same metaphor, President Rios Montt would state that the democratic baby had been taken too rapidly out of its incubator, and "that is why we have [the problems we have today]." Schirmer comments that this transsexual birthing discourse reveals just how much the military saw itself as both Creator (Mother to the Fatherland) and Parent-Guardian and Protector (Father to the Motherland) and "thus retained full birth right to the Nation in terms of the past and the future."[25] This was also the justification for the foundational violence deployed by both Pinochet and the Argentine military government, who described themselves as saving the country from chaos and rebirthing it.[26] The birthing of the nation did not prevent the mutilation of mothers, and the destruction of fetuses in the womb, however, although a carefully managed verbal screen was maintained between declaration of policy and the campaign of eradication. Thus for decades Rios Montt was able to deny any knowledge of atrocities.[27]

In their report, the commission concluded that racism was present "in the most bloody moments of the armed confrontation when the indigenous population was punished as if it were an enemy to conquer" (193). Enrique Dussel described the rationale thus: "Since the barbarian is opposed to the civilizing process, modern praxis must in the end use violence if necessary to destroy the obstacles to modernization."[28] And in a monumental study of the trope of the cannibal from the discovery and Conquest onward, Carlos Jáureguí describes "cannibalism" as "a fundamental trope in the definition of Latin American cultural identity from the first European visions of the New World as monstrous and savage, up to the narratives and cultural production of the twentieth and twenty-first centuries, in which the cannibal is redefined in many ways in relation to the construction of postcolonial and postmodern identities."[29] But in the civil war in Guatemala, cannibalism was more than a trope. It was a practice imposed by some members of the army that forced the perceived enemy to act as cannibals and that likewise, in some instances, required their own troops to prove their domination by eating the enemy.

The Commission on Historical Clarification documented numerous acts of cannibalism in which "the aggressors ate the viscera of victims or forced the victims to drink their own blood or eat their own members," often in public.[30] In one incident after the execution of twenty-two men, the soldiers opened their skulls and ate their brains. When the rest of the population went into the schoolhouse where the execution had taken place, they found plates of brain on the table.[31] The commission cited cases of prisoners being made to eat their own ears or penises. Indigenous members of the PACs were forced to participate in atrocities and, in one incident, made to eat the victim's brains. In this case, to be manly was to be savage. In an incident reported by Victor Montejo, during the torture of one victim "they removed his teeth one by one and forced him to swallow them like pellets. They cut off his tongue, pierced his eyes."[32] Montejo, a schoolteacher who survived the army's attack on the village where he was teaching, described the attackers as "dark-skinned": that is, they were probably indigenous. Officers who later arrived by helicopter were a lighter-skinned elite. What this means is that brown-skinned people on both sides were forced to act as the cannibals they were supposed to be. One of the recruits told Montejo that in the army, "the only thing you are taught is to kill and kill, again and again. Just because you're fed well and warm blood runs in your veins, you soon want to start making the bullets fly, as they say, it makes you feel real macho."[33]

What is most striking in these testimonies is that cannibalism was not only forced on captives but also incorporated into army training. Victims were made to act as they were supposed to act, as savages, while the soldiers were made to become savages in order to kill. The rites of passage employed in training indigenous troops were particularly disgusting: these conscripts were made to swallow all kinds of dirt. Many local traditions in Latin America reenact the Conquest in dance or performance, but in this case the performance of the festive victory celebration involved cannibalism. Carlos Jáuregui argues that the narrative of cannibalism is not about a problem of the diet of Native Americans but speaks to the conqueror and his system of values and beliefs.[34] In these Guatemalan cases, however, we confront the literal interpretation as, in a curious reversal, the army takes on the savagery they attribute to the enemy while forcing their prisoners to behave as cannibals.

The fury against the original peoples knew no bounds. Among the acts documented by the commission were killing defenseless children, often by beating them alive against walls or throwing them alive into pits where the corpses of adults were later thrown; amputating limbs; impaling victims' bodies; covering victims with gasoline and burning them alive; extracting the viscera of still-living victims in the presence of others; leaving in agony for days people who had been mortally wounded; slitting open the wombs of pregnant women; and similar atrocious acts. In a punitive operation, the soldiers sat the men on spikes that penetrated their bodies and came out of their mouths: they cut their tongues, "the noble parts," and part of the head in the shape of a vessel (*huacal*).[35] Such acts of extreme cruelty against the victims also degraded the perpetrators and those who inspired, ordered, or tolerated such actions. The Guatemalan *kaibiles* assumed the role of the satanic and, like the werewolf, were transformed from citizens into messengers of evil, a transformation that would later be performed by members of the drug cartels.

Why was there a need to cause and witness such suffering? Why did the slaughter have to turn into a sadistic spectacle? There was no tactical advantage in sadism, therefore one can only conclude that hatred of the indigenous combined with the perpetrator's absolute freedom to do his worst were contributing factors. As in the Bosnian case, a policy of ethnocide encouraged extreme cruelty. The Comisión de Esclarecimiento Histórico specifically documented attempts to remove all traces of ethnicity from survivors by forbidding them to wear native dress, forcing them to speak Spanish and attacking their religious beliefs.[36] Each indigenous male who was inducted into the civil patrols (PACs) was forced to kill other members of his native group in order to violently repress any sense of solidarity or community.[37] What the army wanted was to create a "new man," indifferent to the suffering of others and free of any solidarity with his community.

The massacres were the orgiastic highlights of the terror campaign. I single out a handful to illustrate the hysteria of the army on these occasions. In 1981, in pursuit of the Army of the Poor guerrilla movement, the army attacked the first village they came across, a place known as Laguna Seca, where many of the children were confined to bed because of a measles epidemic. The adult population, believing the children would not be touched, abandoned the village. When they returned, they found that some children had had their throats cut, others had been shot, and two had been hanged. In April 1998, inhabitants of Chel accused of collaborating with the guerrilla were rounded up. Fourteen adolescent girls were taken to the church and raped. The rest of the population were taken in groups of five to a bridge, where they were made to undress. Their clothes were then burned, and they were executed by different methods: some were beheaded, others shot, and others thrown into the fire. Small children were smashed against rocks and thrown into the river. Ninety-five villagers were killed. Others who had left before the arrival of the army returned to the village to bury the dead and afterward were forced to remain in hiding, some of them for up to nine years.[38] San Antonio Sinache suffered two massacres, the first in March

1982. The men had been ordered into the mountains to search for the guerrillas. During their absence, some old people were tortured and shot; others had their throats cut, among them a Maya priest; women were executed, some of them with their skirts in disarray and without their *huipil*, showing that they had been raped.[39] A second massacre in May occurred when many were shot trying to escape to the mountains. The filmmaker Pamela Yates, who persuaded a general to let her ride on an army helicopter when she was filming the documentary *When the Mountains Tremble*, found herself in Ilom in the aftermath of a massacre the army said had been perpetrated by the guerrillas, although the dead she filmed were women killed by the army.[40] Although the army professed to believe that they were rounding up guerrillas, the killing of children, old people, and women suggests the darker purpose of finishing off the work of conquest. In his book *Massacre in the Jungle*, Ricardo Falla documents mass killings in rain forest settlements whose inhabitants were evangelical Christians. Not only were priests killed but killings took place both in Catholic churches and Protestant chapels. Many of the settlers were burned to death; others escaped into Mexico.[41]

Those of us brought up in the humanities, which rest on a certain concept of the human, find it difficult to confront such a divestment of humanity. In the extreme cases I have mentioned, vulnerability creates an incentive to destroy everything that can be considered human in others by making them devour their own flesh, while atrocity merchants prove their own supremacy by eating the enemy and drinking the blood of dogs. The cultivation of sadism and the deliberate defiance of all taboos challenges any notion of the state as the guardian of the human rights of its population. The deliberate destruction of feelings of empathy in its young men would have effects long after the end of civil war. The ferocity of the kaibiles was passed on to the drug wars when their demobilized members were employed by the Mexican Gulf cartel and reinvented themselves as the Zetas, with consequences that are examined in chapter 9. The temptation to term "ironic" the recent election of Pérez Molina, a former general in the civil war, as president of Guatemala because he is expected to fight the cartels must be resisted. The election of a participant in a brutal war is an act of despair.

Virtual Apartheid: The Peruvian Way

According to the Peruvian Commission on Truth and Reconciliation, the number of indigenous killed could not be attributed to their participation in the war. Not only did they form a majority of the sixty-nine thousand dead, but thousands also had to leave the south-central region. Caught between the Sendero Luminoso, who tried to reeducate them, and the army, who identified them as *terrucos*, they were victims that both sides found it permissible to kill. It was only in 1991, when the army began to organize *rondas compesinas* (peasant patrols) and taught them how to use arms, that the indigenous began to be seen, in some sense, as allies. But the death toll was grim. Of every four victims of the civil war, three, according to Salomón Lerner Febre, the president of the Truth and Reconciliation Commission, were peasants whose maternal language was Quechua.[42] Although denying that the war was an ethnic conflict, he wrote that "the two decades of destruction and death would not have been possible without the profound contempt towards the dispossessed people of the country, expressed equally by members of the insurgent Sendero Luminoso (Shining Path) and the Army, a contempt that is woven into every moment of Peruvian everyday life."[43] On the part of the Shining Path, extermination of entire communities was rationalized as a strategic means to an end. It sought to destroy the infrastructure of the existing society and construct it anew without regard for indigenous organization or government.

As Nelson Manrique points out, "In a country highly fragmented not only by socio-economic ethnic and regional differences where anti-indigenous racism constructs differential scales of humanity, according to which the indigenous are not as human as other Peruvians, there does not exist a general consciousness that the forced disappearance of thousands and the slaughter of tens of thousands of people constitute a national tragedy."[44] There are more than fifty-five ethnic groups in Peru, and about a fifth of the population speaks an indigenous language. Yet when the conflict broke out in the province of Ayacucho, various sectors of the country were seemingly indifferent to what was occurring, before the tragedy struck those who were considered fully citizens.[45] It was less problematic to torture, disappear, assassinate, and exercise differ-

ent forms of violence and extreme cruelty against those who were considered not only different but, more particularly, unreal — those whose
lives have been negated.[46] For that reason, Quechua-speaking peasants,
especially those from rural, distant, and poor communities, became the
principal victims of violations of human rights committed in the name
of the Shining Path's armed struggle and in the defense of the state. In
its report, the Truth Commission emphasized that

> for many years, modern, urban, Limeño Peru treated the regions most
> affected by violence, the most distant and poor with indifference. Even
> when the armed conflict forcefully entered the heart of the major cit
> ies at the end of the '80s and the beginning of the '90s it was difficult to
> unite the experiences and memory of violence of such different worlds,
> so much so that the emblematic icons of victims of the conflict up to
> that point, suddenly changed skin color, language, and place of residence
> when they appeared on television screens. Images of violence experi
> enced in the center of power displaced those taken for so many years on
> the periphery of Peruvian society.[47]

Unlike the Guatemalan massacres, the war was not declared against the
indigenous as such, but there is no doubt that influential sectors of the
population held them in contempt as "primitives." The alien nature of
each side of the divide to one another came to the fore in a well-known
incident of the Peruvian civil war that was carefully scrutinized by the
Commission on Truth and Reconciliation and has since been debated
in books and articles and on the occasion of public commemorations.
It occurred in January 1983, when a group of eight Peruvian journalists
were attacked and killed in the indigenous village of Uchuraccay. Countless pages have been written on this event, but what demands attention
is the way conquest and subjugation entered into the narrative in the
guise of impartial judgment. The journalists, on their way to Huaychao
to investigate the reported killing of members of the Sendero Luminoso
by indigenous villagers, were bludgeoned to death as they tried to pass
through the nearby village of Uchuraccay in a region of the Sierra partly
controlled by the Sendero. Even though they occurred during a time of
civil war, the deaths gave rise to a national outcry because the journalists
were killed in a village of Indians.

The commission appointed by President Belaúnde was headed by the novelist Mario Vargas Llosa, the jurist Abraham Guzmán Figueroa, and the journalist Mario Castro Arenas and also included a number of advisers, including anthropologists, a legal expert, a linguist (the only Quechua speaker), and a psychoanalyst. They arrived by helicopter and spent less than three hours on the inquiry, which, as many critics pointed out, was seriously flawed. Nevertheless, Vargas Llosa wrote a skillfully worded report, gave several interviews, and wrote a number of articles and refutations of critics of the report that were later published in a collection of his essays under the attention-getting title *Sangre y mugre de Uchuraccay* (*Blood and Filth of Uchuraccay*).[48] Of the thousands of pages written on the civil war, no incident has commanded so much attention as this one, whose implications went far beyond the event and raised questions about the roots of violence, about atrocity, about discrimination, and eventually about the system of justice in a multilingual nation.

Although Uchuraccay has been exhaustively examined from every possible angle, I offer no apology for adding to this copious documentation, since it offers a complex example of discriminatory discourse and its effects. It also raises questions about the ethical status of literature and the authoritarian nature of the lettered city. Uchuraccay was one incident in the civil war between the Sendero Luminoso and the Tupac Amaru Revolutionary Movement, on the one hand, and the military and the police, on the other, but assumed extraordinary importance because the victims were journalists, posthumously commemorated as the martyrs of Uchuraccay; because it was investigated by the commission headed by Vargas Llosa, a famous novelist, public intellectual, and eventually presidential candidate and recipient of the Nobel Prize for literature; and because of the subsequent polemic over his report. It also occurred at an early stage of the civil war. One of the slain journalists, Willy Retto, was a photographer and was photographing the confrontation even as he was being attacked. This photo, along with a group photo of the journalists on their way to Uchuraccay and a photo of their exhumed bodies, was included in the exhibition *Yuyanapaq: Para recordar* (*Yuyanapaq: To Remember*) along with blurry snapshots that the photographer was taking even as the group was challenged and attacked.[49] The photos show peasants, men and women, apparently interrogating the photographer. Although one journalist has his hands raised and another is kneeling, the violence cannot be seen, but its results are shown in a photograph of the exhumed bodies strewn among stones and jars in a field, and half stripped of clothing. This and the group picture of the young men as they set out on their excursion were photographs that would divide Peru, making Uchuraccay a key national event in the war. The photographs record a moment just before death. Dramatic as this moment is, however, it cannot tell the whole story. The newspaper that had initially praised the community for killing subversives, *El Comercio*, reported that "consternation and astonishment greeted the discovery of the remains of eight journalists barbarously stoned and hacked by peasants in the locality of Uchuraccay who in a tragic misunderstanding were confused with terrorists."[50] The Vargas Llosa Commission would confirm the barbarism of the attack and describe the inhabitants of Uchuraccay as stubbornly primitive.

In his report, in interviews and polemics, and in "Inquest in the Andes," the narrative Vargas Llosa wrote for the *New York Times* that encapsulated the work of his commission, he again and again represents himself as the rational modern man faced with the alien other. In his vividly written *New York Times* article, he re-creates the thoughts and feelings of the journalists as they set out with no premonition of danger on their taxi ride and later on their hike over arduous terrain toward Huaychao, a route that would take them through Uchuraccay. This part of the narrative is told with a novelist's eye for detail. Vargas Llosa reproduces their jokes; the moment they stopped to take photographs; where they stopped for breakfast; the quarter of an hour they spent in Chacabamba with the Argumedo family, who lent them mules; their encounter with Juan Argumedo, whom they came upon sawing wood and who offered himself as a guide. This empathy with the journalists, this concern for every detail of their last journey, is in sharp contrast to the author's depiction of the Quechua-speaking *comuneros*, to whom he gives the name *iquichanos* (about which more later) and who are depicted as clinging to ancient beliefs in the *apus*, the gods of the mountains, the most illustrious of whom, he writes, is "Rasuwillca, in whose belly lives a pale skinned horseman in a palace full of gold and fruit."[51] The iquichanos, he insists, are monolingual are desperately poor and at times violent especially when their way of life is threatened. During Independence, they fought on the royalist side and refused to accept the Republic. "The few studies of their way of life depict them as jealous defenders of those uses and customs, that although archaic are the only ones they have."[52] In the official report, he describes them as "atavistic."[53]

What is striking about the account is that while the actions of the journalists and the mestizos make sense, those of the indigenous seem absurd. "They have so little understanding of the explanations of the workings of the law," he writes, "that while I explained this (that in Peru, it is illegal to kill and that judges and courts are in charge of the law) and seeing their faces, I felt as absurd and unreal as if I were indoctrinating them in the true revolutionary philosophy of comrade Mao betrayed by the counter revolutionary Dog, Den Tsiao Ping."[54] In one sentence he ridicules both the Shining Path and a millenarian culture, demonstrating the absurdity of Shining Path indoctrination through the dogma of Chinese communism but also presenting the indigenous as utterly ignorant of law and outside global history. Den Tsiao Ping, the Chinese leader who ushered in the overhaul of the Chinese economy, was regarded as an enemy by the Shining Path. But the apparent lack of understanding on display in Vargas Llosa's address is hardly comparable to that of the Shining Path's audiences, captivated by the exotic references. If the villagers did not understand, it was because Vargas Llosa was speaking to them in a language that was not their own.

Nor did he take into account that they might have had previous experience of Shining Path infiltration and had been warned by the army to be suspicious of strangers in the area, or that the community may not have been unanimous. He was clearly keen to identify magico-religious elements in the slaughter, arguing that the wounds on the journalists appeared to be ritualistic. The journalists, he claimed, were buried face down as devils or as those who had made a pact with the devil. Their ankles were broken so they would not return to avenge themselves. Why was he so anxious to identify the killings as ritualistic if not to support a preconceived notion of primitive violence? He concludes that "the violence stuns us because it is an anomaly in our ordinary lives. For the Iquichanos that violence is the atmosphere they live in from the time they are born until the time they die."[55] This is an odd comment, as if violence is anomalous in our daily life, as if our civilization does not offer daily examples of violence, from the shooting of illegal immigrants crossing borders to indiscriminate bombardment and to torture in the name of security. The explanation can only be that he is determined to depict the indigenous as *innately* violent.

Critics have emphasized that in his report, Vargas Llosa does not allow the indigenous to speak, instead assuming the authority to speak for all the comuneros of Uchuraccay, who appear in his narrative as an undifferentiated and mostly male mass. Enrique Mayer's criticism of the report is damning. "Although the testimony given during the one meeting at Uchuraccay that the Commission had was carefully transcribed, not one single complete sentence has been reproduced in the final report. There are only three words from the comuneros that Vargas Llosa directly quotes. The authenticity of their testimony is vouched for by Vargas Llosa alone."[56] But there is one notable exception to this homogeneity. As the commission prepares to leave, a woman (*mujercita*, "little woman") of the community, singing a song they cannot understand, suddenly begins to dance. Vargas Llosa described her thus:

> She was an Indian who was small as a child but with a wrinkled face of the old, with the cracked cheeks and the swollen lips of those who live exposed to the cold of the punas. She was barefoot, and wore various colored skirts, a hat with ribbons and while she sang and danced, she hit us slowly on the legs with a bunch of nettles. Was she saying goodbye according to some ancient ritual? Was she cursing us for belonging to the world of strangers — Senderistas, journalists, who had brought new motives for anguish and fear to their lives? Was she exorcising us?[57]

Vargas Llosa confesses that the incident left him deeply disturbed, for it seemed as if he were discovering "a new and terrible" history of his own country. Never had he felt so sad as

> in the twilight of menacing clouds in Uchuraccay, when we saw this little woman dancing and hitting us with nettles, who appeared to have come from a different Peru from that in which I live, an ancient and archaic Peru that has survived among these sacred mountains despite centuries of oblivion and adversity. This fragile woman was *doubtless* one of those

who threw stones and waved cudgels because the iquichana women are as belligerent as the men.[58]

Vargas Llosa's logic is interesting. The dancer is old and a woman and hence perceived as personifying that ancient and archaic Peru, and encouraging if not perpetrating the murders. At the same time, he offers a spurious generalization: iquichanas are "as belligerent as men."

In a Lacanian reading of the text, Juan Carlos Ubilluz suggests that the woman corresponds to the real as a remnant of the symbolic order, a postsymbolic residue much as industrial waste is the residue of industrial society. "Only in this sense can one say that Vargas Llosa's Indian woman is real: neither natural nor premodern, the Indian woman, like Uchuraccay, is the unwished-for product of Peruvian modernity."[59] The confrontation between a novelist, a man who has devoted his life to a literary genre that has been crucial to the formation of a national imaginary, and a woman whose culture is oral takes us back to the Conquest and the confrontation between Atahualpa and a priest bearing the Bible and what Antonio Cornejo Polar has termed the "ground zero" (*grado cero*) of this interaction, or "the point at which orality and writing do not merely reveal their extreme differences but demonstrate their mutual estrangement and their reciprocal and aggressive repulsion."[60] "Misunderstanding" is an old story in Peru.

The anthropologist Kimberly Theidon points out that the members of the Vargas Llosa commission insisted on the endemic violence of the region and that one could not really blame the villagers —"they were just doing what came *naturally*."[61] The members of the commission could therefore convince themselves that the death of eight journalists in the Iquichano territories provides the most conclusive evidence that even after four hundred years of contact between European culture and Andean culture, it has not been possible to develop a true dialogue.[62] In a searching essay on both the Uchuraccay report and on Vargas Llosas's novel *Lituma en los Andes (Death in the Andes)*, Juan Carlos Ubilluz remarks that it is easier to think of anthropological reasons for the backwardness of the Andes than to think of the state policies that produce it. "It is more comfortable, more familiar, and more convenient to think that the Andean population remains stuck in a pre-modern identity than to think of the state policies that, at the present time, cut off the modern aspiration of the Andean masses in order to favor foreign capital and determined powerful groups in the national political economy." This common sense, he argues, is a fantasy, and "the fantasy of the enclosed nation [*la nación cercada*] is thus an anthropological screen that conceals the antagonisms inherent in the present process of modernization."[63] What I translated as *fantasy* in the above quotation is the Lacanian *fantasma*. Contrary to what is usually understood, the *fantasma* is not a parallel dimension of reality; rather, it supports reality. Far from being a mere exotic fantasy of Westerners, the indigenista paradigm — the belief that the Andean world is radically other — is the support of a national reality based on the segregation of the Andean masses from a modern project that drags along a colonial inheritance, as a consequence of which they are considered less than human.

The idea of a radical separation between the two Perus is at the root of Vargas Llosa's argument, which draws a clear line between primitive violence and civilized life and implicitly between lawless violence and the protection of law through legitimate violence. And it is women, in particular, who embody the primitive. The old woman's actions are inexplicable, her words unintelligible, but nowhere does he acknowledge that his own ignorance of Quechua, a language spoken by thousands of his fellow Peruvians, may be part of the problem. On the contrary, he seems to suggest that the difference between the modern self and this archaic person is inherent in the Quechua language.[64] Twenty years later, the Truth Commission would tell a very different story, one that incorporated Quechua testimony into the account. They pointed out that the Shining Path had previously caused alarm by infiltrating the village and that demands for protection from their attacks had been ignored and continued to be ignored by the authorities. The commission further pointed out that the fear that had led the villagers to kill the journalists was not some archaic throwback but a response to a clear and present danger brought about by the Shining Path's tactics and the army's advice that outsiders should not be tolerated. In fact ethnographers working in other communities have documented the constitution of strategic communitarian identities in the service of survival of which the peasant militia (*rondas*) formed to protect communities are one example.[65]

Uchuraccay was not a community out of touch with the rest of Peru. There was a school, a church, a cemetery, and a cabildo. Situated in a strategic position not far from the center of Shining Path activities, the villagers and members of the guerrilla organization coexisted in a state of tension that came to a head when the guerrillas tried to organize a school to indoctrinate women. It was this move that aroused the hostility of some members of the community, a hostility that was aggravated when the Shining Path executed the president of the community, Alejandro Huamán. This, in turn, led the community to resist and kill five militants with stones and wooden bludgeons, months before the events of January 1983. Approving that action, General Noel, regional commander of the armed forces, sent in a helicopter with fifteen members of the security forces known as *sinchis*, who encouraged the villagers to attack any strangers. Uchuraccay was probably not so different from other communities where some supported the Shining Path and others feared them. When the journalists arrived, the *comuneros* rejected their explanations and bludgeoned them to death, burying their bodies hastily near the central square. The bodies of the guide, Juan Argumedo, and of Severino Huascar Morales, a Shining Path supporter, were kept hidden so that the *sinchis* would not suspect that the Shining Path had been present in the community and take reprisals. The community, hitherto divided, decided on a pact of silence around those two deaths and reported the deaths of the journalists as an act against terrorists. This was not archaic ritual violence but a response, albeit an erroneous response, to an intolerable but thoroughly contemporary dilemma that the Shining Path created when they demanded the support of villagers. They would withdraw from villages when threatened, leaving the inhabitants at the mercy of the army. The deafness of the Vargas Llosa Commission and the Belaúnde government to the community's demands for protection doomed it to destruction. In the wake of the massacre, there were yearly commemorations of the journalist "martyrs" of Uchuraccay, but no mention of the 135 members of the community killed, mostly by the Shining Path, out of a total of 470 inhabitants. The community itself was scattered and ceased to exist until after the civil war, when some refugees returned and settled in the "New Uchuraccay," away from their former homes.[66]

The Commission of Truth and Reconciliation went to considerable pains to underscore the dangerous consequences of misrepresentation and misinterpretation. For instance, the Vargas Llosa commission described the comuneros as iquichanos, a pre-Hispanic group known for their warlike nature. In fact, "iquichano" was not an ethnic identity, and the group's reputation for violence was, according to some historians, a nineteenth-century invention of the elites, not a historical reality.[67] It forms the basis of the divided Peru thesis: on the one hand, modern Peru; on the other, the archaic Peru impervious to modernity advanced by Vargas Llosa and apparently by the anthropologists on the Vargas Llosa Commission, who concluded that betterment and progress must be difficult for them to conceive. Yet some of the comuneros were dressed like any urban Peruvian and wore watches, 30 percent of them were literate, and one of their demands had been for schooling in Spanish, since they were aware of the disadvantages of monolingualism. Nor were they ignorant of the law and the Constitution, for they had often appealed to the Guardia Civil. They also demanded a road, a demand that hardly supports the view that they were protecting their isolation. Misunderstanding plagued the trials of the three comuneros accused of perpetrating the massacre: the proceedings were translated from Quechua to Spanish, but not vice versa, so the accused could not understand all the proceedings. Still less was there any attention to the subtleties of the Quechua language, which requires a suffix to every sentence in order to distinguish what is personal witness and what is hearsay. The Vargas Llosa Commission also failed to realize the effect of fear on communities, caught as they were between two brutal armies — on one side the military, and on the other those they termed *terrucos* (terrorists), *plagakuna* (people of the plague), *tutapuriq* (night walkers), and *malefekuna* (people of bad faith).[68] As the anthropologists Kimberly Theidon and Enver Peralta Quintero commented, after witnessing the commemoration of the journalist "martyrs of Uchuraccay," the idea that the "primitive" people might have been exercising political and intentional initiative in the context of a brutal war was outside the conceptual framework of the reporters and their families.[69]

Despite the work of anthropologists who have distinctly more nuanced assessments of the events in Uchuraccay, there is no indication that Vargas Llosa changed his views. In the novel *Lituma en los Andes* (*Death in the Andes*); in *La utopía arcaica* (*The Archaic Utopia*), a book on the writer José María Arguedas; and in numerous essays, interviews, and articles, he continued to assail indigenous culture as backward. Not only that, he revives the charge of cannibalism, attributed not only to distant ancestors but also, in *Death in the Andes*, to contemporary inhabitants tainted by the old superstitions. Victor Vich is certainly right when he describes *Death in the Andes* as a paradigmatic text for "the discussion of fantasies of power and the way in which conservative thinking goes on producing biased images of the nation, culture and ethnicity in contemporary Peru."[70]

The novel begins with a confrontation between Lituma, the police sergeant from the coast and an Indian woman who appears at the door of the outpost. "When he saw the Indian woman appear at the door of the shack, Lituma guessed what she was going to say. And she did say it, but she was mumbling in Quechua while the saliva gathered at the corner of her toothless mouth. . . . The woman repeated the indistinguishable sounds that affected Lituma like savage music" (1). Quechua is not only compared to savage music, emphasizing its primitive character; in addition, the woman salivates as she speaks, and since spitting is a form of uncivilized behavior, her speech is characterized as primitive. To be sure, the fictional character, Lituma, is not to be confused with Vargas Llosa. However, from the very outset the author affirms a division between the barbaric sierra and the common sense expressed by the man who comes from the coastal city of Piura. Lituma, an army sergeant who was one of the main protagonists of Vargas Llosa's novel *La casa verde* (*The Green House*), has become an honest and conscientious civil guard member from the north, dispatched to an area he doesn't know and can't relate to. Faced with the unexplained successive disappearances of three men, Casimiro Huarcaya, Pedrito Tinoco, and Medardo Llantac, in the middle of a civil war, he sets out to investigate their disappearance and comes up with the baffling web of superstition and fear that deeply affect him and challenge the common sense that he embodies. The novel has many subplots — descriptions of the people's trials organized by the Shining Path and the executions of villagers and foreigners, the army's cruel interrogation of a deaf-mute, and a love story between Lituma's subordinate, Tomás, and a woman whose lover he had killed. The anchor of common sense in the novel, Lituma, is condemned to live and work in this remote part of the sierra, where he learns what it means to live in a culture of fear. This fear, however, has less to do with the civil war than with magical thinking. In Naccos, the village where they are posted, there is an indigenous community, a group of workers building a road and a bar run by the aptly named Dionisio and his wife, doña Adriana, a witch with a murky past that involves the *pishtacos*.[71] The pishtacos are mysterious creatures of Peruvian folklore who suck out the innards of those they encounter.

> The pishtaco would lurk at night on the roads, on a bridge, behind a tree, appear to a lone shepherd, or travelers, or mule drivers, or migrants, or people taking their crops to market or coming back from a fair. He would come out of nowhere, with no warning, in the dark, eyes flashing. His enormous body was wrapped in the flying poncho, and it paralyzed them with terror. Then it was no problem for him to take them back to his cave with its dark, freezing tunnels, where he kept his surgical instruments. He slit them from arse to mouth and hung them up and roasted them alive over pans that collected their fat. He skinned them and made masks out of their faces and cut them into little pieces and crushed their bones to make his hypnotic powder. (182)

Thus the cannibal surfaces once again this time in what is perceived as the absurd belief system of the indigenous.

There are many ways of reading the pishtaco myths that are, indeed, embedded in highland lore, but they all come back to the theme of the exploitation of the victim's body that is transformed into a helpless robot or a body to be consumed. It is a myth about losing free will, and given the exploitative relations that prevailed in the region, it is a way of accounting for loss of will among the conquered. In Vargas Llosa's version, the pishtaco myth confirms the primitive cruelty of the region, the irrational superstitions and cruel actions that include cannibalism. What is interesting is that he does not seem to be aware that modern societies are just as prone to believe in alien creatures, as is evidenced in the current craze for vampires and zombies, which might well be telling us something about our civilization.

Investigating a Sendero attack on a mine, Lituma spends a night there with an engineer, Shorty, and a Danish professor, Red, presented as an authority on Andean beliefs, which he has studied for thirty years. In this way, Vargas Llosa is able to represent his negative views on indigenous belief as if supported by European intellectual authority. Lituma overhears the Dane describing the "religious passion" of the Chancas and Huancas "for human viscera, about the delicate surgery in which they removed their victims' livers and brains and kidneys and ate them in their ceremonies, washing it all down with good corn chicha" (146). "'The Huancas were animals, Red," declares Shorty, "And the Chancas too. You're the one who told us about the barbaric things they did to keep their apus [mountain gods] happy. Sacrificing children, men and women to the river they were going to divert, the road they were going to open, the temple or fortress they were building — that's not what we call civilized" (152). Because a road is being constructed in Lituma's district of Naccos, the reader can anticipate that it will be the scene of human sacrifice.

The Danish professor, the voice of reason and knowledge, asks what seems to be a series of rhetorical questions. "Can any ancient people pass the test? Which of them were not cruel and intolerant when judged from a contemporary perspective?" (153). Lituma, in the light shed by an acetylene lamp, imagines a "golden halo, like the ones in religious pictures, might suddenly appear around his white hair," thus giving him priestly or saintly authority (154–55). Listening to him, Lituma feels nostalgia for his native Piura, "whose outgoing people could never keep a secret, its deserts and mountains without apus and pishtacos" (152). The transparency of the north stands in sharp contrast to the impenetrability, the secrecy, not to mention the cannibal ancestors of the highland people. When one of the engineers wonders "if what's going on in Peru isn't a resurrection of all that buried violence" (153), he is describing the novel's central theme. The old practice of human sacrifice before building a new road will be revived in the present.

What is odd about *Death in the Andes* is that the atrocities of the civil war, although inserted in the novel, are marginal to Lituma's investigation of the three disappeared men — an albino, a deaf-mute, and the former mayor of a village who is in hiding from the Shining Path. While the

Shining Path is an ever-present threat, it becomes clear that the threats that arise from superstition, the cannibalism and witchcraft practiced in the area, are of far more concern. The crazy witch woman, Adriana, wife of the owner of the only bar in Naccos, is the first to tell him that human sacrifice is still practiced in order to appease the apus, although it takes most of the novel to persuade Lituma that studying the customs of the ancient Peruvians might help him understand what is going on (175). As Juan Carlos Ubilluz points out, it is as if Vargas Llosa is claiming "that the sociocultural backwardness of the Andes (the mediate cause) was the only and true cause of violence in that region." He describes it as the novelistic expression of the same ideology that underlies the Uchuraccay report.[72] Like Mexico's heart of darkness, according to which there was an Aztec in every Mexican, this notion of buried violence offers an alibi that absolves modernity, attributing violence instead to primitive elements as if the entire region, its mountains and avalanches and its inhabitants, are not only alien to modernity but also in danger of contaminating the rest of Peru. Indeed, Lituma himself, after surviving the *huayco*, the disastrous Andean storm, thanks a rock for saving his life: "mamay, apu, pachamama, or whoever the fuck you are" (180).

It is even more bizarre that in *Death in the Andes*, women are said to have been the most active participants in the magic rituals, reminding us of the little old woman of Uchuraccay. Doña Adriana describes how in the past, women had taken charge in an annual festival, and it was they who hunted their sacrificial victim, the lord of the fiestas. "Only the women went to hunt him down on the last night of the fiesta. They were drunk too, wild like the wild girls in Dionisio's troupe. . . . They formed a circle and closed him inside, singing, always singing, dancing, always dancing. . . . The circle got smaller and smaller until they caught him. His rule ended in blood" (237–38). Adriana, the bar's owner, is meant to evoke the Bacchae, while her husband is transparently named Dionisio, evoking not the roots of Western thought in Greek philosophy but the persistence of the primitive tribe.

But it is a drunken road-builder who finally reveals the mystery of the three disappeared, a denouement that ties the Shining Path to cannibalistic practices. One of the missing men, Medardo, had been the mayor of a community and in flight from the Shining Path, thus endangering Naccos, where he had taken refuge. He was sacrificed, along with the albino and the deaf-mute, and they were then eaten. "'Everybody took communion. I didn't want to, but I took communion, too,' the labourer said in a rush, 'that's what's fucking me up. The stuff I swallowed'" (275). The stuff he had swallowed was human flesh. Cannibalism is the heart of darkness in Vargas Llosa's imagination. True, he believes that novels reflect the imaginary, not the real, but his imaginative writing also contributes to the deeply embedded prejudices already present in the social imaginary.

So-called archaic and violent pasts exist like a subconscious in many of the novels of the boom. In Carlos Fuentes's short story "Chac Mool," for instance, the Aztec rain god comes alive, and in "La noche boca arriba" ("Night Upturned") by Cortázar, the alien Aztec past, with its cult of sacrifice, engulfs an inhabitant of the modern world who becomes a sacrificial victim.[73] But in Vargas Llosa's Peru, the indigenous represent a danger to the modern nation. He belabored this point in a book in which a political viewpoint is presented in the guise of literary criticism. *The Archaic Utopia* is a study of José María Arguedas, a writer, anthropologist, and Quechua speaker who had traveled all over Andean Peru and spent much of his life writing of indigenous cultures, their traditions and their transformation. He was cruelly caricatured by the Shining Path as a "magical whining nationalist" who sported "a Hitler-like moustache."[74] The Right ridiculed him as a romantic *indigenista*. Twenty years after his suicide in 1969 and after the devastation of the civil war, Vargas Llosa dedicated over three hundred pages to this writer, toward whom he had, at best, ambiguous feelings. Although he granted that Arguedas wrote one successful novel, *Deep Rivers*, "his other works are partial successes or failures but are always interesting and sometimes disturbing."[75] But literary criticism is only part of his interest, a cover story for a more extensive project — that of destroying what he regards as Arguedas's utopian belief in collectivism and his supposed opposition to modernization.

Here I am concerned not with the accuracy of Vargas Llosa's reading of Arguedas but with the sense of urgency in the writing, which comes from a need to demonstrate that the utopian dream of community and collectivity that supposedly sprang from pre-Columbian sources was not only an impossibility but has once and for all been discredited. What lies behind this attitude is a political philosophy that is presented in the guise of literary criticism. *The Archaic Utopia* is not simply a tract. It is an impeccably researched book by a novelist who was trained as a literary critic and who conscientiously explores every document, beginning with the letters Arguedas wrote just before killing himself in 1969. At the same time, there is a clear determination to disqualify the bulk of Arguedas's writing as "a form of understanding literature, that for better or for worse, has become obsolete in most of the world" (17). For Vargas Llosa, a myth of progress hurried on by free individuals underwrites literature as well as politics. Commitment, on the other hand — the obligation of writers toward their own societies — turns writers into ideologues, he claimed. "Writers who force themselves to write committed literature, forcing their true nature and betraying their demons probably produce mediocre works" (28). In Vargas Llosa's vocabulary "demons" refers to the subjective underworld that goads the authors to write, as if there is a clear division between the external demands on a writer and the subjective.

As a folklorist, Arguedas had collected examples of a folk cult around Inkarri, the Inca leader whose decapitated body, it was believed, would someday become whole again. As an ethnographer, he at times espoused versions of theories of development that were widely accepted at that time. As a writer who grew up in the highlands speaking Quechua, he was sensitive to the intricacies and beauty of the Quechua language and deeply aware of the marks left by the Conquest on a people whose culture was by no means primitive or simple. Vargas Llosa's emphatic desecration is disguised as a rescue operation that decontextualizes Arguedas's writing in order to separate what is of literary value from his supposed belief in the absurdly archaic utopia. Referring to the legend of the return of the Inca, he argues that the mutilated god who was remade in his subterranean refuge was "an emblem of the longing for resurrection of that archaic utopia to which he [Arguedas] was instinctively faithful even when his reason and intelligence told him that the modernization of the region was inevitable and indispensable" (163). The book is thorough and well documented but nonetheless single-minded in its determination to resist any positive assessment of indigenous peoples.

Vargas Llosa's own political philosophy, culled from Karl Popper's *The Open Society and Its Enemies,* is presented as not only rational but utterly opposed to the magical and religious world that Popper dismisses as primitive and premodern. Popper argued that the magical or tribal or collectivist society was a closed society, and the greater the effort to return to it, "the more surely do we arrive at the Inquisition, at the Secret Police, and at a romanticized gangsterism. Beginning with the suppression of reason and truth, we must end with the most brutal and violent destruction of all that is human. *There is no return to a harmonious state of nature. If we turn back, then we must go the whole way—we must return to the beasts.*"[76] Reviewing the social aspects of philosophy from Plato to Hegel and Marx, he traces the "collectivist" theories that, in his view, correspond to the horde and the tribe, not to a community of free and sovereign individuals. The problem with Popper's theory is that the tribal system is too rigidly defined, too carefully designed as a foil for the open society, and the generalizations are too crude. Vargas Llosa not only accepts uncritically that tribal societies lead to totalitarianism but seems to think the beliefs of the Peruvian indigenous have no parallel in the so-called advanced "open" societies, even though millions in the United States are still waiting for the apocalypse.[77] In "Questions of Conquest," an essay written just before the Quincentennial celebrations, he reads the Conquest in Popperian terms. The followers of the Inca let themselves be slaughtered, being "incapable of making their own decisions" and "were incapable of taking individual initiative. . . . Those 180 Spaniards . . . did possess this ability."[78] The solution to the ongoing problem of "cultural heterogeneity" anticipates the conclusion of his book on Arguedas: "Indian peasants live in such a primitive way that communication is impossible. It is only when they move to cities that they have the opportunity to mingle with the other Peru. The price they must pay for integration is high—renunciation of their customs, and the adoption of the culture of their ancient masters. . . . Perhaps there is no realistic way to integrate our cities other than by asking Indians to pay that price. . . . If forced to choose between the preservation of Indian cultures and their complete assimilation, with great sadness I would choose the modernization of the Indian population because there are priorities, and the first priority is, of course, to fight hunger and misery." As Misha Kokotovic points out, this argument rests on the assumption that neoliberal development will extend to the indigenous population and that indigenous peoples "live primitive lives in isolation from the modern world."[79]

Vargas Llosa embraces an idea of progress that is not much different from nineteenth-century positivism. Although this attitude is not identical to the cruel racism of the *gamonales* or the attitude of the white mestizo landowners and traders who oppressed the rural population, and it bears little resemblance to the genocidal intent of the Guatemalan military, it amounts to what Hector Díaz Polanco calls "ethnophagy"—that is, a method of eliminating indigenous difference that relies on "the assimilating effects of the multiple forces put into play by the system."[80] Indeed, *The Archaic Utopia* concludes with "ethnophagy," not as a project but as a reality, as the author joyfully celebrates the emergence of a new informal Peru in which emigration from the highlands contributes to "cholification," that is, the conversion of the indigenous into "cholos," the city-dwellers who have shed traditional customs and beliefs. "Thanks to these ex Indians, cholos, blacks, mulatos and Asians," he writes,

> for the first time there has developed a popular capitalism and a free market. What all Peruvians can agree on is that the Peru that is in process of formation will be nothing like the resuscitated Tahuantinsuyu, nor a collective society of an ethnic nature, nor a country at war with the bourgeois values of commerce and the production of wealth, nor closed off from the world of exchange in defense of its immutable identity. (335)

The negatives are intended to throw into relief the positive values of the informal economy personified by the street vendors, who, he fails to note, have no legal protection and often a meager income and whose underground survivalist "culture" was brilliantly captured in the film

October, directed by Diego and Daniel Vidal, in which the main character is a pawnbroker and money-lender, living among an underclass who
survive on borrowing, cheating, and petty crime.

Some of the enthusiasm for this popular capitalism was inspired by
Hernán de Soto's *The Other Path: The Informal Revolution in the Third
World* and its argument that there was an alternative to the discontents
that had helped to fuel the Shining Path's uprising. That alternative was
embodied in a new class of urban entrepreneurs working in the informal economy. De Soto argued that cities have conferred individuality
on their inhabitants and individual effort has come to predominate over
collective effort, an argument that clearly resonated with the novelist,
but he also acknowledged the infiltration of violence and criminality
into everyday life that Vargas Llosa fails to mention. Rather, the mi-
grants and their black-market capitalism, commonly considered symptoms of the decay of Latin America's cities, are presented as bringing
about changes necessary for the achievement of economic and political
modernity. Vargas Llosa believes that the transformation of Peruvian
society "is already under way, made a reality by an army of the current
system's victims, who have revolted out of a desire to work and have
a place to live and who, in doing so, have discovered the benefits of
freedom."[81]

An argument can be made that Vargas Llosa's attitude toward the
indigenous is cultural and not racist, that it does not pertain to the indigenous as ethnically different. Yet it is difficult to separate culture
from skin color, since the latter is a form of distinction, employed both
by sectors seeking to assert their superiority by reason of being whiter
and by indigenous people judging white people to be foreign. But the
underlying problem is what Victor Vich termed an authoritarian place
of enunciation, "which belongs to a Latin American discourse dedicated
to constructing continental reality upon two antagonistic forces that,
following the ideology which governs the enunciation, are always presented as irreconcilable. We must acknowledge," he argues, "that our
modernity is still exercised and conceptualized within a social imaginary that retains a number of colonial heritages that are not at all democratic, that are fundamentally hierarchical, and that in Peru have always
prevented the imagination and the practice of a community of equal

subjects, with the same rights and with enough institutional pathways to demand them."[82] Ileana Rodríguez, following Benjamin Arditi, argues that liberal politics cannot operate in what she terms creole societies, in which slavery, debt peonage, indenture, and many other forms of labor that have actually been sponsored by liberalism prevailed. She argues that the basic tenets of liberalism are inoperable in such societies, and she cites Charles Taylor's question as to whether the supposedly neutral set of difference-blind principles of the politics of equal dignity (rights and freedoms) is in fact a reflection of hegemonic culture.[83] Indeed, the Vargas Llosa solution, which foresees the automatic dissolution of difference in a newly urbanized society while maintaining social inequalities, illustrates her point well.

Madeinusa, the work of the talented filmmaker Claudia Llosa (Vargas Llosa's niece), shows how seductive both the closed-society argument and the solution of flight can be. Set in an indigenous village in the high Andes, it is the story of a girl capriciously named Madeinusa who lives with her sister and would-be abusive father, the mother having run off to Lima. At the beginning of the film, she is shown putting rat poison around the outside of the house and brooding over a box of possessions in which she keeps her mother's earrings. Their town is isolated and clings to a bizarre tradition: the inhabitants believe that between Good Friday and Easter Sunday, when Christ is dead and not yet resurrected, there can be no sin. Awaiting the festivities during which Madeinusa will appear as the Madonna, tensions in her household mount. She sleeps in the same bed as her father and her sister Chona, who cannot help hearing the father's urgent sexual demands (his *droit de seigneur*) on Madeinusa. The incestuous relation seems to reflect village society itself. There is no getting away from the fact that, like her uncle, Claudia Llosa views the indigenous villagers as walled in, utterly separate from the rest of Peru. During the Easter celebrations, no one is allowed in the village (its Quechua name, Manayaycuna, means "the village that no one can enter") for the Dionysian revels, during which the women choose the men they want in an orgiastic dance. In another odd ritual, the mayor (the girls' father) cuts off the ties of the males of the community; it is unclear whether this action is a castration ritual or a severing of the group from civilization. As they prepare for the festivities, a geologist, the allegorically named Salvador (Savior), is stranded in the town, unable to travel to the zone where he works because there is no transport during the festivities. The mayor locks him in a room, since the villagers do not want strangers to be present. Dressed as the Virgin, Madeinusa unlocks the prison and gets the gringo to take her virginity and to promise to take her to Lima. In the melodramatic denouement, after her father has had sexual relations with both Madeinusa and her sister and broken the sacrosanct maternal earrings, she poisons him and puts the blame on Salvador, an accusation that certainly means a death sentence for him, while she takes the bus to Lima, which might be seen as a liberating move. But it is liberating only if we accept the premise of the film — the absolute division between the closed society of the village and the freedom promised by the city. As Juan Carlos Ubilluz points out, "Her liberation is hardly born out by the ending, which shows her hugging a doll as if it were a substitute for her absent mother."[84]

A desire for the end of ethnicity, identified with the archaic and the cannibal, underlies the different solutions to the indigenous "problem." The prospect of a nation without ethnic difference justified the slaughter in Guatemala, while in Peru the modernizing power of the city was supposed to convert the indigenous into citizens who had shed their ethnicity and become "cholos." Such policies assumed that the indigenous were not capable of constituting their own modernities, an assumption that has now been challenged in Bolivia, in Chiapas, in Chile, and increasingly in Guatemala and highland Peru.

"Dead?"

"Dead. Do you know why I am telling you this, because she was tall, white (gringa) and attractive. But she was already in a bad state. She could not satisfy. The troops were raping her."

(With her throat cut)

"Yes, of course. They had her behind the table; they had covered her breast and were raping her." (the soldiers)

There were a lot of them. About 12 or 14. I chased them out with a stick. "Savages. She's dead."

"She's hot, officer," they said. . . .

"Well, we cut off the head and hands and threw her in the river."

—Testimony of "El Brujo" before the Truth and Reconciliation Commission (Peru),
   Informe final de la Comisión de Verdad y Reconciliación

THREE | Raping the Dead

The matter-of-fact language of the officer belies the extremity of the event described — the torture and slaughter of a girl, an insurgent nicknamed "la Gringa," given as evidence by one of the torturers before the Peruvian Commission on Truth and Reconciliation.[1] Although in this instance, the matter-of-fact language cannot disguise the fusion of lust, labor, and death and the perverse desire of dark men for white women, in the civil wars of Peru and Guatemala the vast majority of the victims were indigenous women. In Guatemala, rape was an instrument of genocide, an extreme event, a prelude to the annihilation of the indigenous.[2]

How can rape be described? For the most part survivors use euphemisms that cannot possibly convey the extent of its physical and psychic damage. And what of the rapes that preceded a horrible death and where there was no survivor to tell the story? Rape followed by execution *performs* expulsion from the human by first reducing subjects to a state of abjection when the "I" no longer is sovereign and then disposing of them as so much rubbish. Abjection places the victim outside the bonds of the human for the abject is "inscribed in a primordial chaos, marked by a primary indistinctness or formlessness. Which is to say that, before differentiation, ordering is a relation to lack of distinction. The abject is, in other words, not a pole in a binary distinction but indistinction itself."[3] In other words, rape not only abolishes any claim by the victim to be in the same "human" category as the rapist, who is confirmed in his supremacy, but also annihilates woman as the feared other. Such extreme masculinity is a rage against the womb, and as the Peruvian Commission pointed out, "in the internal conflict men are marked by a model of 'warrior' masculinity characterized by the exercise of violence, aggressiveness and the exhibition of force."[4]

For the raped woman, the sense of humiliation was overwhelming. A witness who testified for Guatemala's Recovery of Historical Memory Project, described how, while one man raped her, others felt her breasts, hit her, and burned her with cigarette stubs:

> It was really humiliating, it was a mixture of hatred, a mixture of frustration, a mixture of absolute impotence. I spent much time here in great pain in the vagina, with great pain in my parts and in the stomach because every time a man had relations with me, it was as if the desire to go on living were diminished more, more and more and of course everyone who had the pleasure beat me afterward, because it was like saying "I used you" and using words such as "whore" and "Piece of shit, I fucked you."[5]

For the victim who survived, the sexual act was transmuted into unbearable and unforgettable torment. Its devastating effect went beyond the individual, for it attacked the family as the very basis of society, inducing feelings of isolation and desperation. Women who survived wartime rape often suffered physical damage and were left isolated. As Diken and Laustsen wrote of former Yugoslavia, "The victim is excluded by neighbors and by family members. Hence the rape victim suffers twice: first by being raped and second by being condemned by a patriarchal community."[6]

Although there are many similarities between what happened in Bosnia and the rapes committed during the civil wars in Guatemala and Peru, it is also important to stress the special circumstances in those countries. The Peruvian Commission cited a significant detail in noting that a young woman used the term "royalist" of the perpetrators, thus linking present-day violence to the Spanish army and the wars of independence.[7] The commissioners also pointed out that the attackers were referred to as *patrones* or bosses, underscoring that for these women, male abuse of power was part of a history of conquest and domination. To rape and then kill suggests more than an act of warrior triumph. Is it too exaggerated to suggest that it is a reenactment of the Conquest itself? — that, like the massacres described in chapter 2, it attempted to finish the work of conquest? Soldiers and police often used guns, which they thrust into the vagina or anus in a kind of symbolic reversal of impregnation. Such symbolic acts of violence combine the utmost cruelty with extreme misogyny.

While there is no knowing the exact number of rapes committed during the wars both Truth Commissions acknowledged that the majority of raped women were indigenous, an estimated 88.7 percent in Guatemala; in Peru 75 percent were Quechua speakers.[8] The Guatemala Commission documented 1,465 cases but estimated the total to have been around 9,411, an estimate that cannot be complete because many women died as a result of rape and torture and because the surviving victims often felt guilt and shame and found it difficult to narrate the experience.[9] The civil wars struck at the very root of a system which, however unjust, had allowed the indigenous to maintain their languages, their traditional dress, and certain customs.

However incomplete or imperfect the commissions' documents, they clearly emphasize that rape is a violation of universal human rights and a form of torture, and support these claims with extensive references to rulings by international organizations, especially the United Nations and the Inter-American Commission on Human Rights.[10] In Peru both the Shining Path and the MRTA (Movimiento Revolucionario Tupac Amaru) committed rape (see chapter 5), but statistics show that 83 percent of rapes were committed by agents of the state; these crimes often took place in barracks and police stations. In Guatemala, soldiers were trained to rape using prostitutes.[11] The Guatemalan Commission on Historical Clarification underscored that the cult of masculinity exacerbated by military training had as its necessary counterpart the degradation of women, stating, "Wars exalt the values implied in the masculine paradigm that assumes the superiority of men over women and violence as a demonstration of macho power."[12] A Guatemalan witness confirmed this, declaring, "In the military career, there is a positive triumphalist mentality as if to teach them that they are unique, that there are no laws, much less dignity and respect. As a result of military service, men become machista and disrespectful, with the result that they violate all the cultural norms of family and community: they always say, 'Here you are going to be a man.'"[13] Thus wartime rape can be understood as a mark of sovereignty acted out on the body of women, a sovereignty that demands the degradation not only of the woman but also of her family and offspring, who were often forced to witness the rape.

A Genocidal Rape

What it meant to be a man was demonstrated in the savagery of the Guatemalan massacres, which were of such a magnitude that "on a first reading, it could even provoke a certain incredulity."[14] The events were made credible through the reiterated details, the exhumations of bodies, and "the images, still vivid in the minds of witnesses — of cut throats, mutilated corpses, pregnant women with their bellies cut open with bayonets or machetes, bodies *strewn [sembrados]* on stakes, the smell of *burnt flesh* of those burned alive and dogs devouring abandoned bodies that could not be buried"; these images were so vivid as to persuade the members of the Commission that they must "correspond to a real event."[15] Children ("the seed") were killed by beating them against the wall or by throwing them alive into graves where they were crushed by the bodies of dead adults. During such operations, girls were separated from the rest, then raped and killed. Mass rape was a systematic and planned practice in what the Guatemalan Commission ultimately judged to be genocide.[16] Describing "shows" with prostitutes that preceded a military operation, *Memoria del silencio* concludes that "it was not a question of isolated acts and sporadic excesses but a strategic plan. The devaluation of women was absolute and allowed the army personnel to attack them with total impunity because they were indigenous women of the civil population."[17] Women were raped in front of their children, and the children were often savagely killed. Old women were raped. In such actions, rape was an act of conquest designed first to debase and then to exterminate the enemy. Nor was rape an isolated act committed by one person; rather, it was the work of a group, a performance for comrades, that was so degraded that it inspired disgust. A witness described a woman who lost consciousness when raped several times by twenty soldiers: "She was in a pool of urine, semen, and blood; it was really humiliating, a mixture of hatred, frustration and impotence."[18] Reading the Truth Commission reports is a devastating experience and questioning every detail seems impertinent. Memories are not photographic and are always partial. But there can be no doubt as to the ferocity deployed, a ferocity that speaks of the overwhelming force of the rapists and the extreme helplessness of the victims.

A mass rape observed by a fugitive shows exactly the overwhelming force deployed by the troops to annihilate a lone victim. "One day I managed to escape, and from my hiding place, I saw a woman. They shot her and she fell. All the soldiers left their backpacks and dragged her like a dog to the bank of the river, they raped and killed her and also a helicopter that was flying overhead came down and they all did the same with her."[19] It is the helicopter that makes the scene bizarre. The technologically sophisticated machine descends to earth so that the crew can rape a helpless, dying, or dead woman. Think of the difference in force and sophistication between the machine, the modernity of technology, and the elemental nature of the act, which, far from being bestial, is all too human in its intent.[20] How much power does it take to conquer a wounded female? What beast would commit such an act?

Army witnesses who gave evidence before the Guatemalan Commission on Historical Clarification confirmed that rape was ordered by the commanders who gave "precise" instructions as to how to inflict the utmost cruelty, for example, by first raping the women and then shooting them through the vagina or the anus.[21] Catharine A. MacKinnon, writing of Bosnia, calls this "rape under orders."[22] One Guatemalan witness stated that the soldiers were thinking not of "excesses," *only* of "pillage and rape," as if violence against women could be counted along with the guaranteed spoils of war. Some of the soldiers who participated in mass rape welcomed the opportunity. "It was a 'gift' from the commanders who announced 'here's meat for you' ['Hay carne muchá']."[23]

Where it was the extermination of a people that was at issue, women's reproductive organs were mutilated in every possible way, their breasts or bellies were cut and fetuses were torn from pregnant women's bodies.

In one case, a woman had her tongue and ears pierced after being raped by a number of soldiers: they "took out her eyes, they took off her breasts and left her on a stone, they cut off the soles of her feet.... They left her hanging on a stake, what was left of her body, naked."[24] This destruction of the body after the rape was a message of extreme hatred.

Many witnesses' accounts described women being raped in front of their children, husbands, or fathers, as a deliberate attack on the family itself. Children and adolescent girls were raped, and in one act of cruelty, two young girls were raped for fifteen days and then forced to dig their own graves before being buried alive.[25] Since members of the family, adolescents and children, pregnant women, mothers, and babies would be killed anyway, one must conclude that such ancillary acts were intended as performances for the benefit of the perpetrators, who were thereby renouncing all social ties to family, to others.

That rape was indeed a weapon of war was graphically illustrated by a Guatemalan episode in which the eighteen-year-old wife of a man who had been executed was raped by forty men, a mass rape ordered by their commanding officer. She was six months pregnant and raped in front of her mother. Troops who refused to participate were punished. The men who raped her dressed her up as a soldier and then went on raping her until, "half dead, she was burned on a hillside."[26] What were the killers trying to express when they dressed the woman as a soldier as if they were playing at dolls? Perhaps she had to be disguised as an enemy combatant so that the final torture could be inflicted. Many equally bizarre scenes are recorded in *Guatemala: Memoria del silencio*. Women were forced to dance, to cook for the army, and were raped to the music of the marimba. It is ironic that the kaibili anthem "Himno al macho patrullero" has nothing to say about the courage it takes to slaughter the defenseless.

In Rabinal, naked women were beaten and told they were cows; "they treated them as if they were cows exchanging the stallion."[27] The very postures forced on raped women were designed to maximize their abjection. "They put them on all fours and then shot them, placing the gun in the anus or vagina."[28] Made to crouch in animal-like postures, their bodies defiled, the victims no longer resembled human beings. "They treated us like animals. They gave us nothing to eat except for three tortillas. They carried big sticks and hit us all as if we were just dogs, and they came in to interrogate kicking us. At night the soldiers came to rape the girls, the youngest."[29]

Rape did not always end in death but survival could be agonizing. A girl returning from the market in Rabinal was raped, and her father was badly beaten and brought into the room where she was lying naked on the table, where she was raped again. When the father did not speak, the captain cut off his penis and put it between her legs, deliberately violating the taboo against incest. As shocking as the act itself was the reaction of the girl's husband, who told her that the army had the power, that it was useless to complain — if she hadn't gone to market, nothing would have happened.[30] Civilian authorities set up by the army and civil patrols all committed rape under orders.

That rape was routine has been documented many times. In the army controlled town of San Bartolomé Jocotenango, widows and women whose husbands were hiding in the mountains were forced to serve in the military bases or in segregated houses, where "they would live under threat and constant surveillance subject to the whims of the soldiers and patrollers who could decide when and how they wanted to 'occupy' them."[31] Attempting to account for such atrocities confronts one with a harsh truth — the truth that humans greatly outdo the animal in acts of cruelty that we then describe as "bestial." The Guatemalan examples show that not only can men be made to kill and rape "under orders" but that they can be persuaded to do so in ways that goes beyond anything in the murder files.

The civil wars struck at the very roots of traditional arrangements and family ties in a bid to abolish indigenous difference either through extermination or by recruiting indigenous people into the state appa-ratus against the insurgency and forcing them to participate in acts of violence against their own communities. The ground was prepared by the state of exception that allowed the army to operate outside any guar-antees of juridical rights, and certainly outside any covenant of human rights. In this light, rape was a calculated act that targeted monolingual women wearing traditional dress and speaking indigenous languages, for women as bearers of tradition must be incapacitated or destroyed in the cause of creating a new Guatemala cleared of the guerrillas and

without ethnic difference. As Greg Grandin argues, the army's genocidal campaign was depicted in the Truth Commission report "not as
state decomposition but state formation, a carefully calibrated stage in
the military's plan to establish national stability through an incorporation of Maya peasants into the government institutions and a return to
constitutional rule."[32]

Demonic Pleasure: The Peruvian Scene

Although the genocidal designs of the Guatemalan army were not repli-
cated in Peru, the Peruvian state offered no respect for either indigenous
women or for the women accused of belonging to the Sendero. Because
of President Belaúnde's initial reluctance to engage the army following
the first Sendero attacks, the Sendero was able to occupy indigenous
villages and indoctrinate their inhabitants. In 1982, the government declared a state of emergency in the city of Ayacucho and eight provinces,
inaugurating the "dirty war" that would escalate during the presiden-
cies of Alan García and Alberto Fujimori.[33] Both the Shining Path and
the MRTA (Movimiento Revolucionario Tupac Amaru) committed rape
(under circumstances that I examine in chapter 4), but most rapes were
committed by the army when they reoccupied areas that had been over-
run by the Shining Path or when they took women to be interrogated
in barracks and police stations. Even old women from the indigenous
villages were not spared, for the army often assumed that the indigenous
supported and aided the Shining Path and were therefore *terrucos* — the
denigrating label applied to the insurgents.

What happened when the army invaded areas formerly occupied by
the Sendero was graphically described by a young victim. The soldiers
came into the house, hanged the family from the rafters, and broke
their arms. They tortured the eighty-year-old grandmother by putting
a heated iron into her vagina and anus "while interrogating her as to
the whereabouts of her Senderista son. They threw kerosene over her,
burned her and then took her off to be killed."[34] In massacres men and
women were separated and the women raped.[35] The supreme torture
was raping women in front of their children or their husbands.

But for the men of the Peruvian army, it was the female guerrilla who
aroused the most ambivalent feelings of desire and rejection. This was

graphically demonstrated in an incident reported by a male prisoner. Hearing weapons being fired and troops shouting, "*Terrucas*, this is how you are all going to die, we're going to burn you," he saw troops in formation and witnessed a demonic scene by the light of fires:

> I saw them bring in a body. I saw that it was a woman. She was naked. They threw her on the ground as if she were just a thing and they began to abuse her in a degrading manner, all the soldiers abused her sexually. At first the woman said nothing but after a number of them, she said, "Don't do it anymore." There were about 30 or 40 men. At the end, they all stood around and began to shoot in the middle of the fire and they told her she should speak and she didn't reply. Apparently she had fainted. Four people masked in black appeared. They crucified her. Apparently they had an instrument, like a dagger measuring more or less 15.20 centimeters, others held guns of normal caliber but with a silencer on the end of the barrel. They crouched between the woman's legs and put the knife in the vagina. The girl woke up, cried out and fainted.[36]

Finally the body was put into a sack and thrown into a truck.

The reader of this evidence might well feel a certain skepticism. How could the person estimate the caliber of the guns?, we want to ask. On the other hand, it is the girl's pathetic "Don't do it anymore" that bestows authenticity on the event and allows us to grasp the essentials of the scene — the difference between her powerlessness and the immense force that operated against her. This goes beyond rape and torture. It is, as in some of the Guatemalan incidents mentioned, a demonic ceremony, an act of solidarity for the soldiers that culminates in the insertion of the dagger into the vagina, an act that amounts to a symbolic destruction of womanhood. Raping the dying or the dead turns rape into *Lustmord*, that is, pleasure in death itself.[37]

The combination of liquor and exaltation no doubt was responsible for orgies of violence like the one that took place in the Capaya base in Abancay. A prisoner saw fifteen or twenty women being chased across the patio by soldiers who tore off their clothes and raped them. "It was a pack of soldiers who threw themselves one by one on the same women, they were hundreds of soldiers. The orgy lasted all night, and some women had their legs broken. On the following day, all the bodies lay there, none of them moved, they had their legs apart, and some were turned over."[38] Could there have been hundreds of soldiers? Perhaps not. But the orgiastic atmosphere and the group hysteria tell us how rapidly rape can become atrocity.

As in Guatemala, Peruvian soldiers adopted rituals both to establish solidarity and to demonstrate their warrior status. Sometimes they identified themselves by nicknames or wore hoods, giving an air of sinister and archaic mystery to the rapes and killings, as if they were performing acts which were outside any human norm. Commenting on the ritual aspect of mass rape, Kimberly Theidon writes that she was told that soldiers anointed their face and chests with blood. "These ties of blood joined the soldiers and the bodies of the raped women and served as a way of forging these ties."[39] But this ritual can also be interpreted as the reverse, as a breaking of ties, as a sign of absolute domination over the abject other. Such group activities must certainly rank among the deadliest of the war.

Many of the incidents of rape reported to the Commission on Truth and Reconciliation, especially those committed in police stations and barracks, were opportunistic, as the rank and file took advantage of women prisoners, who were often naked and shackled, to vent their hatred and anger. Victims were not only raped but also beaten, kicked, and subject to all kinds of humiliation. In one case, soldiers urinated on a woman whom they afterward forced to do domestic labor.[40] Such acts of denigration identified women as inferior. One survivor described being raped anally and vaginally until she was almost dead while the soldiers insulted her, shouting, "Bitch betrayer of Peru, this is how you'll die."[41] During rape, women were routinely insulted as prostitutes or animals, as if the verbalization confirmed the degraded state of the victim and helped spur on the perpetrator to more acts of violence. Police passed their penis over the women's faces and mouths and beat them on their stomachs, as if to emphasize the deadly campaign against the body's reproductive potential.

The Peruvian critic, Rocío Silva Santisteban has described these acts as a "rubbishing" (basurización) of the female body.[42] She relates such behavior to the disgust (el factor asco) that separates those who feel disgust from those deemed impure or dangerous. In other words, they are *basura* (rubbish). Rubbish is what is ejected, dispensable because lacking in form, and is thus related to abjection. The "rubbishing" of women is illustrated in a photograph included in the exhibition and book *Yupanapaq*, published by the CVR. It shows the body of a young woman killed in action, soiled and half naked, being thrown into a truck to be dumped who knows where.[43]

What is striking is that what is pleasure for the man is pain for the woman, for there is no doubt that rape was intended as a form of torture and was usually accompanied by beatings and threats. A witness describes how when she was being painfully raped, her attacker was cheered on by the others especially when "she was groaning more, complaining more." They advised the rapist "to do it this way or that." They put their hands in her vagina. The worst pain was when they grabbed her breast "as if they wanted to pull it off."[44]

Some women were passed around, raped first in their villages, then taken to an army barracks and, as in Guatemala, gifted to the soldiers as *carne* (meat).[45] Giving victims over to the troop was known as *la pichana* or "the sweep."[46] That such incidents took no account of the suffering of the victim or the consequences was illustrated when they reportedly boasted, after raping a thirteen-year-old, "Qué rica que estaba Lourdes" ("How great was Lourdes"), as if the girl had incited them.[47]

That rape was also a theater of punishment was graphically illustrated in the case of María Magdalena Monteza, a nineteen-year-old girl tortured by officers of the DINCOTE (the army intelligence service). She was made to walk naked. They painted her lips, injected her with a substance that made her dizzy, and then raped her. It was the first time she had had sexual relations. On the following day she was raped again. "My body did not seem to belong to me," she said; eventually she confessed, even though she was not implicated with the insurgency. But María Magdalena was unusual because of the legal case she brought against officials of DINCOTE. Because she had "confessed," she was sent to Chorrillos prison, where she gave birth to a child of torture. During her trial, she charged the army with sexual assault. Despite the evidence of sexual acts, the attorney's office declared that "it had not been possible to fully identify the presumed authors of the crime" and that therefore an essential element of the case, "the individualization of the presumed author or authors of the crime," was lacking. The CVR collected its own circumstantial evidence, which included the timing of the pregnancy and the mental state of María Magdalena. They concluded that "rape or the threat of rape of imprisoned women by agents of the prison system and the security services of the armed forces amounts to torture."[48] In 1992, María Magdalena was condemned to twenty years in prison; in 1998, she was finally pardoned. The fact that she was imprisoned at all is a stark demonstration of the way justice worked in favor of the rapist.

Those who survived faced the shame of having been raped and the fear of rejection by their community. "If there is a theme that strikes a person dumb, it is rape," writes Kimberly Theidon.[49] These women were "blamed by their companions, their families and by the agents of the State and even by those who committed rape." They were considered "used" or "wasted." Little wonder that they had resort to euphemism. A Guatemalan witness speaks of "touching," a term also used by the Bosnian rape victims. A Peruvian military officer confessed that it would be difficult for an indigenous woman to say right out "I have been raped": "For them it is shameful."[50] Rape violates the integrity of the body of the individual or of the community to such an extent that it becomes unspeakable. A Peruvian witness speaks of *acoso sexual* (sexual harassment); in Guatemala women used words such as *pasar* or *usar*. Another survivor describes her ordeal thus: "I was beaten many times . . . put into a toilet with excrement, they hung me by the arms, they put me in a bath of water, took off my clothes and humiliated me in the most intimate [aspect] of womanhood [*en lo más íntimo en lo que uno es una mujer*], and they are things that one cannot get over rapidly."[51] In detailed testimony given before the Peruvian CVR, a witness speaks of her rape:

> In the very same headquarters, they threw me down, began to beat me, they beat my feet, legs, sides and breasts, they pulled my shirt and they raped me. They were several, I remember up to the third who threw himself on top of me, even when I was shouting. I shouted all the time that I was innocent, they looked at me naked and said, "Look how thin she is, she won't take it." And one of them, not content with having raped me, put the barrel of the machine gun [*metralleta*] in my anus and said, "You still haven't had it here."[52]

For the military and the police, on the other hand, rape was a public demonstration that the victims were without honor, and *puta* (whore) was the insult of choice. They sometimes marked a woman as raped by cutting her hair.

Indigenous people often chose not to report rape because they had no confidence in state institutions; because of the absolute impunity of the perpetrators, who were often living in their community; and because of shame: "Unlike sin, shame resists verbalization, it [rape] cannot be elevated into a sign of faith or belonging."[53] Furthermore, rape affects the integrity of the family and violates those deeply sedimented norms that are not easily subordinated to national or international law, especially in societies where family custom weighs more heavily than the decrees of the state. "Honor" still functions as an unwritten code in many sectors of Hispanic societies, as it did in Bosnia. In sixteenth-century Spain, the purity of the wife was the guarantee of the male's honor, his standing in society, and had to be defended by husbands or fathers. Honor underscores the gap between individual behavior and legality and indicates a place where the law is ineffectual.

For the Andean people, honor was a question of family and community integrity. In indigenous communities honor is not an individual value but a communal one, such that rape endangered the weft and warp of the social bond. This helps to explain why women rejected the offspring of rape and why the children of rape were generally stigmatized. Indigenous women impregnated after rape tried to abort, while others "allowed" the undesired babies to die, sometimes by leaving them on a hillside.[54] Husbands often abandoned raped wives or abused them as spoiled goods.[55] Indigenous women were even discriminated against by those sent to help them, as Kimberly Theidon discovered. Before undertaking fieldwork in the war-torn region of the Andes, she had met in Lima with an organizer for a civil rights group who told her that the Andean people did not suffer like the rest of the population, that "they" had already forgotten it all, that "we" are capable of abstract thinking and that is why we suffer so. "They only think of their daily bread and their animals. They don't think beyond that. And that is why they have not suffered like us. They're not capable." Quite the contrary, Theidon would show. Quechua speakers understand that the "human" is not a

fixed quality; one can fall out of the human. Her book is a detailed record of interviews and field notes that pay due respect to the intricacies
and specificity of Quechua terminology for the emotions. She notes that
painful thoughts (*llakis*) descend to the heart and take over the body,
suggesting that thinking is not separated from emotion and that bad
memories can invade a person and take over. Theirs are "remembering"
bodies, and those memories can be passed on to the next generation.[56]
Mothers cannot suckle their babies "because they would transmit their
fear and the evil memories and they were afraid of contaminating the
minds of their children with their 'milk of anger and worry.'"[57] It is this
that makes the example of Giorgina Gamboa, extensively discussed by
Rocío Silva Santisteban, so striking. At age sixteen, she was raped by
seven *sinchis* (the special forces), first in her home and then in the police
station of Vilcashuamán, as a result of which she became pregnant. She
spent five years and three months in prison, and her charges against the
rapists were dismissed as a trick. When pregnant she was taken to make
her case to the minister of the interior, who dismissed her with a bad
joke about naming her child: "If a boy, 'Sinchi,' and if a girl, 'Sincha.'"[58]
The degree of insensitivity beggars understanding. She demands an
abortion because she fears she will give birth to a monster, but the authorities refuse. She gives birth to a baby girl, whom she first plans to
put out for adoption but then decides to keep. What is important in this
case is the active repossession of her life and body. In 2002, when she
appeared at a public hearing of the Truth Commission, she was with her
then twenty-year-old daughter. In her essay on the case, Santisteban argues that in refusing the role of victim and giving her testimony publicly,
she inserted her own voice into the national narrative and was able to
overcome the limitations of the Truth Committee, which had adopted
a "tutelary" attitude toward victims. Georgina speaks to the members
of the Commission, to journalists and on behalf of "human rights." Her
testimony was "organized according to the urgent need to highlight her
search for justice and the need that this be situated in a broader public
space than her community."[59] What this demonstrates is that the appeal
to human rights can be a useful tactic against governments and authorities for whom sexual crimes against women do not count as crimes.

Rape is difficult to represent, so Claudia Llosa's feature film *La teta asustada* is unusual in its attempt to depict the trauma from the point of view of an indigenous woman.[60] The *teta asustada* (the terrified breast) is the corporal response to rape that had caused the mother's milk to be contaminated and the distress passed on to her daughter, Faustina, who inserts a potato into her vagina as protection against rape even though the war is over and she lives in the city. But Faustina's home in Lima is the hillside shanty town where she lives with a predatory uncle and an extended family who happily imitate the city-dwellers, even constructing a swimming pool in the yard and arranging elaborate wedding celebrations for their sons and daughters that are modeled according to popular images of sophisticated occasions. The seduction of modernization is contrasted with the power of tradition. Faustina works as a maid for a neurotic woman (Aida) to earn money for the transfer of her mother's corpse to the home village. After inviting Faustina to sing in public, Aida capriciously abandons her on a city street in the middle of the night. Though she arrives home safely, the incident turns Faustina against her employer, and she steals the pearls that were supposed to be awarded to her. In an act of liberation, she has the potato removed from her vagina and sets out from Lima to bury her mother's body not in the village but in the desert sands on the edge of the ocean — a gesture that completes her liberation from tradition. As in Llosa's earlier film, *Madeinusa*, Lima represents the promise of emancipation from the burden of the past and its archaic superstitions. The idea of the movie was initially inspired by Kimberly Theidon's book *Entre prójimos*, although the film does not reflect Theidon's respect for indigenous healing practices.

Both the Guatemalan and Peruvian Commissions cited were able to draw on the numerous declarations on women's rights emitted by the United Nations,[61] underscoring the fact that nation-states had failed to legislate for the human rights of women. Although both commissions recognized and documented the acts of cruelty against women during the wars, peace has not brought fundamental changes except that atrocity is now privatized. Despite the number and strength of women's organizations, including organizations of indigenous women, families of the disappeared, and NGOs under the aegis of UNIFEM (the women's fund of the United Nations), their denunciations have not sufficiently disturbed the deeply embedded attitudes that put women in a lower category of the human. The melancholy truth is that "feminicide," a term coined to describe the rape and death epidemic in Ciudad Juárez, Mexico, is not confined to that country. The rape and extermination of women in Ciudad Juárez and in Central America in "peacetime" raise the uncomfortable prospect that atrocity of this kind has now been "privatized," a possibility I discuss in chapter 9.

Nosotros somos profesionales de la guerra y estamos preparados para matar. La guerra es así. Yo no le puedo decir a un soldado, al que se le ha preparado para matar, "Ahora no mates." ¿Y si mañana existe un problema, le vamos a decir, "Ahora sí mata"? (We are professionals of war and we are trained to kill. War is like that. I can't tell a soldier who has been trained to kill, "Don't kill now." And if there's a problem next day, shall we tell him, "Now kill"?)
—Quoted in Silva Santisteban, *El factor asco*

FOUR | Killers, Torturers, Sadists, and Collaborators

The killer without remorse is a character in video games, films, and fiction, but it took Jonathan Littell's novel *The Kindly Ones* to suggest that we are all potential torturers and murderers. Max Aue, his protagonist, commits plenty of atrocities and at one point comments, "There was a lot of talk, after the war, in trying to explain what had happened, about inhumanity. But I am sorry, there is no such thing as inhumanity. There is only humanity and more humanity."[1] Because I am reluctant to think we are all potential killers, I want to explore in this chapter what makes certain people not only killers but killers who are willing to inflict the utmost cruelty.

I particularly recall the cruelty inflicted on Guatemalan women and children returning from market and who were stopped by a military patrol. "They took their donkeys and everything they had bought. They took the women and children to a place nearby. They stripped the women naked, tortured them and left them hanging with sticks in their genitals for people to see. They broke the heads of the children."[2] The scene, described in matter-of-fact language, horrifies because of the sheer motiveless brutality and because the women were brutalized for no other reason than that they were indigenous women, and the children were killed because they were children. Was the atrocity a regression to a barbaric past or the announcement of things to come, now that any pass- erby can fall victim to a drug gang? Judith Butler suggests that "violence is surely a touch of the worst order, a way a primary human vulnerability to other humans is exposed in its most terrifying way, a way in which we are given over without control, to the will of another, a way in which life itself can be expunged by the willful action of another."[3] While vulner- ability may "humanize" some, for those who entertain fantasies of mas- tery, it invites displays of power that exceed any calculation.

In his book *War and Gender: How Gender Shapes the War System and Vice Versa*, Joshua S. Goldstein argues that men are trained to cultivate aggressiveness from childhood, that misogyny plays a part in that train- ing, and that war is the culmination. But all men do not participate in atrocities and torture, and all women are not innocent spectators. Giorgio Agamben has an interesting commentary on the story of the werewolf, the man who takes off his clothes and turns into a wolf: "The transformation into a werewolf corresponds perfectly to the state of ex- ception, during which (necessarily limited) time the city is dissolved and men enter into a zone in which they are no longer distinct from beasts."[4] But is "bestiality" proper to the beast, or is it human, all too human? The scenes of atrocity that took place in remote villages and the scene of torture in a barracks or a police station have no parallels in the animal world. And though they happen during the states of exception, this still does not account for the willful and opportunistic participation in killing and torture.

Although the end result of atrocity and torture may be the same — the death of victims — they respond to different impulses, the first often being orgiastic and the latter calculating, even though the pleasure of the torturer is involved in both. While massacres are group activities, torture is not practiced in the heat of battle, and the torturer must cal- culate the degree of punishment a victim can support without dying. In the Stanley Milgram experiments (discussed further below), students acting the part of the torturer, when ordered to inflict more and more degrees of electroshock, obediently did so even when the "victims" were at the threshold of death.[5] But laboratory situations are not quite the same as torture chambers. In an interview, a Uruguayan soldier who requested demobilization from the army after going through army courses on torture, acknowledged that "sometimes a little sadism enters into it, for instance when electroshock is applied to the testicles."[6] Alcohol and drugs may have contributed to the savagery of atrocities in which troops attacked bodies, especially the reproductive organs. In Guatemala, the soldiers cut off the penis and thrust it into the mouth of the victim; they jumped on the stomachs of pregnant women to kill the fetus. Victims were impaled by seating them on a spike. Why this need to punish bodies, mutilating them in every possible way? In Littell's *The Kindly Ones*, when faced with the tactical problem of overflowing graveyards and the immense number of victims who have to be exterminated, a kind of mass hysteria develops among the killers. A similar savage hysteria seemed to have taken hold of the kaibiles who massacred the inhabitants of the Guatemalan village of Dos Erres, flinging women and children onto the dead bodies of men in the ditch. As they finished their work, "they were laughing as if nothing had happened."[7] Recording incidents such as this, the members of the Commission for Historical Clarification recognized that this degree of cruelty raised difficult questions. How did the participants come to commit "extremely immoral acts that disturb the civilized conscience"? How could one explain "insulting and attacking the beliefs and symbols both of Christian religion and Maya spirituality that are united in the culture of the majority of our people"?[8] And, one might add, why was the vulnerability of the victims such a powerful incentive? Atrocities can occur only when moral and religious interdictions have been removed and when any awareness of the humanity of the other has been thoroughly eradicated by a process of debasement. It also enacts a fantasy that, in Slavoj Žižek's words, "constitutes our desire, provides its co-ordinates; that is, literally enacts our desire." I am stretching the term "desire" here beyond any Freudian meaning, to include the desire to harm others.[9]

The name of the Guatemalan special forces, the kaibiles, was derived from Kaibil Balam, a Mam indigenous leader who during the Conquest managed to evade the conqueror Pedro de Alvarado and whose name means "he who has the strength and cunning of the tiger." As with the El Atacatl battalion in El Salvador (chapter 7), the appropriation of the names of indigenous heroes and Maya terms such as *cuaz* (brother) was part of a psychological warfare that involved adopting these names not in order to understand the indigenous but in order to take on their powers. One of the kaibili camps was named Xibalbá, "the house of fear," a place inhabited by the dead and by the lords of death and sickness according to the Popol Vuh, the book in which Maya beliefs were recorded.

The recourse to indigenous belief and magic has nothing to do with guilt, remorse, and redemption, much less with ancient cults; rather, it reflects the fantasy of lording over death. The intellectual author of the extermination campaign against the indigenous, Colonel Héctor Gramajo, compared the "Thesis of National Stability" to the *curandero*'s egg, thus relating it directly to indigenous magic. The curandero (the native healer) exorcises evil lodged in the body by drawing it out with an egg. The Thesis of National Stability, which looked to a future without ethnic difference, was a program for exorcising the evil of dissidence and the painful psychic consequence of cruelty. It enables Gramajo to envisage a future without remorse or memory, and it recasts the Thesis of National Stability as a native cure.[10] The appropriation of Indian magic by oppressors was not a unique practice, nor was it an anachronism. Writing of the atrocities on the rubber plantations of early twentieth-century Colombia, Michael Taussig argued that the magical attraction "is not only a cunningly wrought colonial *objet d'art*: it is also a refurbished and revitalized one. It is not just primitivism but third world modernism: a neocolonial re-working of primitivism."[11] He then points out how the word "magic" itself "magically contains both the art and politics involved in representation, in the rendering of objecthood. In the colonial mode of production of reality, as in the Putumayo in Colombia, such mimesis occurs by a colonial mirroring of otherness that reflects back onto the colonists the barbarity of their own social relations, but as imputed to the savagery they yearn to colonize."[12] Such are the fantasies engendered by conquest. But now we are in late twentieth-century Guatemala, not early twentieth-century Colombia, and it is a modern army that is taking on the supposed beliefs of the conquered. Magical appropriation of the kaibili explodes into the present like a nightmarish version of Walter Benjamin's *Theses on History*.

The training of the kaibiles was modeled, according to the Truth Commission Report, on a number of antecedents, including the US

Rangers, the Colombian lancers, Peruvian and Chilean commandos, and the US Army.[13] It also mentions the courses organized at the School of the Americas training camp in Panama, where the instructors were North American officers and petty officers, the majority of whom had combat experience in Vietnam. Training included "techniques of survival in extreme situations of combat, torture techniques of prisoners . . . indoctrination in anticommunist ideology. . . . As part of their training they simulated attacks, penetration and the destruction of villages."[14] The training was brutal, and it was not uncommon for cadets to suffer injury or death.

Originally deployed near the frontier with Belize, which some officers would like to have annexed to Guatemala, the kaibiles' camps were named El Infierno (Hell) and La Pólvora (gunpowder), names that proclaimed their destructive capacity and their proud assumption of evil. According to the Truth Commission, their mission was to prepare combatants and officers of lesser units in the conduct of special operations: "to develop initiative and maintain morale at every moment, principally in critical situations and special operations, and to select by means of arduous training and under physical and mental pressure those elements of the Army who were capable of realizing commando operations."[15] No doubt this training accounts for the extreme brutality during operations such as the Dos Erres massacre, when they bashed children's heads, committed rapes, and forced pregnant women to abort by beating them on their stomachs or jumping on them. As the Truth Commission reported, "At the end of the day, after executing women and children, they rejoiced."[16]

After the peace accords some of the kaibiles were reportedly recruited by Los Zetas, the Mexican enforcement cartel, the paramilitary organization responsible for the spectacular prison break in Zacatecas in May 2009. Los Zetas have also perpetrated numerous killings and beheadings and were recently reported to control many areas of Guatemala, particularly areas bordering on Mexico. They are also involved in immigrant smuggling and extortion. Their methods and ruthlessness have become legendary.[17] They have even been active in the Congo. Postings on the web included videos of their training and brought many responses from young Latin American men who yearned to join them.

The combination of rational planning, magical thinking, and the utmost brutality recalls Hitler's Germany, where language mystified the cruelty. An item in the kaibiles' "Decalogue" stated that "when alien forces or doctrines [*fuerzas o doctrinas extrañas*] attack our country or the army," the kaibil is a "killing machine."[18] "Alien" is a powerful word, one that has an element of the nonhuman or the not-properly-human. Did they believe that "alien doctrines" had entered the indigenous like a succubus and converted them into enemy aliens? Did they believe that alien doctrines had infiltrated children?

The Torturer's Story

Credit (if one could call it that) for expanding the repertoire of cruelty is due to the hysteria of the Cold War, which led the United States to support totalitarian regimes in Latin America as bulwarks against communism. The Doctrine of National Security propagated by the School of the Americas justified the war against an internal enemy, while as Rocío Silva Santisteban has pointed out, the dirty war that ensued was waged without the inconveniences of the Geneva Convention, which had established certain standards for the treatment of prisoners of war.[19] The School of the Americas trained many of the most sinister and notorious figures of the 1980s and 1990s, men like Rios Montt of Guatemala and Hugo Banzer of Bolivia; Colonel Monterrosa, who ordered the massacre in El Mozote in El Salvador; Roberto Viola and Leopoldo Fortunato Galtieri, who both, at different times, belonged to the military government of Argentina; Miguel Krassnoff of Chile, an important officer of the DINA (Dirección de Inteligencia Nacional) who was responsible for torture and disappearance and was finally charged in 2011. It is estimated that the School of the Americas in Georgia, founded in 1946, trained 61,000 Latin American police and soldiers. Clandestine experiments by the CIA during the Cold War included the use of LSD and other drugs, sleep deprivation, and the use of prisoners in potentially deadly experiments.[20]

Of course torturers did not need to be trained in the School of the Americas, but the school provided a good cover story when it designated the war against the guerrillas a war against communism. The guerrillas and left-wing militants undoubtedly felt that they were fighting against injustice and on behalf of the underclass, but the "war on communism" enabled military governments to believe that they were actors in a global conflict and to justify killings on an unequaled scale, as well as torture. Indeed, the Doctrine of National Security, according to the Argentinean Commission for the Defense of Health, Professional Ethics and People's Rights, ensured that "from this perspective, any opponent to the established social order is considered an enemy of the state. As enemies of the state, opponents are outside the bounds of state protection and thus vulnerable to arbitrary treatments, such as torture and, ultimately, extermination."[21] Because the attack on opponents was designated as war, the extraction of information through torture meant not that the torture victims' lives would be spared but rather that they would be killed and their bodies disappeared. Elaine Scarry's essay on torture underscores the fictional justification for the interrogation: "The questions, no matter how contemptuously irrelevant their content, are announced, delivered, *as though* they motivated the cruelty, *as if* the answers to them were crucial."[22] What is crucial is the betrayal, which turns the victim into a traitor. While intense pain obliterates the sense of self and the world, the torturer is free of pain and feels no identification with it, such that he is "able to bring it continually into the present, inflict it, sustain it, minute after minute, hour after hour."[23] Although I have some reservations about Scarry's thesis that I state in chapter 7, it is certainly true that the degree of one person's physical pain measures another person's power and immunity.

Many contributors to the anthology *When States Kill* claim that "contemporary Latin American states have practiced different forms of terror . . . in a politically rational, calculated, modern fashion."[24] In a monumental discussion of modern torture, Darius Rejali argues that state-sponsored terror is "part of a modern political system based on the same rationality that characterizes modern, bureaucratic societies."[25] He also shows that forms of torture that leave no mark have been extensively practiced not only by terror states but also by democracies, including the United States. However, I am not altogether convinced by claims that contemporary torture practices are modern and bureaucratic, for what was more bureaucratic than the Inquisition, with its detailed accounts of interrogation? Jacobo Timerman, imprisoned by the Argentine military, mocked the notion that it was technologically sophisticated in its methods, pointing out that it was as if the torturers were "trying to create another, a more sophisticated image of the torture sites, as if thereby endowing their activity with a more elevated status. The military encourage the fantasy; the notion of important sites, exclusive methods, original techniques, novel equipment, allows them to present a touch of distinction and legitimacy to the world."[26] He found the notion of torture's "modernization" ludicrous:

> That conversion of dirty, dark, gloomy places into a world of spontaneous innovation and institutional "beauty" is one of the most arousing pleasures for the torturers. It is as if they felt themselves to be masters of the force required to change reality. And it places them again in the world of omnipotence. That omnipotence, in turn, they feel assures them of impunity — a sense of immunity to pain, guilt, emotional imbalance.[27]

In Argentina, where the preferred instrument of torture was the cattle prod that had been used for decades, it was not the methods of torture that were innovative but, as I point out in chapter 8, the disappearance of bodies, which was made necessary by the global reach of organizations such as Amnesty International and the United Nations.

The idea that torture was just work is, not surprisingly, supported by the published confessions and the interviews with torturers. Although the publication of such confessions may respond to the need for sensationalism that the market encourages, they *produce* banality as a strategy and downplay any pleasure they may have felt. In an interview with Jennifer Schirmer, a G2 torturer in Guatemala presents torture as a career opportunity, as if he had been a graduate student looking for his first job. "Many young people like ourselves who enjoy living in a better environment [and who enjoy being] able to drive cars and carry pistols, well, we try to get ourselves assigned to the section called G2." He describes the work of G2 as follows: "The reason G2 exists is to kidnap and torture until our subjects are wretched and maimed. They are assassinated, buried, or left by the side of the road. That is the work we do."[28] But this air of normalcy, this pretense of just doing a job, disappears when he begins to describe his training. He was initiated by being thrust into a cell with a captive who would die in any case. Armed only with a knife, the trainee has to figure out "how to torture that person, how to kill that person and if you have enough courage to do so . . . and then, from there, you begin to do your work, making pieces of that person, to do it like one cuts up an animal." The process he says, "lasts only one or two hours" (286), a disclaimer that denies what must have been an agonizingly slow death for the victim.

Although he acknowledges that it makes him uneasy to think about these things, even to the point of asking for God's forgiveness, his claim that one needs "courage" is hardly persuasive when it comes to killing an unarmed man. Between any sense of pity for the prisoner and the power of the military institution, there is no contest. The latter prevails over innocence and justice. For, as he points out, whereas informers are allowed to live, those who do not give information "because they are innocent or because they are rebels and they don't want to say anything, then these people are strangled, tortured, and finally assassinated" (289). The difference between guilt and innocence is unimportant, and torture involves not the judicial task of winnowing the innocent from the guilty but the instrumental purpose of separating the useful from the useless. Page DuBois, writing on a history of extracting truth through torture that goes back to the Greeks, suggests that torture flourishes in "intolerance of difference, inability to permit democratic exchange." Most particularly, she argues that "torture has become a global spectacle, a comfort to the so-called civilized nations, persuading them of their commitment to humanitarian values, revealing to them the continued barbarism of the other world, a world that continues to need the guidance of Europe and North America, a guidance that is offered in the form of a transnational global economy controlling torture as one of the instruments of global domination."[29] The application of the "Doctrine of National Security" illustrates her point exactly. National security justifies torture in military regimes and is used not only for getting information but also as a form of extreme punishment, as was clearly the case in the G2 torturer's training session.

The testimony of the G2 torturer is often contradictory. He enjoyed his work, he says, because it was a form of vengeance for the death of his parents, and yet he wants forgiveness for those he has hurt. He is fatalistic, knowing that at thirty-one it is too late for him to change and that he will die young. He recognizes that "when you are no longer useful to this section, your own comrades will be the ones who are going to kill you" (293). He is a mere instrument, someone who has sacrificed free will to an external imperative he knows to be flawed.

Torturers are essentially middlemen who execute orders from higher officials against whom they feel resentment. Discussing the testimony and an enactment of remorse given before the Peruvian Truth and Reconciliation Commission by a former army torturer, Rocío Silva Santisteban underscored his resentment against superior officers who remained immune from punishment. El Brujo had not only tortured and killed but had also sold information to the families of prisoners and the disappeared. Silva Santisteban lists as his crimes against humanity the practice of group rape, bribes (money bribes from men, sex from women), tortures accompanied by orgies, psychological tortures (e.g., threats to cut off the penis, or in the case of women to kill their children, or in the case of children the threat to kill their mothers).[30] Although Santisteban cites El Brujo as an example of the banality of evil, I would make a distinction between the men who try to normalize torture in their discourse, and torture itself, which can never be banal for the tortured.

As León Rozitchner stated in his introduction to the testimonies of a group of Argentine women who had survived the ESMA detention center in Buenos Aires, "We believe that . . . crime and murder, whether individual or collective, by the state or by society, although they may be 'normalized' and bureaucratic, are not and can never be banal."[31] He goes on to affirm that "those who practiced it were well aware that they were performing dirty work for superior officers who could rationalize the methods without ever being implicated." That is why one of the recurrent motifs of the torturers' confession is that they were scapegoats for the upper-echelon officers who gave orders. This, rather than remorse, is what motivated so many testimonies, as was spectacularly demonstrated in Argentina in 1995, when retired navy captain Adolfo Scilingo broke ranks and publicly denounced his superiors, declaring, "The Naval Mechanics School turned me into a criminal, used me and then threw me away. Why should I be complicit in their cover up?"[32]

Scilingo had been an ESMA officer who put prisoners onto planes, where they were anesthetized by a doctor, stripped of their clothing, and thrown to their death in the ocean. He was told that it was "a Christian, and a basically nonviolent form of death," an interesting indication that the superior ranks were sensitive to the charge of cruelty, while failing to recognize that throwing people from planes was a cruel form of murder.[33] In 1976 and 1977, between nineteen hundred and two thousand prisoners were killed in this way. Scilingo's determination to give the interview was motivated not by any lofty design but by a feeling that it was an injustice when two fellow officers and friends who had engaged in torture were refused promotion by the Senate while superior officers were protected. What was wrong, in his view, was the unfair treatment of officers, not the cruel deaths of subversives. When his interviews with the journalist Horacio Verbitsky were aired on television and published in the book *El vuelo* (*The Flight*), they caused a sensation because they revealed what many already suspected but had never been public knowledge — that the disappeared had been ruthlessly slaughtered.[34]

One of the most detailed accounts of the apprenticeship of a torturer was written by the Peruvian journalist Ricardo Uceda, who interviewed the disgruntled secret service agent Jesús Sosa. After the downfall of Fujimori in Peru, Sosa gave Uceda an extended interview and made the case that he was fighting an enemy in which all methods were justified.[35] At the age of twenty-one he was selected for undercover work during the early stages of the campaign against the Shining Path guerrillas at a time when the secret service knew very little about intelligence gathering, much less about the guerrilla organization. As a recruit he went undercover as a street vendor in Ayacucho, even though his undercover disguise was totally unconvincing: the agents were immediately recognized as strangers to the region. Soon afterward the subalterns were given a different task — that of digging graves and finishing off prisoners. This would become Sosa's métier. He was sent to Totos, a remote outpost in Shining Path territory that was nicknamed "Fantasy Island" because there, it was cynically claimed, the insurgents fulfilled their desire of dying for the revolution; it would acquire a sinister reputation, since no prisoner came out of the barracks alive. Sosa was left to deal with captives as he saw fit. In one of the first groups to be tortured, he first tried hanging them from a beam and beating them; when they did not confess, he shot them. He was a believer but did not think God would disapprove of what he was doing.[36] Silva Santisteban points out that all his actions corresponded to an instrumental logic and that when he began his career, he was operating under a government that was democratic, unlike the military governments of the Southern Cone.[37] Execution evidently came easier to him than interrogation: executions became routine, as he himself was the first to admit. "Torture had become a work. At times you understand it as a challenge and as a disagreeable form of labor."[38] His duty was clear. All those suspected of terrorism merited death — even Elvira Munaylla Morales, who had become a captain's mistress after being taken prisoner and confessing that she had participated in Sendero executions. Even though the captain pleaded for her life, Sosa was implacable. He shot her when the captain was away from the base.[39]

When it came to killing, he was an efficiency expert, especially when the number of executions began to increase. "It was essential that the prisoner die instantly, from a single shot in the forehead and if possible when he or she was not expecting it. . . . As for burials, they needed to be planned — ditches dug beforehand — and with an impeccable finish, with a thick layer of stones and earth."[40] Because of the need to cover up the huge numbers of executions, bodies were often hastily buried near the barracks. In 1985, he was forced to supervise the removal of between five hundred and fifteen hundred decomposing bodies that had been buried too near a barracks, a nauseating task for him and his troops. This incident reveals the problem of concealing killings on a massive scale. In the many television interviews he gave after Fujimori's flight from Peru, he explained what he did without any indication that he regarded his actions as wrong. His efficiency, the rapid executions, his ability to locate suitable burial grounds, his foresight in bringing supplies of shovels for excavation made him a valuable asset. Uceda attributes his acceptance of his job as executioner to the obedience inculcated in army training and to his religious beliefs, which assured him that he was doing God's work "because I don't believe God supports these shitty terrucos."[41] It was only when things began to go wrong that he had doubts. Transferred to Lima, he was incorporated into the notorious Colina group under Major Enrique Martín, which committed a number of extrajudicial killings for which President Fujimori would later be convicted as the intellectual author.[42] These included an attack on a fund-raising party in Barrios Altos in 1991, in which a nine-year-old child was among those killed, and the notorious arrest and execution of nine students and one professor of the University of La Cantuta. On this occasion he claimed not to know that the group would be executed. Although he denied having participated in the execution, in a television interview he insisted the executions were justified because the victims had helped plant a car bomb that had exploded in Tarata Street, Miraflores. Not only was this not the case; the fact that there was no attempt to bring the students to trial and charge them was also a clear indication of the lawlessness of the Peruvian state at this point. Sosa rationalized such murders and executions on the grounds that Peru was at war and the victims were the enemy. The slaughter of a child in Barrios Altos was simply collateral damage. Three of the executioners of the Cantuta professor and students interviewed separately by Uceda assured him that

> at the moment when they pressed the trigger, they did not feel pity, fear or enjoyment or any other sensation supposedly connected to having killed someone. They did not feel satisfaction for having avenged innocent people nor remorse because the students had not been judged. They were Senderistas and ought to die, they believed. Most of all it was an order and the important thing was to finish the job as quickly as possible.[43]

According to this statement, the executioners were anaesthetized against feeling remorse, pity, or horror for what they were doing because they were acting under orders.

Uceda comments on the fact that the La Cantuta operation was an ongoing affair. Twice they dug up the bodies they had buried because the burial places were not safe enough. The story of how maps of the burial ground found their way to the newspapers *El Diario* (a pro–Shining Path paper) and *Sí* (of which Uceda was editor) illustrates the conspiratorial atmosphere of the Fujimori presidency. The Colina group were tried by a military tribunal, and Sosa was condemned to fifteen years imprisonment but was released in 1995 when an amnesty law was passed.

Sosa's career shows how obedience becomes both the justification for cruel acts and an alibi when the legitimacy of those acts is questioned.

Even when put on trial, he did not question his own actions, only the judgment of superior officers, especially Major Martín. Nor does he mention that torture went on in the Colina headquarters, despite the discovery of the horribly mutilated body of Mariela Lucy Barreto Rioganda, a Colina employee accused of divulging information about the burial site of the Cantuta students. Interviews with Sosa were conducted on television by a young woman who did her best to show outrage. Such interviews like those with Osvaldo Romo in Chile situate the viewer or reader in a dubious no-man's-land between curiosity and titillation, in which truth becomes secondary to the sensation. To accept that the killer is only doing his job is to become the accomplice. What can be garnered from the torturers' tales is that, although the torturers uniformly defended themselves as workers obeying orders, this was nothing more than an alibi for their own enjoyment of power. Ever since the trial of Adolf Eichmann, those responsible for torture and extermination have claimed to be doing a job, obeying an order. It is a standard defense, even though it didn't work in the Eichmann case. Yet there is a substantial difference: Eichmann sent people to their deaths in their thousands even during the final days of the Reich, but he himself was not an executioner.

The defense of the Latin American torturers was that there was a state of exception, an ongoing war, and that the "terrorists" were enemies of the state. Yet even in war there are international laws governing the rights of prisoners. The concealment of their methods, the secret burial grounds, the rapes, and the use of torture by military governments were so many admissions that what was being done was a crime and that they knew it. Neither Romo nor Sosa nor the G2 executioner was forced to become a torturer. Romo was a civilian and the others could probably have transferred to another unit, as was the case of the Uruguay torturer.[44] Moreover, Sosa not only executed prisoners but became a member of two clandestine groups, first the Scorpions and later the Colina group, that were engaged in rogue activities, allegedly with the connivance of President Fujimori. What distinguishes these men is not the banality of doing a job but their enthusiasm for it. The role represented an injection of power for people who would otherwise have had none. Their willingness to give interviews on radio or television or for newspapers and books suggests not only the need for self-justification but also their need to believe, like Max Aue in *The Kindly Ones*, that everyone, given the circumstances, would have acted the same. Nevertheless, their power was acquired at a price. Sosa had moments of nausea and disgust. El Brujo and the G2 torturer felt the need to clear their consciences. Romo was the only one of these torturers who justified his role to the very end, although he too refused to confess to raping women.

Becoming Cruel

Atrocity committed by those not usually considered mad demands elucidation. Since Dostoevsky's *Crime and Punishment* (or even earlier in Shakespeare's *Macbeth* and Mozart's *Don Giovanni*), authors have explored the psychology of evil. But many contemporary films and novels are less concerned with the metaphysical question of evil and more with the mechanics. The Brazilian film *Tropa de elite* (*Elite Squad*)[45] and the Salvadorian novel *El arma en el hombre* (*The Weapon in the Man*), by Horacio Castellanos Moyá, are different versions of how men become killing machines.

The Brazilian film follows the career of a thoughtful mild-mannered black student named Matias, who turns into a ruthless killer and member of the Elite Squad fighting the drug war in Rio's shanty towns. Its success with the public was phenomenal and may have contributed to the public's support for the cleanup of the favelas in preparation for the Olympic Games. The music, especially "Rap das armas" ("Gun Rap"), became major hits.

The film opens by citing the psychologist Stanley Milgram, who found that "an extreme willingness of adults to go to almost any lengths on the command of an authority" makes ethics irrelevant.[46] The idea for the experiment Milgram performed in his Harvard laboratory occurred to him during the Eichmann trial, when he heard Eichmann's plea that he was obeying orders. The researchers were divided into those who ordered and administered simulated shocks that they gradually increased from 50 volts to 400 or more — enough, in a real situation, to cause death — and those who received them and who were instructed to cry out as if in pain. The majority of those administering the voltage obeyed the orders without protesting, even when the voltage reached a very high level, enough to cause death, leading Milgram to conclude that ordinary people following orders would not hesitate to inflict extreme pain. His experiment was met by a storm of protest and criticized as being unethical. Because of the photographs of American soldiers torturing in the Abu Ghraib prison in Iraq, interest in the experiment has been revived, and its thesis, that "ordinary" people will torture under orders, has gained currency. In effect, what converts Matias, the aspiring law student who in the course of *Elite Squad* will become a ruthless killer, is not simply a willingness to obey orders but the desire to avenge a friend's death and assuage his feeling of guilt. Loosely based on a book by Luiz Eduardo Soares, André Batista, and Rodrigo Pimentel, the film won the Golden Bear award in Berlin and was immensely popular, though critics were divided into those who believed it eulogized a violent and deviant institution, those who saw it as an artistic depiction of reality, and those who praised the film for showing a Brazilian institution that really worked.

The BOPE, whose symbol is a death's head, is an actually existing elite police squad that has recently engaged in cleansing favelas of drug gangs in preparation for the Rio Olympics. Captain Beto Nascimento, who narrates the voice-over in the English version, refers to this task of cleansing the favelas as a "war." In this war the favela drug dealers and the population that supports them are subversives, the enemy to be killed. The favela leader, Baiano (from Bahia, from the poverty-stricken Northeast), embodies a rebel tradition that glorified bandit heroes. His opponent, the officer Nascimento, is under extreme stress because the pope is due to visit Brazil and has elected to stay near a favela, and it is important that blatant trafficking and violence not be allowed to disrupt his sleep. Given the absence in the film of Christian forgiveness, charity, and sympathy, this is deeply ironic.

Nascimento's wife is expecting a baby and wants him to retire from the troop and resume some kind of normal life, which the BOPE mission has made impossible. When the mother of a slain son comes to reclaim the body and tells him that the boy had been killed for squealing to the police, he feels sympathy, a dangerous sentiment for the leader of the Alpha unit. Nascimento's psychological conflicts between his need for family life and his ruthlessness as a policeman articulate the narrative.

Searching for a successor so that he can retire, he focuses on the two recruits Neto and his friend Matias, who is still undecided between police work and a career in law. A student at the university, Matias attends a class on Foucault and argues in opposition to the majority of students that sometimes force is necessary.[47] Nevertheless, the upper-class Maria befriends him and becomes his lover and introduces him to their charity work helping the favela population.

One of the pivotal moments in the film is the training of the BOPE recruits led by Nascimento just two months before the pope's visit to Brazil. These sequences show the tipping point that will either break or make the potential squad member, "even the training of the Israeli army is not as tough as this," we are told, though without any acknowledgment that this is an internal war. First the prospective recruits undergo a process of humiliation and dehumanization. They are told to forget their souls and to realize that their bodies are now the property of the squad; they are addressed by number rather than by name and assured that they will never survive the course. During their initiation, they are violently attacked by "skulls" (the BOPE squad), treated as scum, told they are corrupt, and ordered to go back to where they came from, all of which is supposed to train them to resist pressure.

Nascimento acknowledges that BOPE is a kind of cult, and this is confirmed by its death's-head emblem and its marching song, which boasts of skinning and eating the guerrilla, making explicit the genealogy of a corps founded for political cleansing that is now engaged in the drug war, in which it takes on the enemy's supposed "cannibalism." For lunch the recruits are forced to lick food off the ground, and one of them, the corrupt cop Fabio, is humiliated in a particularly brutal manner. He is ordered to eat his own vomit, beaten, made to demonstrate his incompetence, and finally shamed and expelled, as are all who waver. A cemetery with crosses "commemorates" the symbolic deaths of these aspirants. Matias and Neto and one other recruit are the survivors of the training that culminates with a BOPE invasion of a favela. "Our men in black go in to kill and not to be killed," Nascimento says. Once "graduated," the new members of the squad are let loose, and Neto kills thirty men in his first week on Operation Holiness. He is fearless and is the recruit temperamentally closest to Nascimento, but in his enthusiasm for the kill he disobeys orders and can no longer be promoted as commander of the squad.

The training sequences show Nascimento as a ruthless and cruel leader, in contrast to the scenes of family life, which depict him as a concerned husband and then as a father with a newborn baby. Suffering from the conflict between family and his violent "work," he is a protagonist whose dilemma is clearly intended to inspire sympathy. Portrayed as a defender of the family, it is significant that at one point he mentions, among the scourges of contemporary life, not only drugs but also abortion clinics, as if these belonged to the same category of social evil, voicing the filmmaker's political preferences for the fetus over the mother's welfare. Although he acknowledges that what the BOPE does may seem inhuman, he defends it as the only solution to the drug problem. This Manichean division between good and evil allows no place for charity or reform. Indeed, Matias's good deed in arranging to give a pair of glasses to a short-sighted favela child is what precipitates the violence that brings about tragedy. Charity is dangerous. After seeing a photograph of Matias in BOPE uniform in the newspaper, Baiano violently extracts information from the student drug dealer and plans to kill Matias when he returns to the favela to hand over his gift of glasses. But Matias is due to be interviewed for an internship, and Neto offers to replace him. He drives straight into the trap and is fatally wounded. The dealers recognize the BOPE death's-head tattoo on Neto's body and immediately understand the consequences. In revenge, they turn on the students, seizing the NGO couple who had brought students into the favela. They beat the woman up. They pour gasoline over the man and burn him alive in a spectacular bonfire at the highest point of the favela. Meanwhile, Neto is given a solemn funeral, during which Nascimento defiantly places the BOPE flag on the coffin. Matias feel responsible for Neto's tragic death, which becomes a turning point in his life. Maria, who has escaped the favela, finds that Matias is now unapproachable in his grief, and at the funeral, perhaps as a conciliatory gesture, she gives him the name of Baiano's lover as "someone who can help him" and asks him not to harm the girl. The squad immediately bag the woman, torture her, and shoot Baiano's right-hand man. Nascimento now takes on

the urgent task of finding Baiano. They go from house to house spread-
ing terror and come upon a boy wearing a pair of expensive sneakers
probably bought with drug money. They "bag" this boy, then threaten
to rape him with a broomstick wielded by Matias. The kid puts them on
to Baiano, showing them where he lives. As Baiano nervously leaves the
house, he is shot and wounded. He begs Nascimento not to shoot him in
the face because he wants to look good in his coffin at the wake. Nascimento gives the gun to Matias, who aims at Baiano's face, thus claiming
his right to be Nascimento's pitiless successor.

What accounts for Matias's transformation from peaceful law student to merciless killer and torturer is grief over the death of his "soul
brother," Neto, and his desire for revenge. The film supports the old argument that the end justifies the means and can be considered a retro-
active defense of the Brazilian police state repression of the 1960s and
1970s, which used torture unto death as a means of suppressing liberal
and left-wing opposition. The fact that students and NGOs are depicted
as superficial and misguided at best, and protected by the drug lord at
worst, discredits them and their concern for the inhabitants of the favela,
while Nascimento, despite his brutal behavior, is a caring family man.
Unlike another popular Brazilian movie set in a favela, *Cidade de Deus*
(*City of God*), there is little attempt to depict the favela dwellers as individuals. In *City of God*, one of the children, Rocket, has nonviolent aspirations, and in the course of the film, aided by a newspaper reporter, he
becomes a photographer; because he lives in the favela, he is at hand to
become the chronicler of violence. At least, in this film, there is a slender
possibility of recuperation.[48]

That the use of torture and terror is the only possible solution to violence in the favelas, is also the thesis of the book on which the film is
based. The English translation by Clifford E. Landers often adopts a
jocular tone quite out of line with the subject matter. Unlike the film,
the book is episodic, each section ordered around a triumphant story
and written ostensibly as a tribute to a friend, Amancio, who had been
shot by fellow policemen in friendly fire. After the funeral, the narrator
vows to tell the story of the "best urban warfare troop in the world," a
significant statement that takes as given that war is the only solution to
drug trafficking. The introduction signed by the writers presents it as a

condemnation of extreme practices, citing Nelson Mandela on the need for truth in order to achieve reconciliation and citing psychoanalytic literature on the need for mourning. Yet neither the book nor the film unreservedly supports this thesis. A tone of righteous indignation draws a curtain over the horror, over a vision of Rio in a state of permanent warfare in which both sides are equally brutal and there is no possible positive outcome. What is the significance of the fact that the film was extremely popular and a sequel has now been released? It has given the BOPE a kind of glamour, so that now as they engage in their war on the favelas, they have citizens' support. At the time of writing, the success of an alternative policy of clearing the favelas "without firing a shot," advocated by Robson Rodríguez da Silva, head of the Units of Pacification Police (Unidades de Policia Pacificadora), is still in question.[49]

What is lost in these media versions are the antecedents of Brazil's violent history, the war on guerrillas in the 1960s, the authoritarian state, and the long silence over the past. It was the state's negligence that allowed the favelas to grow; and it has taken decades for Brazil to confront its dictatorship, so the archives of repression are only now being scrutinized by scholars. *Elite Squad* is just one example of popular culture's collusion with cruelty and repression. The myth of the heroic bandit has given way to fictions that narrate the apocalyptic war without end, exemplified by the "Yorkshire Ripper" novels of Donald Peace, in which criminals and police share a common culture of extreme violence. *El arma en el hombre* (*The Arm in the Man*), by the Salvadorian novelist Horacio Castellanos Moyá, shows how this violence destroys the "human," illustrating the process by following the transition from civil war to criminal violence and from criminal violence to policing. The protagonist, Robocop, is inarticulate and uncommunicative, unless the barrel of a gun can be said to communicate. He has no remorse and makes no attempt to justify his brutality. A former special forces foot soldier and member of the Acahuapa battalion (whose name recalls that of the infamous Atlcatl battalion mentioned in chapter 6), Robocop is discharged from the army after the return to democracy.[50] Without any skill except killing, he joins Bruno, also a former fighter, and makes a living of sorts stealing cars for a "powerful network." He is well armed with guns and grenades that he appropriated during the war, and it doesn't take long for him to start killing again. With his comrade he undertakes a burglary at the home of a German couple that goes wrong when the old man defends himself with a pistol. Robocop shoots him, and his accomplice, Bruno, shoots the wife. Their only booty is the old man's pistol. The futility of crime and violence establishes the predominant note of the book. With the help of Saúl, a comrade alongside whom, during the civil war, he had ambushed and killed a guerrilla commander and his men, he links up with one of his former officers, Major Linares, who is now engaged in secret operations against former guerrillas. The clandestine group formed by the High Command is well equipped: they have a van with radio transmitters and monitoring equipment. Their orders are to kill an ex-guerrilla who is now a member of the National Assembly. Robocop kills him with a shot to the head in his own driveway and in front of his school-age daughter. The murder has consequences, forcing Robocop into exile in Guatemala because "things had changed." "Some years ago nobody would have said anything against liquidating a terrorist, but now, with that chatter about democracy, types like me encountered ever more difficulty doing our work" (39). By describing killing as "work," Robocop deprives it of ethical baggage, as did the Germans of the Einsatzgruppen that eliminated Jews, and as did Captain Nascimento when he described the BOPE squad's "work," and as did the death squads during the dirty war in the Southern Cone, whose *tarea* (task) was to kill. It is worth reflecting that work in Marxist terms forges the class system and makes the worker a potentially revolutionary force. But the work of the killer is precisely the opposite. It is to preserve the status quo by any means.

On his return from exile, Robocop has become dangerous even to the people who had employed him. Captured and interrogated as a dangerous delinquent and heavily drugged, he has visions in one of which he sees a Guatemalan indigenous kaibil who teaches him how to destroy the will and intelligence of the enemy and take out their brains. Like the kaibiles of the Guatemalan civil war, he needs this indigenous "savagery" as an alibi for his actions. With the collusion of Major Linares, he escapes from prison and is flown out of the country by private plane on what the major has planned as his death flight. On the plane Robocop's former partner, Saúl, turns on him. Robocop is able to take control and kill him, then orders the pilot of the rescue plane to land on a deserted beach, where he kills the pilot and blows up the plane. He finds his way to a fortified compound on the borders between Guatemala and El Salvador, where he joins the "Tio Pepe gang," some of whom are ex-guerrillas under the command of El Viejo and who engage in illegal activities, particularly drug smuggling. Ordered by El Viejo to carry out an operation in Guatemala City, Robocop is ambushed by a rival gang but fights his way out, then kills his former mistress after spending the night with her. He returns to El Viejo's compound, where a group of gun traffickers has taken refuge, exposing it to the US antinarcotic operations. Robocop is captured by the US squad, which is indifferent to his criminal past, seeing him only as a useful collaborator who can be incorporated into their organization. What Castellanos Moyá has condensed in this novel is the trajectory that leads from civil war to rogue activities, and from criminality to reentry into society as a US agent. His survival in the deadly war games has been achieved at the price of surrendering every last trace of what is usually regarded as the human — that is to say, he has stripped himself of empathy, joy, tenderness, and love in order to become a killing machine. The price of survival has been the death of the self.

Collaborators

Normal life under the military dictatorships was an elaborate pretense in which sectors of the population, including some of the intelligentsia, willingly or unwittingly collaborated. Fear contributed to a breakdown of social responsibility, although there was a difference between the everyday fears of ordinary people and active support or collaboration. In Chile, the name Mariana Callejas came to stand not only for collaboration but also for cover-up of torture and the complicity of the literary institution in atrocity, shattering the notion that literature was, by its very nature, uncontaminated by the dirty work of the state. She was the wife of the CIA agent Michael Townley, who afterward was imprisoned for organizing the assassination of Orlando Letelier in Washington and was also guilty of many other violent crimes, including the car bombing that killed General Prats in Buenos Aires in 1974. His wife had an active role in the car bombing and his other activities. A paid agent of the secret service, she took a creative writing course at the University of Miami and organized literary meetings in her home in the prosperous Lo Curro section of Santiago, meetings that were attended by writers who had remained in the country after the coup. Meanwhile, her husband was experimenting with sarin gas and torturing prisoners in the basement, among them Carmelo Soria, a Spanish citizen, who like other victims was afterward transferred to the Grimaldi detention center, from which he disappeared. The Spanish prosecutor Baltasar Garzón would later try unsuccessfully to have Townley extradited for the crime. The family house became a potent symbol of the complicity of literature, or at least literati, in the collective refusal to acknowledge what most people must have suspected: that behind the cultivated facade, torture and execution were daily practices. In Pedro Lemebel's chronicle "Las Orquídeas Negras de Mariana Callejas o el Centro Cultural de la DINA" ("The Black Orchids of Mariana Callejas or the Secret Services Cultural Center"), the writer imagines the literary soiree at her villa and the guests who recited T. S. Eliot and danced "inebriated with the funereal orchids of Mariana Callejas."[51] The garden, scented with honeysuckle and jasmine, shaded "the laboratory of my chemist husband Michael who is working late on a gas to eliminate rats" (14); Lemebel describes this project as "that swastika labor whose stink evaporated and wilted the roses that died near the garden windows" (14). After the end of the military regime, when the secret was out, Callejas went on attending literary events. "Surely," Lemebel writes, "those who attended the evening of cultural banality in the years after the coup, could remember the troublesome power surges that made the lights blink and interrupted the dance music. Surely they could not know about that other parallel dance, in which the contortion of the cattle prod made the tortured human flank arch with the voltage."[52] In that innocent house, he concludes, "literature and torture coagulated in the same drop of ink and iodine, in a bitter festive memory that asphyxiated the syllables of pain" (16).

The conclusion that literature is not neutral or innocent was shared by his friend Roberto Bolaño, to whom he told the story of Mariana Callejas, which in turn inspired the novel *Nocturno de Chile* (*By Night in Chile*), whose narrator, a priest named Father Urrutia, is a thinly veiled stand-in for Ignacio Valente, a priest and literary critic who gave Pinochet lessons in Marxism. In this story what is at stake is an ideology of literature that disconnects it from the political. Narrated as the deathbed confession of an Opus Dei priest, writer, and critic who wrote under the pseudonym H. Ibacache, it relates the life story of a man who, as a youth had enjoyed the patronage of a major literary critic, who wrote under the pseudonym "Farewell" (a transparent reference to the once famous Hernán Díaz Arrieta, who wrote under the pseudonym "Alone"). Withdrawing from social life during the Allende presidency, he returns to literary gatherings after the 1973 coup and becomes a regular at the literary salon of Mariana Callejas (María Canales in the novel). What characterizes Urrutia is his abdication of responsibility either as priest (he refuses to visit the home of peasants to administer the last rites to a dying child) or as a writer who visits María Canales's salon because there's nowhere to go during the curfew and she is "pleasant and likeable" and "a generous host" whose guests stay until the curfew ends in the early morning. He admits to having had only two conversations with María, although he cherishes her son, who, like him, is named Sebastián. The child has a "wan little face. He is a silent child," "his lips sealed, his innocent little body all sealed up, as if he didn't want to see or hear or speak, there in the midst of his mother's weekly party" (115). This description reminds us of the *imbunche*, a creature from Chilean folklore whose orifices were sewn up; in Catalina Parra's art this creature becomes a symbol of the silencing of the population. The story can be read as that of either the degradation of the avant-garde or perhaps its extreme realization.[53] The priest can claim ignorance of the sinister goings-on because he was not present at the *tertulia* when a stray guest came upon the torture chamber and the tortured man lying on the bed. When the story of María's husband becomes public, he asks himself a series of questions, one of which is "Why didn't anyone say anything at the time?" The answer was simple: "Because they were afraid. I was not afraid I would have been able to speak out, but I didn't see anything. I didn't know until it was too late." For Bolaño, the obscenity is not only the torture but also the willed blindness of the priest. "Not seeing anything" absolves him from speaking out and thus from responsibility. Visiting María after everyone had abandoned her, he still refuses to see. When she asks whether he wants to see the basement (as if the torture chamber were a tourist attraction), he refuses, because for him it is important not to see. As they say goodbye, she utters the enigmatic remark

"That is how literature is made in Chile." "While I was driving back into Santiago," he comments, "I thought about what she had said. That is how literature is made in Chile, but not just in Chile, in Argentina and Mexico too, in Guatemala and Uruguay, in Spain, France and Germany, in green England and carefree Italy. That is how literature is made. Or at least what we call literature, to keep ourselves from falling into the rubbish dump" (127).

The implications are grim: it as if the ivory tower depended on "not seeing" the extermination camp. That is why the priest's alter ego, his conscience, is described as a "wizened youth": it is underdeveloped, and since he admits to no sin, he cannot ask for absolution. The final words of the novel are "And the storm of shit begins," indicating Bolaño's own conviction that the breakdown of all civility and social responsibility in Latin America had been the advance warning of global disaster.

The even more devastating view that literature is implicated in atrocity is advanced in the novel *Distant Star*, which explores the artistic avant-garde's implication in crime. Narrated by Arturo Belano, the story follows the infamous career of Carlos Wieder, who writes poetry under the name Alberto Ruiz-Tagle: Ruiz-Tagle is the surname both of a real-life activist horrendously tortured and killed by the Chilean secret service and of Chile's president from 1994 to 2000, Eduardo Frei Ruiz-Tagle.[54] Death and sovereignty are combined in the life and work of Wieder, who was a well-regarded poet. Indeed, he embodies to the point of parody the avant-garde dream of uniting life and art. He kills the aunt of the beautiful Garmendia sisters, both of whom are admired poets and with one of whom he supposedly is in love, then lets four men into the house to sequester the sisters, one of whose bodies is later found in a mass grave. The narrator happens to be in a detention camp after the Pinochet coup, and from the prison yard he sees Wieder crossing the sky in a small plane he uses for writing aerial messages. It is a sly reference to the poet Zurita, who wrote his poem "La vida nueva" (after Dante's "La vita nuova") in the sky over New York in 1982. Although Zurita believed he was launching an avant-garde action against brutality, by attributing skywritten poems to a supporter of the dictatorship, Bolaño suggests that the avant-garde were not always above politics and could collude with the dictatorship. Wieder's skywriting farcically aspires to

God's omnipotence, inscribing phrases from Genesis in Latin, as if the act of creation is now being reformulated not only in terms of Western Christian tradition but also in terms of the re-creation of Chilean society by dictatorship. Phrases such as "God created Heaven and Earth" are followed by the disciplinary command "Learn," which is what the civilian population will now be forced by the military to do: that is, they will be forced to reset their lives. In another of his aerial exhibitions, he evokes sadism and death as he "conjure[s] up the shades of dead women." After one such skywriting exhibition, performed during a thunderstorm before an audience of military officers, he inaugurates an exhibition of photographs for twenty or so people in a private apartment. Only one visitor at a time is allowed into the exhibition: for maximum impact the viewing has to be private, since what he is showing is a kind of pornography of death. But what the viewers experience is not enjoyment. The only woman among the guests comes out of the exhibition vomiting uncontrollably. Only Wieder's father seems to have no reaction. The photographs, it is revealed, were of women who looked like "broken, dismembered mannequins in some pictures." They had all been taken in the same place (clearly a detention center or death camp), and some of the women may still have been alive when photographed. In other words, the photographs are meant to have the "pleasurable" effect of a snuff film. What Bolaño brilliantly underscores is the failure of the sadist Wieder to convert his pleasure into a ludic spectacle.

The exhibition comes to an abrupt end when the secret service enters the apartment and confiscates the photographs, although it is not the photographs themselves that bring about Wieder's dismissal but their revelation of what was happening in the secret prisons. Political murder cannot be translated into art, but Wieder's connivance in cruel forms of repression does not stop. At the end of the military regime, Wieder disappears, and he is thought to be dead, although his name appears "in a judicial report on torture and the disappearance of prisoners of war" and "in 1993, he was linked to an independent operational group who were responsible for the death of various students in and around Concepción and Santiago" (108). The fact that Wieder is "discontinuous" (an aspect supported by the structure of the novel, in which he makes spasmodic appearances) turns him into a grotesque version of Georges Bataille's description of the Marquis de Sade's Sovereign Man.[55]

Years after the end of the Pinochet regime, Wieder once again returns to haunt Belano, who is living in Spain. A former police detective named Romero, now acting privately on behalf of an unknown client, turns up to ask Belano's help in tracking Wieder, who he believes had recently been the cameraman for a number of pornographic films whose actors and camera man had been murdered. Researching this mysterious career, Belano has the dream-revelation that he and Wieder have been traveling on the same boat "but I had done nothing to stop it going down" (121). Hence Belano sees himself as tacitly complicit in the degeneration of the human (and perhaps of literature), a process that, far from coming to an end with the military regime, was still going on. The fictional Belano believes that killing Wieder at this stage would be fruitless, a conclusion that Gareth Williams considers "a melancholic paralysis on the part of the writer."[56] This is certainly a credible conclusion, although it seems to me that the "melancholic paralysis" has now become a general state that wishful thinking cannot overcome and that no individual can heal. If the fact that Wieder was killed by a private operator and not by the state underscores the dissolution of the state as executor of law, it also indicates the end of state-operated justice.

The torturers in the dirty wars were men, which does not necessarily rule out women. We know that in some instances recorded in Nazi Germany women participated in the cruel treatment of prisoners, but in most of these Latin American scenes, it is men who are doing the torturing and sometimes feeling an erotic pleasure as they reduce the other to a screaming mass. In postdictatorship societies, the reckoning has been slow to come, and sometimes it does not come at all. In the Bolaño novel, justice as dispensed by the state has given way to the atavism of private vengeance, suggesting that society is regressing. The liberal state had been overthrown by the totalitarian state, which in turn collapsed into a neoliberal state, in which the memoirs of torturers caused hardly a stir and in which only a few were belatedly brought to justice. This leaves me wondering about *Distant Star*, the title of Bolaño's novel: does it refer to a star light-years away from the sad present?

FIVE | Revolutionary Justice

The red thread of violence runs through Marxist thinking from the Paris Commune onward. It binds many different left-wing movements from Leninism to the anticolonial struggle as theorized by Fanon, and by Mao's *Little Red Book*, with its catchy slogans: "If we have no guns, we shall get them and if we do not have power, we shall conquer it."[1] But the enemy was not only external. There was the danger from within, from weakness and error that must be eradicated.[2] In the guerrilla organizations founded after the Cuban revolution in many countries of Latin America, the character of the guerrilla, the new man who must be ready to sacrifice his own life, was seen as the crucial factor in the revolutionary war.[3] The photograph of the dead Che taken in Bolivia in 1969 is still the ghost that haunts the social imaginary, reminding us that the price of dedication may be death, that rebellion does not necessarily triumph nor does success depend solely on human will but on a complexity of more mundane circumstances.

It was Castro's success in Cuba that made the guerrilla *foco*[4] the model for many other insurgencies, some of which, like the Sandinista insurgency in Nicaragua and the guerrilla movement in El Salvador, would eventually form governments.[5] Guerrilla groups in Argentina and Peru were defeated by the army: others were discredited by failure or corruption as in the case of the Colombian FARC (Fuerzas Armadas Revolucionarias de Colombia) with its dubious reliance on kidnapping and the drug trade; its survival in jungle terrains was stripped of any glamour as former hostages told stories of hardship and death.[6] The strategic and tactical failures — such as underestimating the power of the state and the military and overestimating the magical power of charisma — are well documented. That theirs was a predominantly masculine ethos that trumped traditionally feminine attributes such as "tendresse, devotion and self-sacrifice" has been argued by two critics, Ileana Rodríguez and María Josefina Saldaña Portillo, in their studies of the guerrilla in Central America and Cuba.[7] Ileana Rodríguez writes, "Vanguard parties, political leaders and engaged writers neglected, demeaned and marginalized women therefore disparaging and omitting all that was synonymous with Woman."[8]

In this chapter, I discuss two incidents in Argentina and El Salvador and the more significant Shining Path in Peru to examine notions of sacrifice and masculinity. Although the Argentine and Salvadorian examples are minor and involve only one or two instances, they illustrate the link between ideals of extreme masculinity and cruelty. At first sight, the Shining Path appears to be a counterexample: not only did women serve as prominent members of the Shining Path Central Committee, but 40 percent of its army were said to be women. But though compelled to kill like men and thus defy traditional gender roles, the ruthlessly hierarchical organization limited them in all kinds of ways. Women found that they could not oppose marriages that were forced on them, and when they got pregnant, they were made to abort.[9] Examining "masculinity" and "femininity" in these contexts exposes the fact that revolution did not extend to gender relations and that weakness came to be seen as a crime that merited the death sentence.

The (Female) Enemy Within

Commenting on how Che Guevara viewed the guerrilla group "almost as if it were a sect" in which there was always "a risk of abdication, of being picked up or infiltrated," which led to "that terrible tradition of *Guevarismo*," the novelist Ricardo Piglia describes "the tendency to discover the traitor within the weak, within those that waver within the group itself." Thus, "the notion of the friend as the one that can potentially desert and betray is the extreme result of this theory—and we already know the consequences. . . . Politics thus becomes a practice oriented toward the inside of the group itself through distrust, accusations and disciplinary measures. There is never a politics of alliance. In any case, the possibility of alliance is defined by distrust and the shadow of betrayal."[10]

Nowhere was this more evident than in the much-discussed incident that took place in Argentina in 1964 when the Ejército Guerrillero del Pueblo (Guerrilla Army of the People, or EGP) executed two of its members, an incident that, more than forty years later and with the benefit of hindsight, is still debated. Under the command of Jorge Masetti, known as Comandante Segundo, and with the distant support of Che Guevara (the Comandante Primero), the EGP planned to ignite revolution in the impoverished Argentine province of Salta in anticipation of Che's campaign in Bolivia. Before the EGP left Cuba, Che gave a grim send-off that was all too prescient: "From this moment on consider yourselves dead. Death is the only certainty in this: some of you may survive, but all of you should consider what remains of your lives as borrowed time."[11] The trajectory of the group is described in a *testimonio* by one of its members, Hector Jouvé, and in comments by the painter Ciro Bustos, who was later imprisoned in Bolivia along with Régis Debray and became discredited as a supposed informer.[12]

In September 1963 the EGP entered the Argentine province of Salta. Given their minimal political impact, the lack of popular support among the impoverished inhabitants of Salta province, and the fact that the uprising took place when the civilian government of President Illia was in charge, it was at best ill-timed and would be scripted for failure. The operation was significantly named Operación Sombra (Shadow Operation); the name adopted by the group alluded to the Argentina gaucho epic *Martín Fierro* and the novel *Don Segundo Sombra* by Ricardo Güiraldes, both of which focused on the hero as independent loner. The group was eliminated long before Che's campaign in Bolivia, and its last month was a cruel odyssey in which members died of starvation and Masetti himself marched off into the wilderness and disappeared.[13] The irony is that the group's notoriety depended not on its achievement but on the infamous execution of two of its recruits.

Before leaving Bolivia, Masetti had issued a code of conduct, or rather a list of crimes for which the death penalty would be exacted — betrayal, cowardice toward the enemy, insubordination, "torturation," murder, theft, banditry, desertion, and the crime *contra natura*, in other words, homosexuality; the code could be extended to insubordination, ill treatment of the population or a prisoner, and negligence with arms or political material. The strict disciplinary code meted out severe punishment for petty crimes and sexual deviance.[14] The latter is particularly significant for homosexuality transgresses the neat ideological division between the disciplined male and the unruly feminine.

Hector Jouvé (also spelled Jouvet or Jouve), a guerrilla from Córdoba who was favored by Masetti, was disturbed by the execution of Pupi (Adolfo Rotblat), whose childish nickname underscored his lack of experience. Perhaps attracted by the glamour of the guerrilla ideal, Pupi turned out to be ill equipped to survive long marches and semi-starvation. Jouvé had not been present when the decision was made to execute him on the grounds that "he was not functioning, at any moment he was going to betray them, that he was noisy and out of his mind." When Jouvé remarked that he didn't see Pupi as a danger, Masetti ordered him to perform the execution, and when Jouvé refused, the task was given to another comrade. Jouvé was present at the second execution, that of the "young banker" Bernardo Groswald, an event that he described as "incredible": "I believe it was a crime because he was destroyed; he was like a psychiatric patient. I believe that in some way we were all responsible, because we were all in that, in making the revolution."[15] His comment "we were all in that" means that despite misgivings, they accepted a flawed leadership.[16]

Despite the time lag, Jouvé's 2004 memoir shocked his contemporaries. The philosopher Oscar del Barco, a former guerrilla sympathizer, published a response that judged his generation harshly for forgetting the ethical maxim "Thou shalt not kill."[17] The subsequent controversy involved several participants and was fraught with guilt and recriminations, although the participants never explored the tendency to discover the "traitor within the weak" or the feminine within the male body.[18]

Whereas Che, in his writings, acknowledged his moments of weakness and incompetence before he became a "new man," Masetti had no patience with the sufferings of his recruits or with dissent. In the long wait before leaving their training ground in Algiers for Bolivia and Argentina, he had one of his companions, Miguel, shot for insubordination.

The novel *Muertos de amor* (*Dead from Love*), by the journalist Jorge Lanata, draws on the memoirs and documents that chronicle the lamentable story. The book cover shows a hand grasping the red star of revolution, from which a sliver of congealed blood runs across the forearm like the mark of a suicide. And this is indeed a suicidal story that relates the hunger march across inhospitable and sparsely inhabited land. Lanata uses citations from historical documents and from Masetti's letters, along with the imagined interior monologues of the combatants. Inserted in the narrative is the history of Salta province, particularly the founding of the city of Orán, a center of the sugar industry that prospered on the backs of exploited laborers. The guerrillas, possibly out of ignorance or because the area could be entered from Bolivia, had chosen to operate in a region whose politics were determined by an industry that was underwritten by foreign investors working hand in glove with corrupt local officials. The work force was an illiterate and impoverished peasantry who were unlikely to respond to calls for armed struggle. The letter addressed to the workers from Comandante Segundo (Masetti), far from establishing communication displayed the ideological gulf that separated the guerrilla from the laborer. Claiming that the members of his guerrilla group were also exploited, Masetti talks of taking the guns out of the hands of the rich. Like Che in Bolivia, Masetti underestimated the enemy, misjudged the local population, and overlooked the considerable counterinsurgency and surveillance capabilities of the state.[19]

Seeking fulfillment in a totally alien environment, the guerrilla group was constantly frustrated. As Rozitchner comments, the entry into Argentina marked the passage from fantasy to "crude reality."[20] They never engaged with any enemy other than the terrain across which they marched and the climate that they suffered. In isolation, their weaknesses were accentuated, especially those of their leader, Masetti, who was both paranoid and sadistic. Lanata's novel *Dead from Love* continually emphasizes this gap between the image of the guerrilla (the slogans, the uniform), the goal (to seize the government), and the grim everyday life on the mountain, whose native inhabitants had no higher ambition than obtaining a new pair of pants. The shifts from narrative to interior monologue, registered in italics, convey the scattered thoughts and doubts. "What does it feel like to kill another human being? . . . Fear of killing is not very different from fear of madness: it is not fear of madness so much as never being able to escape from it: the terror of not being able to go back, the panic of solitude where borderlines cross" (59). Thoughts registered without attribution, possibly Pupi's, are increasingly gloomy chronicles of desperation: "If God exists, he has never noticed this place. This jungle can only be a punishment from hell. Here only suicide takes off, although this is not what is going to happen unless it is understood that the Revolution itself will take its own life" (64).

One of Pupi's companions describes him lying down during a rest stop, "buried among the backpacks that were full of saucepans and his image was pathetic: he was a sort of *ekeko* replete with presents, with his thick dirty spectacles and a book in his hands" (70). In Peruvian folklore, the ekeko is the god of prosperity, quite the reverse of the pathetic Pupi, who could never match theory (for example, Clausewitz's reflections on the role of chance in wartime) with practice —"practice" being the daily confrontation with the negative judgments of his comrades. Forced as a punishment to carry the kitchen equipment, he is thereby marked as "feminine," and also as a theorist who prefers to read about war but is too clumsy to fight efficiently. One of his comrades describes him as

> extremely anxious and perhaps [he] stuttered a little in consequence. He was the type of person who is in physical disagreement with the world: they open a box of matches upside down. They stumble in level places; they lose things only to find them again a moment later. If anyone saw him coming from a thousand meters on a foggy day they would know he was a student from his deliberately rumpled clothes, his pianist's hands, his pen tucked handily inside his shirt pocket. (70–71)

Ciro Bustos, who later joined Che's expedition in Bolivia, where he was captured along with Régis Debray and was interviewed by Jon Anderson, said "he lived in a state of terror, wept, fell behind in the marches, and slowed everyone down. Men had to be sent back to drag him forward. The others felt disgusted by him." On one march, he refused to cross a river and asked Bustos to kill him. "Finally I pulled out the pistol and put it against his head and I made him walk like that, more or less by force . . . kicking him in the ass."[21] In the novel, Lanata underscores the fact that behaving in an "unmasculine" way posed a problem for a group whose very identity was based on its idealized version of masculinity. Pupo was baptized "Manuelita" by the coarse Pelado, who pronounces "Pupo" as if it meant *puto* (male prostitute). Though keeping his thoughts to himself, one of the group in Lanata's novel reflects that "the New Man would not be born of the vices of the Old Man: "Putos were treacherous and women and druggies too. If a woman managed to be incorporated into the column it would be ordered to give her special protection from harassment by the men. But all that was theory, the only thing we came across was a tapir, and we didn't have time to notice its sex. We ate it almost raw" (71). The unfortunate Pupi, ostracized as "feminine" and hence a burden, does not conform to the image of the guerrilla, and for this he is condemned to death, given tranquilizers and tied to a hammock. When Jouvé refuses to kill him, the task is given to Pirincho, who becomes distressed at the sight of Pupo's dying body in convulsions. Bustos finishes him off. Pirincho is so disturbed by the event that on a mission to Buenos Aires, he decides to abandon the guerrillas.

Astonishingly, the tiny group needed one more victim. Nardo (Bernardo Groswald) was a bank clerk from Córdoba. A group member named Henry Lerner, whom Masetti suspected of wanting to desert, was ordered to monitor him. The report was not reassuring:

> Nardo asked if we gave talks, if we had meetings . . . as if he were coming to some kind of flower show. He was done for after two days. He had flat feet, was frightened of going down slopes, and he began animalizing. It was truly repellent, and as the days went by he began physically to look more like an animal. To go down a hill, he went down on his ass, walked on all fours: a pathetic image for a guerrilla. . . . He was dirty, unclean and finally he was punished, given the hardest jobs, that kind of thing.[22]

While Pupi had been killed because he was not masculine enough, Nardo was killed for not looking like a human being and not conducting himself in accordance with the imagined guerrilla ideal. Or, as León Rozitchner observes, Pupi was "broken" and Nardo went mad. And they were both Jews.[23] "When they ask us for our life and we are given up for dead, then the other disappears as the other because we have disappeared for ourselves."[24]

In Lanata's novel one of the narrators comments on the fate of Che Guevara, who

> climbed the mountain as a volunteer and descended as a myth and spent months staring at the map like one seeking the exit. . . . There is nothing more boring than a Revolution. There is nothing more forced, slow, laborious, contradictory, dirty, illusory than a Revolution: it has to be made every minute of every year of every eternity, times in which the struggle is with oneself. To be human is never enough, is always shameful and one must always be more human and always lose and the day one manages to become a giant, you wake up surrounded by pygmies and everything begins over again. (79)

The end of the group was ignominious. Masetti disappeared; one of the guerrillas, Antonio, fell into a ravine and died; Jouvé was captured and tortured. He would be questioned by General Alsogaray, one of whose sons had joined the ERP (Ejército Revolucionario del Pueblo) only to be savagely killed by the army.

The story of Masetti, as told by Lanata, is a story of stupidity, although he does not get to the core of the problem that was exposed in León Rozitchner's response to Del Barco's article "Thou Shalt Not Kill," that is, understanding the difference between voluntary sacrifice and Masetti's decision to kill members of his own group, thus assuming supreme power over their life and death. Del Barco's response, "Thou Shalt Not Kill," overlooks the lived trajectory of Jouvé, "who takes on the experience after having lived it to the extreme limit of his sacrifice [*entrega*], his valor, his love of life, his credulity, his good father, his innocence." In a critique of Emmanuel Levinas, who provides the theoretical basis for Del Barco's "Thou Shalt Not Kill," Rozitchner contrasts God the Father's renunciation of the body in the cause of an abstraction with the mother-derived material ethics.[25] The entire Masetti incident is a case study of a masculinity that can only be fully realized through death.

Not surprisingly, the copious comments anthologized in *No matar* are, except for one instance, written entirely by men.

In an essay on the incident, Patrick Dove comments,

> The ground of militant reason is thanato-politics, a politics that goes in search of death. It is the sacrificing of existence to the transhistorical telos or cause of history. Sacrifice is something subjects do (one cannot be a militant unless one is prepared to sacrifice everything for the cause) and it is a preparatory step that clears the way for that true subject whose arrival would coincide with the elimination in ourselves and in others of everything that is false or improper.[26]

This is also an apt description of the thanato-politics of the Shining Path of Peru, although in that uprising, women played a crucial role.

Beware of Irony

The Argentine incident produced a discussion and critique of the absolutism of the guerrilla. The murder during the Salvadorian civil war of the poet Roque Dalton at the hands of his comrades revealed how quickly the friend becomes the enemy and hence disposable. For years before joining the guerrillas Dalton had agonized over Communist Party policy that during the Popular Front period and during the Second World War had put revolution on hold, leaving militants waiting because conditions were not ripe for revolution, or to put it plainly, upheaval did not suit the policies of the Soviet Union. The guerrillas, on the other hand, did not wait. In exile in Cuba, Dalton made the decision to join the Salvadorian guerrillas. After being rejected by the Farabundo Martí group, he was accepted into the ERP, which included Joaquín Villalobos, who eventually became its military leader and who in 1975 helped condemn Dalton to death apparently because of a disagreement over strategy that was a struggle for power within the small guerrilla group.

Dalton grew up in a time of political paralysis, when El Salvador was haunted by the ghostly shadow of the 1932 massacre in which General Martínez and his army quelled a revolution and had thousands executed. His novel *Pobrecito poeta que era yo* (*The Poor Little Poet That I Was*) traces the history and frustrations of his generation who had to endure the restrictions of a totalitarian society.[27] The title of his novel is borrowed from a poem by Pedro Geoffroy Rivas, "Vida, pasión y muerte del antihombre" ("The Life, Passion, and Death of the Antiman"), first published in 1936, in which he encapsulated his self-loathing:

> Ah my 25 years on the streets
> 25 stinking years that were no use to anyone
> I, the Poor little poet, bourgeois and good
> Spermatozoid of a lawyer with clients
> the Worm of a Landowner.[28]

Dalton's novel registers the banter, the jokes, the arguments of a group of friends during nights of drinking at a time when the military dominated the political process in El Salvador. In this novel, he expresses all the ideological confusion, desperation, and pent-up desires of male intellectuals in a censored society. It culminates with an episode based on Dalton's own experience in prison, his interrogation by a CIA agent, and his escape from the jail, fortuitously aided by an earthquake. The multiple voices reflect not only the opinion of friends from his university days but also Dalton's own vacillations as he attempted to balance being a writer, a young professional, and a revolutionary. The mood of the novel swings from bitterness to irony, from skepticism to militancy. "We belong to a generation that was cut off by bullets in 1932 and who knows if it will reach its limits by the end of the century. Because the limit we are hoping for will be the Revolution."[29] The novel's protagonists are young men preoccupied with sex, literature, politics, and the viability of the party. In a significant outburst, one of the characters asks,

> What is the image of a Communist for me? A brilliant young poet who wants to be imprisoned though not totally imprisoned? Or a primary school teacher wearing glasses with bad breath, impotent and abstemious, originating from Gotera or one of those frontier towns on the border with Honduras, and always ready to borrow money? Or a textile worker or railroad worker who is always right and has studied for a year in Russia? Or an old peasant who — poor thing, and have a cup of coffee and forgive the poverty of my home — and which he serves in a bowl, but

who has a machete behind the door? Or a political activist who hates intellectuals? A practicing revolutionary who only belatedly reaches a theoretical understanding?[30]

Pobrecito poeta is not only a reflection of the frustration of a generation but a serious critique of the stagnant left-wing politics that helps us understand the attraction of the guerrillas because of their determination to spark an uprising even when the "objective conditions" were not in place. It also reveals the intellectuals' contempt and impatience with the rank and file and reproduces the lengthy discussions of the political dilemma facing intellectuals and the reasoning that led young men to join the guerrillas. After his escape from prison, Dalton found his way to Cuba, where he worked in the cultural center, Casa de las Américas, before resigning from the party to join the guerrilla movement. The questioning and doubts about the party were no doubt exacerbated in Cuba, where the whole notion of a revolutionary vanguard meant something different from that of the Stalinist party. During his time there, he was putting together his book based on the life story of Miguel Mármol (discussed in chapter 6), which involved him in an intense reflection on the party's mistakes. He came to the conclusion that the true revolutionaries were not necessarily workers but those ready to take up arms in the guerrilla struggle and the example was no longer the Communist Party still waiting for the "objective conditions" but the *foco*, the guerrilla group. However, when Dalton applied to join the Salvadorian guerrilla group, the FPLFM (Fuerzas Populares de la Liberación Farabundo Martí), its leader, rejected him on the grounds that he was more useful as a writer than as a fighter. But for Dalton the guerrilla movement was now the only place for the true revolutionary. After being accepted by the ERP (Ejército Revolucionario del Pueblo), he worked underground using the pseudonym Julio Delfos Marín before being killed by his comrades on 10 May 1975.

There are various accounts of this death. Ben Ehrenreich summarizes them as follows:

He was injected with a sedative because the executioners could not bring themselves to shoot him with his eyes open; he was given poison, for the same reason; he was stood against a wall and shot in the back by a firing squad; he was shot in the back of his head, a joke dying on his lips. In almost every version — and there are more — his killers could not bear to look him in the eye.[31]

Roberto Bolaño, who many years later met some of those responsible for the execution, mentions the poet Cienfuegos as one of the men who gave the order to kill Dalton and wondered "whether there wasn't even a bit of literary animosity there."

> They killed him while he slept. They didn't wake him; he never knew they were going to kill him. They debated all day long, because Roque Dalton was opposed to an armed uprising and the *comandantes* said the time was now and that they had to start the revolution. They didn't reach an agreement; Roque Dalton went to sleep, the *comandantes* kept debating and said: "We have to kill him." As though they were a band of gangsters. And they said, "Let's kill him now that he's sleeping, because he's a poet, so he won't suffer."[32]

Bolaño also offers a Freudian interpretation, declaring that it was "basically in the manner of children enacting the ritual of killing the father."[33] The rumor that he was killed while sleeping contributed to his posthumous martyrdom. The Mexican poet Efraín Huerta wrote,

> Let it be while he is sleeping
> The poor poets are very sensitive.
> They drugged him to kill — because for the beasts the best poet
> is a dead poet.[34]

The Mexican poet and critic Gabriel Zaid documented in detail the political rivalries that led to the execution in a collection of essays titled *Colegas enemigos: Una lectura de la tragedia salvadoreña* (*Enemy Colleagues: A Reading of the Salvadorian Tragedy*), first published in *Vuelta*.[35] Based on documents published by the guerrilla organizations, he judges Dalton severely, charging that he was no different from his executioners and that both sides advocated violence. "Who sacrifices whom? . . . Every combatant who does not accept simply being cannon fodder is a contender for the internal struggle for power," adding, "In the discourse of the pistol, the one who has the pistol wins."[36] Dalton was doubly dangerous because of his dissident opinions and the threat he posed to the leadership. A report by the Armed Forces of National Resistance (FARN) included in Zaid's article describes the internal struggles that led to the decision to eliminate Dalton, a decision that was probably determined when Dalton advocated building up grassroots support before beginning the armed struggle, in opposition to Rivas Mira and Villalobos, who wanted to initiate armed struggle.[37] Although the ERP responded to criticism by admitting that the execution had been a mistake, they attacked the petty bourgeois intellectuals "who think themselves the thinking head, leader, critic and rector of Latin American revolutionary processes" and who were now making Dalton a hero "when in all honesty he was victim and creator of his own death." Unlike the hundreds of humble women and men who had given their lives,

> Dalton poet and writer lived his life where the publicity and cult of individualism is the norm and now [he is] dead, they have gathered to condemn the assassins of such an illustrious poet and a good and cordial friend. For these gentlemen, it does not matter that he was responsible for a fratricidal struggle and they have converted him into the heroic poet and writer, standard of petty bourgeois thought, "revolutionary of revolutionaries."[38]

This condemnation in the guise of an apology confirms that within the revolutionary group dissent had no place. Zaid, who had no sympathy for the Left, believed that these armed groups were children of the upper class and the intellectual elite, but "those above do not agree on how to deal with those below: that is the conflict that makes Salvadorian blood flow."[39] What seems obvious, however, is that jealousy and personal factors were masked by putatively impersonal ideological arguments.

Ehrenreich, who has spoken to several of the actors, argues that, indeed, there was an ideological struggle and that "the revolutionary goal of the Rivas Mira, Villalobos and Rogel factions who opposed Dalton was short-term and militaristic. . . . The emphasis was on taking power, and doing it quickly."[40] Villalobos, who became commander of the ERP and turned it into an efficient military organization, was probably the one who pulled the trigger. He admitted being present when Dalton himself opposed his death sentence, "signaling . . . that it was going to be a grave error, that it was an injustice."[41] Unlike the Argentine victims, Roque Dalton was sacrificed not because he was an incompetent guerrilla but because he was a rival and rivalry was always a threat to the band of brothers. The absurdity of Dalton's death continues to haunt the Left. Former guerrillas helped form a postwar government but when, in 2010, the Salvadorian secretary of culture announced that it was "the year of Roque Dalton," Dalton's sons were enraged and "asked that officials of El Salvador's Leftist government never again mention their father's name or allude to his work in public."[42] Zaid's criticism underscored the fact that the personal can undermine political judgment, although he has more to say about the death of the poet than about the thousands of "unpeople," to use Noam Chomsky's term, who died at the hands of an army trained, financed and supplied by the United States. One percent of Salvador's civilian population were killed between 1978 and 1984.[43] Unlike Roque Dalton, the majority of these people cannot be mourned.

The River of Blood

The two incidents in Argentina and El Salvador are minor when compared with the sacrifice the Sendero Luminoso (Shining Path) of Peru expected of its followers. Under its leader, the philosophy professor Abimael Guzmán, the party was committed to "revolutionary violence" as defined by Lenin, Mao Tse Tung, and Guzmán himself, who, like Mao, confidently expected his followers to start an armed uprising even when they had no arms and to recruit and train forces in a reorganized countryside to prepare for taking over Lima and the cities.[44] And unlike the Guevarist warriors, a substantial proportion of the Shining Path's supporters and warriors were women, some of whom were killed.

On the cover of Santiago Roncagliolo's biography of Abimael Guzmán are the bars of a prison behind which Guzmán wearing a striped convict jumpsuit on which is imprinted his prison number raises a fist in defiance. Bearded and wearing dark glasses, he presents a picture of caged fury — caged, that is, like an animal, although the fury he unleashed was a human violence rationalized in dozens of speeches and communiqués.[45] Despite the crimes for which he has been charged, he has not paid with his life. Rather, he has become a trophy of the state, a bogeyman for frightening would-be revolutionaries. A photograph included in the collection *Yuyanapaq: Para recordar* (*To Remember*), published by the Commission of Truth and Reconciliation, shows him in the court-yard of a police intelligence unit, the DINCOTE. The courtyard is open to the sky and guarded from a rooftop by men with guns. On each side of the cage there are groups of men in business suits. Curtains that no doubt had shrouded the cage have been dropped to the floor, reveal-ing Guzmán pointing to a chair, not so much the caged beast but more the actor on stage.[46] The sidebar informs us it was in this manner that he was presented to a group of national and international journalists, for whom he did indeed put on an act, giving a speech and singing the Internationale. The photographs of the caged leader were intended to destroy his mystique, to cast him out of society, to exorcise him. After his imprisonment he declared peace with the government, as if he were a sovereign or the president of a nation.

The Shining Path was never populist and never a mass movement. It was organized from the top down, with its absolute leader and a Central Committee of his comrades that issued the directives. Guzmán, the il-legitimate son of an Ayacucho landowner, had taught philosophy at the University of San Cristobal Huamanga at a time when the explosive ex-pansion of the university population brought first-generation students into the institutions of higher education but without tangible prospects for advancement.[47] As a member of the Red Flag (Bandera Roja) Com-munist Party, he learned armed struggle at the Maoist fount in China, studying at the School for Foreign Militants in 1965 and again in 1967 at the height of the Cultural Revolution, when Mao was purging the party and when, in Guzmán's words, "all militants had to prove that they had sufficient credit to be communist."[48] At a time of massive internal struggles that culminated with the killings and tortures that consoli-dated Mao's power, Guzmán was learning how war could be started and won against the military might of the state and how to build a force with scarce resources. When he broke with the Red Flag and started a new party, his group was quite small. The Report of the Truth Commission put the number of militants at only 520 in the year the armed conflict started in 1980 and only 2,700 in 1990.[49] But figures alone do not account for the initial success of the call to arms and the attraction of a revolu-tion in the Southern Highlands that directed its fury toward Lima and "dependent modernity" and which offered young men and women some degree of authority and leadership but also the prospect of dying a heroic death. Guzmán's break with the Red Flag Communist Party hinged on his plan for the initiation of an armed struggle that would go far beyond guerrilla warfare and aim at the complete reorganization of social and political life, and even human life altogether.

While citing Marx and Lenin, Guzmán adhered closely to Mao's script. Describing the courses Guzmán followed in the school in Nanking, Santiago Roncagliolo in his biography of Guzmán noted that he later would emphasize that the education he received there began with "politics, popular war, the construction of armed forces, strategy and tactics, and the corresponding practical aspect: ambushes, assaults, retreats [*desplazamientos*] and how to prepare artifacts for demolition."[50] The idea was that the uprising should start from scratch. Students at the Chinese military school were told to take up arms and when they protested that they had no arms, the instructor replied, "Wrong. You haven't opened your eyes. A tree is an arm: it can be a shield. A stone is an arm: it can be a garrote. A ballpoint pen is an arm, it can be a dagger." Anything could be an explosive.[51] This is what Guzmán would put into practice. He had his followers steal dynamite from the mines, and kill with stones, machetes, knives, and guns captured in raids on police outposts. His revolution attracted young people impatient for change and lured by the novelty of the slogans, the drills, and even the exoticism of the rituals. When Deng Xiaoping assumed power after Mao's death and proceeded to undo many of Mao's policies and move China in the direction of a market economy, the Sendero took a fervent stand against this revision. In one of their most spectacular acts, they hanged dogs on Lima lampposts as effigies of the "son of a dog, Deng Xiaoping," an action that early on lent a certain exotic patina to their politics, marking their distance from other parties. A photograph in the book *Yuyanapaq* illustrates this exotic intrusion into everyday life. It shows a policeman untying a dog that had been hanged from a lamppost on a drab street. A group of young men stand by, watching him. On the dog is a partly visible sign that reads "Teng Hsiao Ping," just below a poster advertising commercial decorations, children's parties, and wedding showers. Behind the policeman is another poster announcing courses run by the

Asociación César Vallejo.[52] The photograph encapsulates the many aspects of everyday life in Lima from the street corner, the flashy clothes of one of the watchful youths, the wary glances toward the policeman and the drab surroundings that help to explain the pull of the exotic. Like the "estrangement" attributed to literary texts by the Russian formalists, the scene forces awareness of something beyond the everyday.

Naming himself the fourth star in a constellation that included Marx, Lenin, and Mao, Guzmán became the supreme leader, and *Pensamiento Gonzalo* (*Gonzalo Thought*) became the Bible of the party. The name "Comrade Gonzalo," some critics believe, was inspired by a character in Shakespeare's *The Tempest*[53] who dreams of lost and recovered sovereignty, and in this play Gonzalo, "the honest old counselor," is mocked for his utopian vision, which could not be more distant from that of Guzmán: Shakespeare's character imagines a country where there is no work and where women are innocent and pure and where there was

No Sovereignty. . . .
. . . .
. . . Treason, felony,
Sword, pike, knife, gun, or need of any engine
Would I not have: but nature should bring forth,
Of its own kind.[54]

Guzmán, an eclectic reader, liked to use literature in his teaching. The readings of the First Military School that was organized in 1980 included Shakespeare's *Julius Caesar* and *Macbeth* as lessons in conspiracy, but Guzmán also cited Mao, Lenin, and an essay titled "Mahomet" by Washington Irving. And despite his declared admiration for the Peruvian Marxist José Carlos Mariátegui, it was Mao who served as the principal ideological guide. Orin Starn argues that Guzmán's debt to Mao was the "relentless politicization of personal behavior and public life."[55] The borrowed rituals, "the wall-poster, dunce cap, street theater and the sung paeans to Mao (which they memorized in Mandarin) suggests that their very difference from Peruvian everyday practices was what attracted him and his followers."[56] He used Mao's trick of turning policy into catchy slogans and at meetings he targeted internal enemies, in particular those who did not believe Peru was ready for armed struggle. What he termed "the two lines" was the thesis and antithesis that always culminated in the victory of his thought. Although the name Shining Path acknowledged José Carlos Mariátegui as the Peruvian avatar, what he borrowed from him was only the slogan "shining path of communism." Guzmán, in fact, had no interest in the indigenous as such.[57] Nor did he assume the dress or attitude of a guerrilla fighter. Commenting on a photograph taken when he was arrested for demonstrating against General Velasco's plan to reform the university, Roncagliolo comments "that from this arrest dates the only photograph that shows Guzmán with a more or less guerrilla-like look — a hard look, badly shaved, disheveled hair, the prison environment. At this point he still merited respect as a professor and was speedily released. In the event, he would never be a fighter on the front line but rather a man who addressed from the cathedra, using the power of words."[58] This was spectacularly demonstrated when he launched the armed struggle in 1981, with a speech that concluded the business of the First Military School and proclaimed the revolution. It was a performative speech act that announced and brought into being, "a new moment: the strategic offensive of World Revolution." "Like the Deity creating the world," he announced, "from the darkness will come the light."[59] The language resonates with the evangelical fervor of a biblical prophecy that admits neither questioning nor discussion. But the debate was merely a preliminary to action, for what comes after the debate is preordained and is nothing less than global revolution: "The trumpet begins to sound. The roar of the masses grows and will continue to grow. It will deafen us. It will take us into a powerful vortex, to a single note. We will be the protagonists of history: responsible, organized, and armed. And this is how there will be a great rupture, and we will be the makers of the last new dawn."[60] The clash of metaphors is deafening, the tone prophetic, making him sound like an evangelical preacher. There is no need to define tactics given the preordained outcome:

> Infinite iron legions are rising, and more will rise and more and more. They will multiply inexhaustibly to encircle and annihilate the reactionaries. [The reactionaries] will seek to satiate themselves with the blood of the people. But the blood will rise like pulsing wings, and that bruised flesh will turn into the powerful whips of vengeance, and muscles and

actions will turn into a steel battering ram to destroy the oppressors who will be irretrievably smashed.[61]

This is prophecy on a grand scale that makes vengeance the motor of war and bloodshed inevitable. No doubt it had a strong appeal to the young graduates of universities who had no job prospects and whose future was blocked by the privileged. His party, he promised, would

> put the noose around the neck of imperialism and the reactionaries, seizing them and garroting them by the throat. They are strangled of necessity. The reactionaries' flesh will rot away, converted into ragged threads, and this black filth will sink into the mud, and that which remains will be burned and the ashes scattered by the winds of the earth so that only the sinister memory will remain of that which will never return, because it neither can nor should.[62]

Although this is the implacable language of biblical prophecy, there is nothing abstract about the punishment. Garroting, hanging, and strangling are methods of killing in which life is squeezed out of an "enemy" for whom there is no possible outcome but death. This enemy is identified as a class, never as an individual. During the Shining Path campaigns, people were killed because they were mayors or officials and whole villages condemned because they had been occupied by the army and his followers were expected to sacrifice themselves even though they could only be promised that the "bruised flesh" would be resurrected, not only in the form of the "pulsing wings" but as powerful "whips and battering rams" to scourge the enemy. The rank and file of the hierarchically structured party "figured as malleable objects of revolutionary truth, who, in the characteristic vehemence of an *El Diario* editorial would need to have ideas pounded into their heads through dramatic deeds."[63]

Christian and revolutionary discourse share the ideal of sacrifice. The Sendero leadership asked of their followers "a quota of blood," for, like the early Christians, they were marked for martyrdom. What is inexplicable is how young people were persuaded to accept their own deaths in the cause of a future that was not yet in sight. Carlos Iván Degregori argues that generations in the southern highlands had felt themselves deceived by the ruling class and looked to education as a tool of redemption. He finds that "the emergence of a caudillo-teacher like the leader of the Sendero Luminoso is not surprising," nor was the moralizing character of the party, which punished drunkards and adulterers or the use of Marxist textbooks in the universities, which in this period were crowded with first-generation students.[64] "Young people wanted *coherence*, a worldview that substituted the traditional Andean world that was no longer theirs," and "the party offered a coherent *intellectual* explanation of the physical, social world, of the history of philosophy and welcomed the very young giving them mission and an identity."[65] According to Orin Starn, the promise of escape "from a national history of corruption, poverty and despair forms a major foundation of the party's attraction to all of the cadres, male and female. Not so very different in this respect from evangelical churches, which grew with explosive rapidity in the fraught years of the 1980s."[66] But it is a big step from the evangelical mission promising salvation to the acceptance not only of martyrdom but also of criminal assassination. Vengeance was the drug that drove young people some as young as twelve and enrolled at an age when anger, passion, and resentment are not hard to arouse, to kill with stones and clubs, that is, the weapons at hand.

From Mao, Guzmán had learned that "war is the highest form of struggle to resolve contradictions between class, nations, states and political groups."[67] Like Mao, he always depicted the enemy as less than human — as animals or dirt. Although the cry for blood, as Orin Starn argued, took on a particularly Peruvian patina in its "preoccupation with written documents, elaborate greetings and official titles [that] reflected the Peruvian tradition of exuberant enchantment with legal protocol and formal ceremony,"[68] it was the language of violence and revenge that was used to persuade the masses, who must be taught "with decisive deeds in order to hammer in ideas."[69]

As the party's absolute leader and ideologue, Guzmán did not personally carry out cruel acts. In this sense, he was similar to other major authoritarian leaders, although, unlike Stalin and Mao, he was absolute leader *before* the revolution had taken place, assuming the title of president and making "Gonzalo thought," borrowed from an amalgam of Leninism and Maoism, the absolute guide to a "people's war" and violence the only method for replacing one class by another. Because he suffered from Ayacucho's altitude, his base was not in the southern highlands, which suffered the worst of the violence, but primarily in Lima, where he wrote and studied in a rented house. A captured video that acquired some notoriety showed him dancing to the music of Zorba the Greek along with his "high command," among whom were several women, including his first wife, Augusta, who died under mysterious circumstances, and Elena Iparraguirre, the woman who would succeed her as his companion.[70]

In effect, the Shining Path created a kind of cyst or tumor within the Peruvian state. Like the nation-state, the party had flags. It also had commemorative dates, such as 4 March, the date when two hundred prisoners were sprung from the Ayachucho jail; 17 May, which marked the start of the armed struggle; Heroism Day, on the anniversary of the massacre of Shining Path prisoners held in jail; Mariátegui's birthday on 24 June 1895; and 3 December, the birthday of Abimael Guzmán; and there were no less than twenty-seven "Chairman Gonzalo greetings."[71] The party, headed by Guzmán, was the nucleus around which a new state was to develop as the People's Guerrilla Army conquered and restructured its territories and set up "people's committees under commissars each in charge of a different function — security, production, communal affairs, and coordinating people's organization. "Action" committees were responsible for graffiti and explosions and special detachments were responsible for punishment and assassinations.[72]

In the early days of the uprising, when the Sendero cleansed the Ayacucho region of inefficient and corrupt authorities, they could still be seen as justified avengers, as the Robin Hoods of the Andes. Their first actions became legendary — the burning of ballot boxes in Chusqui on the eve of the general election of 1979 that elected the civilian government of President Belaúnde; and then the spectacular prison break from the Huamanga jail, which freed 78 Shining Path prisoners and about 169 criminals. Among the freed prisoners was the nineteen-year-old militant Edith Lagos, who soon afterward was killed in an attempt to steal a police truck. Her funeral in Ayacucho attracted thousands of mourners, up to thirty thousand, by some estimates. Lagos was one of the first of the women to give their lives for the cause. In a poem addressed to "wild grass," "the friend that flowers on my tomb," she prophesies that "in stone everything will be engraved." It is a telling mixture of metaphors that contrasts an ephemeral life with the permanence of death.[73] Indeed, the Shining Path women not only had a higher level of education than the men; they also formed a substantial percentage of the Central Committee and a substantial percentage of the warriors. Those in the "forces" killed and sometimes tortured. The courage of the women guerrillas was admired even by enemies. The executioner Jesús Sosa singled out the imprisoned militant "Carlota" for her spirited defiance. But what was striking was their acceptance of death. Carlota refused to collaborate, saying, "I am already dead, but the party will never die. When I am dead, the party will annihilate you. Besides, I die knowing that we will win. On the other hand, you will die without knowing why." In the same group was Clara Tello, the number one leader in the region. "She died from a bullet from Jesús Sosa's PPK [handgun]. He didn't attach much importance to it and they killed her with the rest of the prisoners, almost without interrogating her." Sosa watched Clara, wearing her hood, walk to her death with dignity, "conscious that it was her last walk, the moment that would arrive in any case, because they never thought to live to see communism."[74]

If anything was more bizarre than this willingness to be sacrificed, it was the massive suicide of members of the Jonestown congregation in Guyana. Such mass suicides are not uncommon, but they are almost always backed by religion, by expectations of an afterlife. Not so with the Shining Path. Gustavo Gorriti, in his essay on the "quota," reproduces a pamphlet with an illustration showing unarmed or inadequately armed Shining Path guerrillas facing the enemy and some of them falling in combat. Behind them is a conflagration. Gorriti attributes the willingness to die as a "secular fervor" that "allowed its believers not only to explain self-sacrifice but to desire it, and made not just understandable but permissible crimes and excesses."[75] The closest parallel to this sacrificial philosophy is the suicide bomber's grim determination.[76] As Achille Mbembe comments, "What connects terror, death and freedom is an *ecstatic* notion of temporality and politics. The future, here, can be authentically anticipated, but not in the present." The present itself is but a moment of vision —"a vision of the freedom to come."[77] Not only did followers accept the idea of the bloodbath; they even sang about giving their quota of blood:

Ahora la cuota hay que dar
Si nuestra sangre tenemos que dar
por la revolución, que bueno será.

(Now we must give the quota
Yes, our blood we must give
for the revolution,
how good will that be.)[78]

Gustavo Gorriti argues that as the war became more intense, "for many Shining Path militants, hunted and anguished, the idea of dying — 'snatching laurels from death' — took on the intense attraction of an experience both mystical and sensual. It was the perfect escape from unbearable anxiety, ceaseless work, and the ever imminent threat of capture, with its horrific consequences."[79] After most of the Central Command was captured and imprisoned during the uprisings in the prisons of San Juan Bautista (El Frontón and El Lurigancho in 1986), they were methodically killed by the military.[80]

Commenting on a collection of poems cobbled out of Guzmán's speeches and signed "Rosa Marinache," Victor Vich contrasts the Shining Path followers' lack of interest in the concrete situation of Peru and its culture with their devotion to an abstraction: "For them as Senderistas, 'what is written' and the teleological vision of history is what matters, that is now a totally seismic image, one according to which different cultural identities will have to be erased by a command that is always conceived as an homogenizing force."[81] Indeed, Shining Path strategy, like the slogans they attached to the hanged dogs, has no connection with life on the street. There was, however, a distance "between the Party (masculine, that included women leaders) and the masses [las masas] (feminine and plural)."[82] Vich cites one of the "poems," to the effect that the Party is supported by

las masas
que es la fuerza
de la tierra

porque la dirige
el partido que es la luz
del universo.

(The masses
that are the strength
of the earth
because directed
by the party that is the light
of the universe.) (27)

This tutelary and charismatic party, 40 percent of whose members were women made it a condition that women militants should act like men. Indeed, they rivaled the men in their implacable dedication, their discipline, and their acceptance of probable death.

They also accepted their role as ruthless enforcers. By 1983, in occupied areas, there were Popular Committees, that, with the aid of the Shining Path army, would found the New State.[83] At the Fourth Shining Path Plenary in 1981, the policy was to increase violence with the goal of provoking "blind, excessive reactions from the state."[84] The military plan was to progress from the first minor actions and the inauguration of the guerrilla war, to establishing support bases, and the formation of the nucleus of the New State that would finally bring about the conquest of power. The scope was grandiose, embracing world revolution. But the practice was less glorious. In the first year, it was directed toward weeding out representatives of the old order and the disciplining of the population, a process that, in the invaded villages, aroused hostility against the arrogant young militants. This would be demonstrated in Lucanamarca. The area of Huancasancos, Sanco, Lucanamarca, and Sacsamarca had been one of the earliest to be liberated. The "authorities" were forced to resign, and young militants were appointed to organize the life of the community. The Popular Committees, thus formed, carried out the policy of autarchy. They secured their authority first by executing Alejandro Marquina, a prominent member of the community, and seizing his cattle and then by reorganizing the community into a self-sufficient unit. To this end they prohibited markets and travel outside the community, even to visit families. As the Truth Commission

Report commented, this radical reorganization of communal life caused much resentment. People chafed at the numerous meetings, denunciations, and the slogans, and eventually, in frustration, they ambushed and killed the leader, an action that brought about their terrible reprisal when eighty "avengers" entered the community and proceeded to massacre men and women:

> The population concentrated in the square are laid on the ground, prevented from turning their eyes. Then the execution is ordered, beginning with the men whose faces they cover with ponchos so they cannot see how they will be executed. The women wait at the side, witnessing these scenes of death in which the men are victimized with axes, machetes, sticks, and pikes. The wounded are finished off with a shot so as not to leave a survivor.

A witness reported that, at the moment when the women were being drenched with kerosene before being burned, a child cried out from the church tower, "Comrades: the guards are entering, escape." This cry of alarm may have saved the population from being completely massacred. One of the victims, Alberto, who survived the massacre, had lost consciousness, and when he regained consciousness, he moved, at which point they again attacked him with axe and knife.[85]

The massacre acquired such notoriety that years later President Gonzalo tried to justify it in his "interview of the century," given to the newspaper *El Diario*, in which he described the action as strategically necessary in order to strike "a decisive blow to subdue them, to make them understand that it's not so easy in some occasions like this." Citing Lenin and Clausewitz on war, he argued that in battle the mass can express all its class hatred. To term Lucanamarca a genocide, he says, was propaganda rubbish: "Yes, we can emit a series of restrictions, demands and prohibitions: at bottom what we needed was for the waters to overflow, for the *huayco* to arrive, certain that when it arrives it overflows but then returns to its source."[86] The *huayco* is a devastating Andean flood, a force of nature, here used as a metaphor for the unstoppable consequence of class hatred. By describing the event as "natural," Guzmán reveals himself not as the intellectual he would like to be but as no different from any rabble-rouser who gave great promises. Perhaps he really believed what he said in one of his statements: "Other than Power, all is illusion."[87] But for the villagers who had not signed on for the great journey, the Shining Path was indeed the *huayco*.

At least 215 massacres were recorded by the Commission on Truth and Reconciliation. The report's section on crimes and violations of human rights is headed by the testimony of a Quechua-speaking survivor from Huanta, who quotes the assassins as saying, "Now we are going to finish off these miserable dogs. We are going to reduce them to ashes"; they then finished off the wounded by setting them on fire.[88] The words are a form of self-justification, assuring the speaker that these are lives not worth living, not worthy of the New State. When the Shining Path descended into jungle areas and attempted to take control of the Asháninka people, they herded them into settlements that were described by escapees as concentration camps.[89] They committed many acts of cruelty against the indigenous peoples. One of the most infamous of these, a massacre that was reported to the United Nations, occurred in 1993 in the Tsiriari Valley days after the capture of Abimael Guzmán. The massacre was committed with knives, arrows, and machetes, and some of the victims were hanged by their feet. There were five women among the dead, two of whom appeared to have been raped.[90]

From a punitive force that tried and executed thieves, rustlers, and corrupt officials, the Sendero became an avenging scourge as it undertook the forcible liquidation of the Old State to make way for the New State. This sounds fine in theory, but in practice it meant sending badly armed units who often had to resort to machetes and stones against an army equipped with helicopters, up-to-date weaponry, and eventually an intelligence apparatus that used torture to extract information. Against this overwhelming force, the Shining Path gambled the lives of its followers. While soldiers in a national army are expected to risk their lives to defend their country, that risk is not simply in the cause of an abstraction but embodied in family and place. For the Shining Path, on the other hand, sacrifice was made on behalf of an as yet invisible future, for an abstraction that was hard to imagine.

It was not only that revolution was necessarily violent but that violence must be provoked. The Shining Path's actions were designed to bring an avenging army into the field and effectively succeeded. The savage response of the military, which used torture, rape, and slaughter to retake areas occupied by the Shining Path, led the revolutionaries to call it a "white terror" and to charge Belaúnde's democratically elected government with initiating the great bloodbath that Guzmán had promised. For the Shining Path, the "valuable lesson" of the democratically elected government was that it unleashed extreme force against the insurgency, thus publicizing its extreme nature and justifying the insurrection.[91] But the state, which had an army equipped for counterterrorism, was more than a match for the Shining Path, and despite the Mao Tse Tung assertion Guzmán quoted — that "from the dawn of history, in revolutionary wars, those with inferior arms have always beaten those with arms of superior quality"— the army's resources, their terror tactics, and the intelligence gathered by the police units, the DINCOTE, and the special intelligence Task Force (GEIN) led them to prevail on both the military and the intelligence fronts. The discovery of Abimael's hiding place in Lima, his capture, and eventually his proclamation of peace, while weakening the leader, did not totally destroy the Shining Path.

The Sendero proclaimed their willingness to die as a challenge to the entire existing order. Yet the sacrifice was not equally shared. While the Central Committee was in a Lima safe house, the "masses" underwent arduous marches and the inadequately armed "parallel popular committees" were set up near military bases. It was a policy that contributed to the massive numbers of victims. And since many of the Sendero army killed with machetes or stones when they had no guns, the killings were especially cruel. But cruelty was also directed against their own followers. Any violation of discipline was punished with greater or lesser severity. Communities organized by the Shining Path constituted "the mass" and were under the command of the local force, which in turn was subordinated to the principal force. When the army approached, the "mass" were made to retreat often in conditions of extreme hardship. There were forced marches. Pregnant women, hungry from lack of food, gave birth in caves, and babies who cried were killed. Even the sleeping arrangements were rigidly organized. Children of both sexes were recruited as "young pioneers" who helped carry water and food and had also to attend the schools where they were taught guerrilla songs, how to draw the hammer and sickle, and strategies for evading the military.

At the age of twelve they were separated from their parents and incorporated into the local force where they would be trained as militants and eventually incorporated into the principal force. By recruiting the very young and women, the Shining Path targeted groups that had hitherto been deprived of power. Those who were recruited into the principal force, during retreats, slept apart from the "mass," confirming their superiority. Many of these were described as "white" by the indigenous, who understood the meaning of racial difference. Women, trained along with men, were expected to perform like them and did. Slogans were battle cries that consolidated the group and a heroic narrative was reiterated in song and in paintings. A dynamite attack on the police station in Vilcashuamán early in the conflict was commemorated by Senderista prisoners in the paintings that decorated the cells, showing women along with men aiming guns at prostrate prisoners.

Like the Church, the Shining Path leaders were experts in indoctrination, but where they departed from the Church was in giving the power over life and death to young boys and to women captivated by a discourse that offered them power and equality. What did it take to turn them into executioners who used machetes, knives, and stones to smash bodies? Were the victims regarded merely as physical obstacles on the path to the future? Like other cases examined in these pages, the influence of the group was crucial to the performance although it did not always work. Carlos Iván Degregori and José López Ricci recorded the memories of a young cadet who had taken part in the judicial executions and confessed that "it was scary and painful to kill in front of people." When the army intervened, he became convinced of the futility of the struggle and managed to escape to Lima.[92] Toward the lower ranks, the "mass," the Shining Path acted like any authoritarian regime, exacting absolute obedience to orders. The *retiradas* (retreats) were especially arduous for young girls, who, despite the official policy that prohibited rape, were often raped or forced to become the partner of one of the leaders. One witness recalled with bitter sarcasm that "under the pretext that it is a revolution, they forced girls and children or whatever to give them 'tierna' (flesh). That is to live with a comrade in the name of President Gonzalo, and then marry."[93]

But many others remained unshaken, especially those in the upper

ranks, the university-educated men and women who parroted the slogans with firm conviction. After interviewing Guzmán's partner, Elena
Iparraguirre, in prison and noting that she never lost her cool, Santiago
Roncagliolo commented, "The great strength of the Shining Path was
always an almost religious ideological conviction that allowed them to
run risks that would have been impossible and to think as a single brain.
They acquired such an identification with their discourse that different
people responded to questions using exactly the same words."[94]

In her book on the women of the Sendero, Robin Kirk struggles to understand their discipline and loyalty. On a visit to a prison she watched
the women marching under banners in front of a huge mural of comrade Gonzalo, shouting slogans in unison. It was impossible to interview
them as individuals.[95] The iron discipline was what enabled the command to remain aloof against charges of atrocities and genocide. Maritza
Garrido Lecca, the dancer whose studio was a cover for Guzmán's hiding place in Lima, stated flatly that "everything that was said about us
ordering extermination commandos or that we were bloodthirsty is a
lie."[96] Guzmán kept himself aloof from the sordid details, surrounding himself with solicitous women and sticking to a program of reading
and writing. When arrested in his Lima refuge, he was sitting calmly
at home, protected by his partner, who waved a red flag as she tried to
prevent the police from touching him.[97]

When questioned about atrocities, the leaders attributed them to "excesses" or described them as "errors," even though the actions became
increasingly indiscriminate when the Sendero escalated guerrilla warfare and began car bomb attacks and other operations in Lima. In 1992,
the Sendero assassinated María Elena Moyano, a well-known community organizer from Villa El Salvador, a shanty town where she organized
milk distribution for the children of the poor. Accused of informing on
a Senderista, she was shot at close range and her body dynamited, an
action that aroused outrage. In her testimony before the Truth Commission, Guzmán's partner, Elena Iparraguirre, would claim that Guzmán
had not ordered the dynamiting and that the operation had been taken
over by *inexpertos* (people with no expertise).[98] The most notorious and
outrageous of the Lima street bombings was also said to be a mistake.
The original plan was for a car bomb to blow up a bank, but the car was

unable to park nearby and instead veered into the busy Tarata Street in Miraflores, where an explosion killed 25 people and wounded 166. Again, according to Guzmán, it was an "error." The remoteness of the high command allowed them to deny responsibility or claim that failure was the work of incompetent subordinates. When the report of the Truth Commission was published, they termed it a misrepresentation.

The Shining Path's worst miscalculation was their violent incursion into and reorganization of the Andean communities, choices that eventually led villagers to form peasant defense units (*rondas campesinas*) to prevent the incursions and helped ensure their defeat by bringing about cooperation between the army and the villagers. Despite all the triumphant talk and the description of the war as if it were a popular uprising, the Sendero tactics alienated the very base they were supposed to attract because of their total indifference to the views of the "mass" and their hostility to indigenous difference. This happened not only in the Highlands but also in the selva, where Shining Path units initially attracted some Asháninka leaders and were drawn into the drug trade. After gaining control of a region along the rivers Tambo and Ene the leaders established strict discipline in the communities, organized the drug trade and according to the Truth Committee report even restricted family gatherings "thus undermining every kind of elective relation that was not based on discipline" (5:253). The "Popular Committees" were described by those who escaped as "concentration camps" where infractions were judged by members of the Fuerza Principal. It was the group psychology and not the petty bourgeois individualism that prevailed, and nowhere was this more evident than in the prisons.

The government had reopened the notorious prison, El Frontón, just off the coast. It was here that Shining Path prisoners established a "shining combat trench" (*luminosa trinchera de combate*) by gaining control of the prison and making it "a training center, an internal selection process, and a planning and indoctrination center."[99] On a visit to the prison, Gorriti was treated to the slogans, each chanted three times, and an hour of singing and was astonished at the way the Sendero had taken control of the prison. The words of the songs expressed absolute faith in the party and in Gonzalo. In an interview with some of the leaders, Gorriti asked how they justified their assassinations of governors, mayors, and owners of small businesses. They replied, "we kill them because they betray the people's cause. There is no outcome for these individuals other than execution." He added, "Besides, this is revolution, and all who opposed this revolution will simply be crushed like one more insect."[100] The date when Alan García's government responded to a coordinated uprising in the Frontón, Lurigancho, and Callao jails with a wholesale massacre, 19 June 1986, was commemorated as the "Day of Heroism."[101] As one of the epigraphs to his novel *Red April* (*Abril rojo*), Santiago Roncagliolo cites a quotation from Helmuth von Moltke reprinted in a Sendero pamphlet. It reads, "War is holy, its institution divine and one of the sacred laws of the world. In men, it maintains all the great sentiments such as honor, disinterestedness and valor. And in a word, it prevents falling into the most repugnant materialism." Each of these claims was negated in the Peruvian civil war.

The Commission on Truth and Reconciliation clearly placed the blame for the ferocity of the war, on the "armed violence" of the Shining Path. Yet the army made use of the war to commit atrocities, particularly rape. The problem is complex and troubling. For to describe all those who died as "victims" suppresses differences between the foot soldiers in a war and the "collateral damage," just as to describe all Shining Path recruits as "terrorists" accentuates the division of Peruvian society, where "reconciliation" is just a word. As I write, there is news that the Shining Path is reorganizing in the Highlands. If true, it indicates that the problems that drove many young people into their ranks are still in place.

The rival guerrilla organization, the MRTA (Movimiento Revolucionario Túpac Amaru), was less powerful and presented a more conciliatory front when occupying an area. One of their major tactics for accumulating resources was kidnapping and the confinement of captives in harsh conditions in so-called "people's prisons." Among their most spectacular actions was the organization of an escape from the Miguel Castro prison in Lima and in 1990 their fatal takeover of the Japanese embassy, which allowed President Fujimori to televise his victory and execute the perpetrators. Like the Shining Path and the FARC of Colombia, with whom they were associated, they became involved in drug trafficking, exacting tolls from planes flying over the zones they occupied in the selva. Their deeply contradictory mission is epitomized by a photograph included in the collection titled *Yuyanapaq*, which shows a MRTA couple seated on a kitchen floor, their faces mostly covered with a red cloth with "MRTA" printed on it. The man is holding a gun with one hand and has his other arm around the girl, who is holding a baby on her knee. Beside her is an automatic rifle that has been wrapped with white cloth. The baby looks up at the mother's masked face as if fascinated. The couple are identified as Nestor Carpa Carolini and Nancy Gilvonio. But the juxtaposition of death symbols with signs of homeliness, love, and family is jarring. What is it supposed to tell us? In 1989, MRTA killed transvestites in the bar Gardenia in Tavapoto because it regarded them as *lacras sociales* (social scabs). Among such social scabs, they numbered homosexuals, drug addicts, thieves, and prostitutes. In 1989 they assassinated an Asháninka leader on the grounds that as a child he had informed on a MRTA leader named Máximo Velando; they referred to it as an act of "historic justice," but it sparked an Asháninka uprising against them.

Roncagliolo, who managed to interview many Senderistas, wrote that "the great strength of Sendero was always the almost religious ideological conviction that allowed them to take impossible risks and think as with a single brain. . . . Their mind was equipped in such a hermetic fashion that no leader has broken or sold out in two decades. But what gave them strength was also their greatest weakness. They could not control love, hatred, treachery."[102]

All around, in a belated glance, the known, the sum of feeling and perceiving, the most abstruse and the clearest are slowly displaced, although it is a vertiginous and intense trajectory in an endless flight toward nothingness. Such is the experience of death, say those who have lived it and have come back to the world of the tangible. They have experienced the future of all of us. The amnesia of which we are ignorant.

—Sergio González Rodríguez, *El hombre sin cabeza*

SIX | Cruel Survival

Surviving can be as cruel as dying. The Chilean novelist Diamela Eltit, in the introduction to Cherie Zalaquett's book *Sobrevivir un fusilamiento* (*Surviving an Execution*), challenges Primo Levi's assertion that nobody witnesses their own death:

> We who were favored by fate tried, with more or less wisdom, to recount not only our own fate but also that of the others, indeed of the drowned; but this was a discourse "on behalf of third parties," the story of things seen close at hand, not experienced personally. The destruction brought to an end, the job completed, was not told by anyone, just as no one ever returned to describe his own death.[1]

For Eltit, on the other hand, the survivors of executions "represent an extreme exception inasmuch as they were assassinated but nevertheless went on living."[2] She is referring, of course, to the Chilean case, but by examining the testimony of other survivors of executions, it is clear that while the moment of horror was followed by a long and tormented afterlife, there were available forms of representation that allowed them to speak of the event. The "impossibility of experiencing and subsequently memorizing an event" in the aftermath of trauma has been a topic of Holocaust studies.[3] But whereas Holocaust victims had lived in the camps, sometimes for years on the threshold of death, the survivors whose afterlife I examine in this chapter were abruptly separated by a single event from their former lives, and they lived the trauma very differently. Miguel Mármol, a communist organizer "executed" during the 1932 massacre in El Salvador, was able to convert his experience into a communist allegory.[4] Rufina Amaya Márquez, a mother who lay hidden while her children were killed along with nearly all the inhabitants of El Mozote in El Salvador, would tell her story over and over again as a maternal lament, often with slight variations.[5] The eight survivors, whose stories are recorded by Cherie Zalaquett, were rural workers; they were executed by the Chilean army in the aftermath of Pinochet's coup in 1973, victims of "the method," the often random annihilation of all those seen as a threat to the state. The very fact of their survival in 1932 seemed uncanny to them, for they could not reconcile their survival with the death of others. The singular event is reconstructed as allegory by Mármol, as a maternal lament by Amaya, and, by the Chilean workers, as a violent dislocation of selfhood in the aftermath of Chile's "caravan of death."

Mármol's account, transcribed years after the event by Roque Dalton, not only exemplifies "crystallized, perfected, adorned memory installing itself in the place of raw memory and growing at its expense" mentioned by Primo Levi,[6] but also reveals the massive repression and selection that ruptures the coherence of the story. Rufina Amaya Márquez, like the Ancient Mariner, was forced to repeat her story for decades, which was met with official denial.[7] The eight survivors were so deeply traumatized that they could not be interviewed before their execution by the Chilean army in 1973.

Execution as Allegory

During the massacre in El Salvador in 1932, the communist shoemaker Mármol stood before a firing squad, but survived by chance. More than thirty years later he narrated the story of his survival in the form of an interview with the Salvadorian poet Roque Dalton. Dalton, who had himself barely escaped execution in El Salvador, had initially thought of writing a novel based on the survival story.[8] But in the 1960s, the testimonio had become the privileged genre for the representation of the subaltern classes. Socialist realism had been discredited, while tape-recorded life stories were seen as truly the voice of the subaltern, as Oscar Lewis had triumphantly proclaimed.[9] But although the testimonio was often considered an expression of the underclass, it was by no means a transparent category.[10] It involves a negotiation of sometimes divergent points of view, even of divergent cultures. Dalton's book was not a tape-recorded memoir but a book based on notes he took during the interview in Prague into which he inserted his own commentaries. The book cover shows the two men sitting on a bench and Dalton taking notes by hand. The published book was not only a description of the events of 1932 as seen by a communist militant but a heavily edited version of the events from the perspective of the 1960s and the early 1970s, when Dalton finally completed the manuscript. During this period the Communist Party's tactics of waiting for the revolutionary moment had ceded to the impatience of the guerrilla movements. The time lapses between the massacre and the interview, and between the interview and publication spans a period when Dalton himself was in the process of shedding his Communist Party affiliation and joining the guerrillas, a process that must have affected his interpretation of events that had happened decades before.[11] Between the 1932 massacre and 1965, between Mármol and Dalton, there was a temporal and an ideological gap. The published account is a much-edited compromise and was intended to illustrate communist causality, even though the communists did not initiate the rebellion. Mármol would narrate it as allegory.

The executions and the massacre (La Matanza) ordered by General Maximiliano Hernández Martínez, who had seized power in 1931, effectively repressed two insurgent forces, that of the nascent Bolshevik Party and that of an indigenous peasant movement that demanded the restoration of lands. The mass execution of communists was one incident in weeks of slaughter that left thousands dead, the majority indigenous peasantry. Mármol/Dalton's testimonio is a version of the uprising interpreted as a workers' revolt that did not and could not document the indigenous rebellion. It raises questions not only about the narrativization of experience, but also about the interpretation of history and about the difference between the carefully edited written record, and the oral tradition of indigenous peoples. More nuanced and detailed versions of the rebellion became possible through the archival work of the historians and the memories of witnesses who told of scenes and events that Mármol could not have known about. Jeffrey L. Gould and Aldo Lauría-Santiago, the authors of *To Rise in Darkness*, have provided a detailed account of the historical precedents and the rural strikes and uprisings. The historians who authored *Remembering a Massacre in El Salvador* investigated the sometimes conflicting histories that went into the Mármol-Dalton collaboration. While they acknowledged that Mármol's testimonio had been important in breaking the silence around the massacre and had become "the master narrative of 1932" and a canonical text in El Salvador,[12] by bringing the indigenous and peasant revolts into the picture, they were able to refute "communist causality," in particular, Mármol's account that made the Communist Party the main protagonist and instigator of the rebellion. To set the record straight, they exhaustively researched the archives comparing Dalton's notes of the interview with the published book, pointing out the discrepancy between the 59 pages of the original manuscript, the 80 pages of additional documents, and the 395 pages of the final version.[13] What this tells us is that Mármol was not only *remembering* the massacre but narrating it as an exemplary story of communist brotherhood, courage, and faith in victory after death.

Mármol represented himself as an exemplary character and more particularly, an exemplary communist who was self-educated, thanks to peripatetic teachers, the schooling in prisons and popular universities, and a plethora of newspapers and publications for those who could read, among them *El Machete* in Mexico and *El Martillo* in El Salvador and *The Bolshevik Submarine*, a journal that was distributed from Panama. Marxist theories freely circulated. Pamphlets, books, and manuscripts of every conceivable left-wing tendency were distributed by the Workers Federation of New York, including Lenin's pamphlets *Left Wing Communism: An Infantile Disorder* and *The Proletarian Revolution*. Bukharin and Preobrazhensky's ABC *of Communism* was an indispensable primer that summarized the basic concepts of Soviet communism — the dictatorship of the proletariat, the question of nationality, and explained the Soviet Union's policies on industry, agriculture, banks, and even hygiene.[14] The authors of a text that declared that "in extreme cases the

workers' government must not hesitate to use the method of the terror"
would themselves fall victim to the terror machine after being sentenced
during the Moscow trials. But in the 1920s and early 1930s, the Soviet
Union was still the glowing example of a successful revolution achieved
in the name of the working class. During this period, the devastating effects of the world economic crisis of 1929 spurred rebellions and protest.
The unpopular government of Arturo Araujo was unable to stem strikes
or stop demonstrations, nor could it satisfy landowners clamoring for
a military solution. General Martínez, Araujo's vice president, was the
landowners' chosen candidate to deal with the unrest, and in December 1931 a military junta headed by Martínez took power, even though
municipal elections in which the Communist Party expected to win
seats were imminent. When the elections were suspended, there were
uprisings in the countryside, especially among the indigenous, who demanded the return of communal lands and became a potent element in
the uprising, allying themselves with the Socorro Rojo Internacional
(International Red Aid),[15] a front organization for the Soviet Union that
was set up in New York and other cities to aid imprisoned comrades. In
El Salvador, International Red Aid mobilized peasants in demonstrations on behalf of prisoners and became the de facto revolutionary force,
so that in fields and villages thousands of miles from the Soviet Union
the imagination of peasants were captivated by the hope of taking back
the land. Yet, as Jeffrey L. Gould and Aldo Lauría-Santiago point out, the
Communist Party itself interpreted the unrest solely in terms of class
obfuscating "relevant local histories and relationships, in effect contributing to the left's blind spot with regard to ethnic relations and the
complex local histories of ethnic factionalism in local politics."[16] The
machete-wielding rebels briefly occupied some dozen small towns in the
west of the country. Meanwhile inspired by the success of the Bolshevik
Party in the Soviet Union the small and recently founded Communist
Party of El Salvador voted to join in a rebellion they did not initiate, believing it would pave the way for the workers' revolution. The historians
Héctor Lindo-Fuentes, Erik Ching, and Rafael A. Lara-Martínez argued
that for decades both the Right and the Left persisted in ascribing the
rebellion to "communist causality," a view that was shared by the Right,
who used "communist" indiscriminately to refer to Indians, peasants,

and the poor.[17] Practically speaking, the party that was predominantly ladino lacked familial and personal ties to the western countryside, especially to its Indian communities.[18] Rather than a vanguard, the party was caught up in a struggle whose impetus initially came from other quarters. Indeed, though a majority at the Central Committee agreed to join the rebellion, several members disagreed.[19] After fixing the date of 16 January for the uprising, and at the urging of their leader, Farabundo Martí, the party postponed their participation until the 19th and then further postponed the uprising until the 22nd despite a warning that the "government knew practically everything." Yet recollecting the insurrection from the vantage point of 1965, Mármol still insisted that "we [the Communist Party] had more than enough strength in the Army, together with the active support of the insurrectionist masses in the countryside and cities, to smash the bourgeois state apparatus" (243), an optimistic assessment that seems to contradict his description of their disarray, his acknowledgment that

> instead of a party that was on the point of initiating a big insurrection, at least that's how all the cadres in San Salvador talked about it, we had the appearance of desperate, persecuted and harassed revolutionaries. From the first moment, it was clear that rivers of blood were flowing, that the fighting was completely lopsided and the people were losing, due to the better organization and total superiority of fire power of the government forces. (247)

The leaders, Farabundo Martí, Alfonso Luna, and Mario Zapata, were captured and executed even before the uprising. Mármol was captured and interrogated, imprisoned in a crowded cell with his comrades and beaten as he was being marched off to the truck, which he soon realized was taking them to their deaths.

Andreas Huyssen points out that "the past is not simply there as memory but it must be articulated to become memory."[20] In Mármol's story, the ignominious failure of the insurrection is transformed into an allegory of communist solidarity and faith in a cause that they believed would inevitably triumph. As the trucks bore them to their execution, he was comforted by the folkloric reflection that he had been lucky "because I was going to die close to my village, close to where my umbilical cord is buried" (58). But this reversion to some ancestral acceptance of death is quickly transmuted into a narrative of solidarity, sacrifice, and brotherhood. In the truck, Mármol had been thrust against the legs of a Russian (who knows how he got there?), the embodiment of universal comradeship. When they were lined up before the execution squad, he said, "I will die alongside Comrade Mármol," a significant gesture that was sealed by their clasped hands. "As best as we could, we joined hands behind our backs, uniting us, and we stood against the wall together feeling proud" (59).

Everything in the account is meant to underscore the ideal of a collective and voluntary resolve, in contrast to the nervous firing squad. "When Captain Alvarenga asked 'Let's see, which one of you, wants to die next?' 'Me,' I shouted, and I took a step forward." After repeated salvos, he was knocked down but helped up by the policemen. "'Fuck it,' I said, 'you'll never put an end to me this way.'" Mármol commented, "I don't know where the serenity, the feeling of invulnerability came from." Wounded after another salvo, he fell. "The Russian's body was over mine and still dripping warm blood. . . . Some of the brain matter fell over my head, making it look like it was my brains coming out of the wounds on both temples" (60). The Russian thus becomes not only his brother but also his savior. Seriously wounded, he nevertheless escaped the slaughter to become the sole and authoritative witness in a belated testimony that was an allegory of death in which he personified secular resurrection. It was as allegory that *Miguel Mármol* broke the silence around the year 1932, which had been effaced from "the official record of Salvadorian history."[21]

What made Mármol's post-trauma experience so different from other survivors of executions is that he is able to fit his experience into a narrative. As he lay wounded but still alive, Mármol felt that he had "been born again" and describes his task and that of other revolutionaries as seeing to it "that justice is done on earth. Not vengeance. We are not romantic avengers, rather we strive to be scientific revolutionaries who work with the laws of history" (311). During his flight from the place of execution, Mármol could no longer sustain the heroic narrative. Now he was totally dependent on the help of others, especially the help of women. The revolutionaries were men. "When it comes to women," he said, "there was nothing to be said," even though it was women, his wife, his sister, his lovers, his children who faced the burdens of hunger and hardship. Women were treacherous. One female comrade later told him she believed he was a cop (396).[22] During his flight, desperately hungry, he comes upon fishermen who are having very little luck. In the darkness they see a girl whom they take for the legendary Ciguanaba,[23] in whom, as a communist, he cannot believe. "However, just in case, I decided not to go on in the darkness" (338). Hearing from a cook that General Martínez had conjured him up during a séance, he dismisses it.

> Like many things that have happened to me in my life to which I've never found a common thread and which I decided to forget, because, on the one hand, their solution doesn't put food on the table and, on the other, why go looking for a tiger without stripes. Being a communist and having an understanding of the problems of society is enough for me. When the people make their revolution, there will be time to delve into the mysteries of nature and death. (395)

This self-censorship, the determination to ignore all that escaped Marxist analysis, may well have been what kept him mentally stable, but it also prevented him from understanding that it was often not science but human weakness that motivated his comrades' actions. After being recaptured in 1934, he was released and then forced to report every two weeks to the police, which made him suspect in the eyes of his comrades. This he describes as one of the worst blows. "The bullet and machete blows are marks that fill me with pride but these ones I'm talking about are scars deep in my soul and maybe even in my ideology, and that's why I prefer to hide them, to bury them off someplace where no one will see them. Someplace where they can't hurt" (401).

Whereas Mármol stresses the confusion, the indecisions and dubious tactics, and describes the heroism of individuals, the editor and critic Roque Dalton, speaking from the viewpoint of the Leninist intellectual of the 1960s, judges Mármol's account to be simplistic, revealing only a crude knowledge of Marxism and inadequate analysis. Thus, *Miguel Mármol* is not only about the events of 1932 but also a judgment on those events viewed in the light of the Cuban Revolution as seen by Dalton and laced with his own view of communist causality and his prejudices.

For instance, in his introduction, Dalton comments critically on Mármol's language, which mixes "that everyday-colloquial, almost folkloric expression, the gamut of *popular speech* with a style of language charged with the catchwords and clichés of traditional Marxist-Leninists of Latin America; and even with a new kind of political-literary language of undeniable formal quality" (31). In a revealing comment he admits that he had refrained from imposing stylistic uniformity on the text, although he himself had to make an effort

> to accept that there was nothing incongruent in that the very man who told me about his childhood with the style of a bucolic-*costumbrista* poet, was also capable of structuring, with an extreme, indispensable verbal harshness, an analysis of the military errors of Salvadoran communists in '32, or the examination and characterization of this or that Salvadoran government on the basis of the state of the relations of production and productive forces at a given moment. (31)

For his part, Mármol described Dalton as "an intellectual of petty bourgeois origin" and made the possibly ironic comment that "an intellectual comrade is always more radical and extreme than a worker." In a farewell letter to Dalton, included in the testimonio, he emphasizes the role "we workers play *as a class.*" The party "emerged from the bowels of our working class" (149), he states, as if to underscore an authenticity that the intellectual could never claim. Nevertheless, in an interview with the English translators in 1986 included in the English version of the testimonio, Mármol does not make any criticism of the edited book, or comment on the additions, possibly because it represents him as he wanted to be represented, as an exemplary communist.

What turned the defeat into a genocidal massacre was not only the execution of communists but the participation of the indigenous who because of their ethnic origins bore the brunt of the landowners' anger.[24] Many were killed because they had signed the list of communist candidates in the municipal elections. In Nahuilzalco, 3,888 Indians who had asked for identity papers certifying that they were not communists were executed.[25] In some places the army killed all males older than twelve. The killing lasted for two weeks, and there were so many dead that the unburied bodies became a health crisis.[26] The indigenous leader

Feliciano Ama was lynched by landowners and hanged from a tree as a warning to others. The massacre was not only followed by repressive measures and the foundation of the notorious National Guard but also led the landowners to join paramilitary organizations and terrorize the indigenous even after the army had suspended military activities.

Repression of indigenous peoples caught up in civil war was not a unique event. The Army of the Poor in Guatemala and the Sendero Luminoso similarly brought collateral damage to indigenous communities. In El Salvador, the Matanza and its aftermath left the country in a state of amnesia that lasted for decades and led indigenous peoples to suppress their ethnic identity. Moreover, in El Salvador, the indigenous had been protagonists in the fight for ownership of the land and the massacre silenced a significant sector of the population. The survivors only began to record their memories after the signing of the Peace Accords in 1992. Jeffrey Gould's documentary film *Cicatrizes de la memoria* (*Scars of Memory*) records the memories of aged survivors.[27] In these indigenous narratives, the ladinos are termed *particulares*, in contrast to the *naturales*. The epithets speak volumes as they differentiate between the private person (the "particular") versus original communities. They also demonstrate that even slaughter was not enough to satisfy the landowners. The widows of the dead were forced to sign over their land, and the survivors stopped speaking Nahuatl and wearing native dress. Yet indigenous peoples found ways of expressing their deep resentment. Indigenous women would turn their backs whenever a ladino passed, and within the communities there was doubtless no amnesia, nor was there anything like Mármol's heroic version of the events. Because of these indigenous memories we know that massacre involved an immense killing machine, whose effect on the perpetrators (army and landowners) seems to have left no guilt or regrets. In the cause of "civilization," everything was fully justified. The self-righteousness of the victors stands in contrast to the tactical silence of the indigenous, which covered and concealed bitter memories. Indeed, it is significant that when civil war broke out in the 1970s, the struggle was less intense in the areas that had been decimated decades earlier. The 1932 uprising had brought together disparate groups — the indigenous, whose demands were fueled by injustice; poverty-stricken artisans and workers; and a handful of liberal army officers. There was no place in El Salvador for negotiation. For Mármol and those who survived the indigenous massacre there was a full stop on political organizing that lasted until the civil war of the 1980s. But the damage to the indigenous community was far greater than the damage to the Left, which later was able to reorganize, albeit not under the control of the Communist Party.

La Llorona

Rufina Amaya's account of her survival of El Mozote massacre in El Salvador is both lament and testimony. It was documented by the journalists Raymond Bonner and Alma Guillermoprieto, who, despite the US government's skepticism and the Salvadorian government's denial that a massacre had taken place, visited the site of the massacre and drew on Amaya's account for the *New York Times* (Bonner) and the *Wall Street Journal* (Guillermoprieto). They had crossed separately into El Salvador from Honduras guided by members of the guerrilla army and had heard Amaya tell her story, which was ignored in El Salvador and only confirmed in 1992 when an Argentine team began to exhume the bodies. An amnesty declared by President Cristiani in 1993 effectively prevented the massacre from entering the public consciousness. Only in 2012 did the Inter-American Court of Human Rights state its intention of taking on the case.[28]

Guillermoprieto arrived in El Mozote a month after the event and interviewed Amaya in the guerrilla camp where she had taken refuge. Mark Danner, who visited the site of the exhumation and also heard Amaya tell her story, wrote that "though she had told her story again and again, much of the world had refused to believe her. In the polarized and brutal world of wartime El Salvador, the newspapers and radio stations simply ignored what Rufina had to say."[29] The exception was the Tutela Legal, the organization headed by the archbishop of El Salvador, which interviewed her in 1990 and published a book on the massacre in 2005. An amplified version of her interview was recorded in 2006 and published after her death in 2007. As the editors comment, "For more than 25 years, Rufina repeated her testimony in the most diverse spaces of national life and in various parts of the world. The recuperation of the historical memory of the event in El Mozote is largely due to Rufina's

Exhumed remains of El Mozote victims. Photograph by Susan Meiselas, courtesy Magnum Photos.

courage in relating the terrible memories of her existence."[30] Her eyewitness account was also recorded for the Memory Museum in El Salvador with the title *Sólo me embrocaba a llorar.*[31]

El Mozote, Rufina's home in the Morazán province of El Salvador, was inhabited by Adventists, evangelical Christians, and Catholics and had remained essentially aloof from the conflict, a fact ignored by the army command when they set out "to drain the sea" of guerrilla support or, in other words, eradicate their support networks. Although the residents of El Mozote were not active rebel supporters, they lived in a zone that the guerrillas frequently used as a corridor. The executioners were the soldiers of a specially trained battalion, the Atlacatl battalion, commanded by the US-trained Colonel Monterrosa.[32]

Both the army and the insurgents were conscious of historical precedents. The army cited 1932 as a precedent when they adopted the name of General Maximiliano Hernández Martínez for one of their brigades. The year 1932 was also important to the insurgent groups that formed the FMLN (Frente Farabundo Martí de Liberación Nacional), an alliance named after the Communist Party secretary executed during the 1932 insurrection. It was the strength and the superior strategy of the later insurgency that prevented the civil war from becoming a repetition of 1932, one of the major factors being the improvement in communications. The radio station Venceremos transmitted from Morazán province news about army atrocities and insurgent victories. These stories were picked up and forwarded by foreign correspondents to the world at large, and they no doubt were the incentive that brought the army to an area it believed was a support base for the guerrillas. After the massacre, the Venceremos report of what had happened in El Mozote brought the US journalists to the Honduran border, from which they were guided to the site by members of the guerrilla organization to view the heaped bodies of those unfortunate enough to have been the victims of the punitive expedition, known as Rescue Operation (Operación Rescate). As Raymond Bonner described it, "The carnage was everywhere. I saw skulls, rib cages, femurs, tibias protruding from the rubble of cracked roofing tiles, charred beams, children's toys, crushed sewing machines, and kitchen utensils."[33] Guillermoprieto's account of arriving at the site of the massacre guided by guerrillas was seized on by the government as proof that reporting on El Mozote was a propaganda exercise. In the months that followed, the Salvadorian army would admit only that El Mozote had been the site of a battle with the guerrillas, and at congressional hearings in Washington, officials repeatedly denied that any massacre had taken place.[34] In 1993, the report of the Comisión de Verdad stated that the accounts of witnesses had been fully corroborated by the results of the 1992 exhumation of the remains.[35]

The commander of the Atlacatl Battalion, Colonel Monterrosa, who was responsible for Operación Rescate, had been specially trained for counterinsurgency under the supervision of US military advisers.[36] When they arrived by helicopter, they set to work methodically. The enormous labor of killing hundreds of people as well as raping the women took hours. When killing with bayonets proved too laborious, they began to shoot them. In Rufina Amaya's account, these "violence workers" sat down after a day of slaughter to gossip as if it were a lunchtime break in a factory. She was struck by the fact that "the soldiers had no fury. They just observed the lieutenant's orders. They were cold. It wasn't a battle."[37] This training, perfected by the military under the control of the US advisers, ensured a killing machine that would function rapidly and efficiently, a kind of Taylorization of murder. Although the cold calculation and methodic separation of the victims by sex and age seem to support the contention that this kind of killing was a peculiarly modern phenomenon, performed by "violence workers," setting children on fire with flamethrowers suggests something beyond cold-blooded execution. South of El Mozote in the village of La Joya, a seventy-year-old woman, a mother, and her three-day-old baby were killed. "On the adobe walls, the soldiers had scrawled, 'The Atlacatl Battalion will return to kill the rest.'"[38]

Rufina saw a good deal, but not all, and clearly some of her first interviews given to Bonner and Guillermoprieto differ in detail from the interview that Mark Danner drew on in 1992 and from her testimony to Tutela Legal and the Truth Commission report.[39] She saw some of the men, among them her husband, being killed. When killing them with machetes proved too laborious, the remaining men were herded into the chapel (*ermita*) and were shot, a labor that seems to have taken from five in the morning to midday. At five in the afternoon, the women were lined up for killing, and some were taken to be raped before being killed. Rufina was rounded up with a group of women, her baby snatched from her. At the back of a line of women, she managed to slide into a hiding place under a crabapple tree, from which she could hear not only the cries of the other women and those of the children but even the conversation of soldiers taking a break from their exertions. The conditioning of the soldiers was so thorough that obedience to army orders took precedence over pity. From her hiding place, Rufina heard one of the men wondering what would be done with the children, some of whom were "pretty," but a comrade reassures him. "The order we have is that we shouldn't leave any of these people because they are guerrilla collaborators, but I would not want to kill children." Yet the army orders prevailed, and the children were killed in particularly cruel ways.[40] A young boy who managed to run away saw the soldiers throw a three-year-old into the air and stab him with a bayonet. "They slit some of the kids' throats, and many they hanged from the tree."[41] As she crawled to the relative safety of a manzanal, Rufina heard children calling out, "They're killing us. They're hanging us, they're knifing us."

Memories are not set in stone, and Rufina's story changes slightly with each telling. In the account given by Bonner, her nine-year-old son screamed, "They're killing me. They've killed my sister. They're going to kill me" (338). The account given by Danner reads, "They were crying, 'Mommy! Mommy! They're hurting us! Help us! They're cutting us! They're choking us! Help us!' Then I heard one of my children crying. My son, Cristino, was crying, 'Mama Rufina, help me! They're killing me! They killed my sister! They're killing me! Help me!'" (75). Whether she in fact heard her children screaming these exact words is not the point. She was putting into words a cry for help that, if not actually uttered, became registered in her mind. Her enforced passivity as she crouched close to the ground, the inability to answer her children's appeal for protection, was agonizing. "I could hear the children screaming still, and I lay there with my face against the earth and cried." The Spanish title of Rufina's story, "Sólo me embrocaba a llorar," combines weeping with decanting, pouring from one vessel to another, as if there is no end to weeping. She at first persuaded herself that the children were not dead. It was only when the army had left and she saw the houses filled with the dead that she knew they had been massacred.

What makes the story especially harrowing is that Rufina's own struggle for survival in order to be able to tell the tale meant going against every instinct of motherhood. While Mármol, dry-eyed, seems unable or unwilling to mourn, Rufina's public mourning is a form of expiation — a confession, not an allegory. Mármol wove his survival into a story of communist courage; for Rufina, repeating the story would be her perennial task. She becomes La Llorona, the mythical woman forever lamenting the loss of her children.[42]

The US administration did its best to suppress or minimize accounts of the massacre, a suppression that was crucial to US certification policy, according to which military aid could only be given as long as El Salvador complied with internationally recognized standards for human rights, controlled its armed forces, and made progress in economic and political reform. Between the 1932 Matanza and the civil war, the techniques had become more brutal. The executions of 1932 were bad enough, but in the 1980s, executions resembled work in a slaughterhouse enhanced by torture and acts of cruelty. El Mozote was only one event in a civil war in which there were many other atrocities, the most publicized being the assassination of Archbishop Romero, the killing of four American nuns, and the slaughter of Jesuits priests who had compiled documentation at the José Simeón Cañas University. In 1981, during the first six months of the Reagan administration, 7,152 Salvadorians met violent deaths, many of them after torture and many at the hands of death squads that operated under the protection of either the army or civilian organizations. Hundreds of their bodies were abandoned in El Playón, a region of lava rock and a dumping ground for garbage that became a macabre cemetery, as if the dead were so much rubbish. But because the killings at El Mozote were witnessed by Rufina Amayo, her personal loss and perpetual grieving voiced the anguish of the dying. After the signing of the Peace Accords in 1993, the monumental task of recording atrocities committed by both sides was undertaken by a Truth Commission chaired by the Colombian Belisario Betancur, whose report was given the title "From Madness to Hope" ("De la locura a la esperanza"). The report carefully documented the historical roots of the civil war, beginning with the 1932 massacre and the establishment of the military's domination over civilian society. It investigated the formation of both civilian and clandestine military death squads and their infiltration into state structures and army intelligence, noting that they constituted "the problem *par excellence* of that dirty war which ultimately destroyed all vestiges of the rule of law during the armed conflict."[43] In giving the document the title "From Madness to Hope," the commission members implied that truth could cure a pathological situation and that the end result would be national reconciliation buoyed by hope. The final sentence of the report, notwithstanding its optimism (or perhaps because of it), rings hollow: "As in classical painting, over the tribulations of war, there prevail the superior categories that make the law the agreed limit to the unbridled liberties and the consecration of madness."[44] The optimistic wording is so abstract when contrasted with the accounts of atrocities that this conclusion reads like a mockery.

A Long Dying

Diamela Eltit questions Primo Levi's assertion that no one can witness death. Reading the accounts of eight survivors executed by the Chilean army in the wake of the 1972 coup, she refers to them as the extreme exception, since "they were assassinated and yet went on living."[45] Beyond justice or recompense, she writes, "the situation requires the reinforcement of thinking that neither erases the horror — the inhumanity of the human — but rather lays it within the social surface as latent, as an underlying imperative that challenges and watches us" (14). The executed citizens are warnings that "force us to listen because they correspond to limit discourses extracted from a space traditionally without speech. A double site of silence. The silence that death brings and the social silence that surrounds the powerless citizen" (15). The witness here speaks to reclaim the humanity that had been denied him or her. The seven men and one woman who survived the executions were reluctant to talk for reasons that become clear in Cherrie Zalaquett's compilations of the survivors' stories. Thirty years after the event, they still suffered the effects of trauma: sleeplessness, nightmares, and a sorrow so deep that some are incapacitated. Most of them were agricultural workers, among the lowest-paid and most exploited sector of the population. Unlike Mármol, who was ready to sacrifice himself for a cause, these witnesses did nothing more revolutionary than join in the agrarian reform initiated by the Frei and Allende governments and take part in land occupations. Some of them were random victims, like a group of boys and a fourteen-year-old girl helping at a fairground. One executed woman was mayor of a commune. Land reform under Allende and land occupation had exacerbated the class war but it is still hard to credit that this alone brought on the fury of the executioners, many of whom came from the same social class as the victims. Yet during the first days after Pinochet's coup in September 1973, the carabineros and, in some case, civilians acting on behalf of landowners as "the Caravan of Death" exacted a ferocious revenge. "When I was imprisoned I sensed that they felt a terrible hatred toward us that I as a campesino never felt," Antonio Maldonado said, unable to account for the savagery (64). Although Patricio Guzmán's film *La batalla de Chile* captures some of the fury of the opposition to

Allende, what astonishes is that the passion could so easily be directed to murder their fellow citizens. The executioners (in some cases civilians) appeared to revel in the absolute impunity and the power that the state of siege had given them. The prisoners were tortured, beaten, insulted as *culiados* and *huevones*,[46] and interrogated about supposed arms caches or their connections to Cuba — a story invented by the opposition to discredit the Allende government. Propaganda was interpreted as reality. The fury of the executioners was in sharp contrast to the disbelief of the victims. Alejandro Bustos González was given electroshock to the testicles and anus, but even when he was transported to the place of execution, he could not believe that it was to be anything more than a charade. Nothing, not even the last violent months of the Allende regime, had prepared them for the fury of their aggressors.

The group of young men and a girl helping in a fairground on Independence Day were captured by the local carabineros, and the girl was raped by several of them before being killed. Most of the soldiers seem to have been willing executioners and torturers, though there were exceptions. Blanca Esther Valderas, mayor of the commune Entre Lagos, was lined up to be shot, but in her case the executioner trembled and couldn't get the trigger to work and she was able to fall from the bridge into a river and swim to safety. Luck is what saved the survivors. Alejandro Bustos González, his face covered with blood from a fellow victim, was thrown into a river and fell down on the bank, still conscious, along with a dying comrade, and from there he could hear the executioners' trucks driving off. Others were saved when a dead body happened to fall on them and hide them; sometimes they were helped because the executioners were in a hurry to leave the place. Daniel Navarro González managed to knock his executioner over and escape down a ravine. Luis, one of the young men from the fairground who was badly injured, managed to walk away from the site but never knew how he wound up in the hospital, where he was repeatedly interrogated but eventually "freed." José Guillermo Barrera was not so lucky. He escaped one execution only to be caught again and killed. What makes the reading of *Surviving an Execution* so harrowing is not only the cruelty of the executioners but the cruelty of the inexplicable.

Zalaquett ran into difficulties when she tried to interview these survivors, for unlike Mármol and Rufina Amaya, they could not narrativize their experience. The one female victim, Blanca Esther Valderas, refused to be interviewed, so her execution had to be reconstructed from previous accounts given to the press (27). Passing the site of the executions, Alejandro Bustos González, who was wounded but fell under the body of a comrade and thus escaped, said, "My mind never rests and I have never felt happiness" (175). Rescued by members of his family, he passed the execution place and saw "eyes hanging from the thorny branches and I went mad" (172). Only one man, Enrique Patricio Venegas Santibáñez, nicknamed Pato, agreed to be interviewed. The photograph of him shows a man with a deeply lined face, gripping his lapels tightly and staring in anguish into the camera. Illiterate, solitary, living without electricity or running water, and surviving on a minimal pension, Pato was brought up in poverty, with no schooling; he lived with his mother and his communist stepfather and only eventually learned that his real father was a soldier in the army. Pato had earned his living selling sweets. He had no interest in politics, although that didn't stop him from being rounded up, along with his half-brother. "They're taking sheep to the slaughterhouse," someone explained to Pato as they were taken up to the top of the hill "in the midst of insults, shouts and ferocious beatings." When the executioners fired, he fell and was covered with the blood of executed comrades. With another survivor, Willy, he managed to find help and, after months in hiding, returned to his native Curacaví, where he lived a solitary, impoverished life: "More than thirty years have gone by. Everyone asks how I survived, what happened" (116). In his sleep he sees the dead and the brother whose body was never found: "Imagine what it is to say goodbye to your brother, hold his head to kiss him and see that he only has half a head" (119). The survivors would endure deep psychological pain, and sometimes physical pain, for decades. Luis González Plaza, who was arrested along with several other young people at a fairground, survived the execution badly wounded but "lived haunted by a terror that left him with the adrenaline permanently at the maximum level. At the slightest suspicious sound his heart was in his mouth" (89). He did not dare walk alone, and a brother had to accompany him to the doctor. It was not until 1999 that he could be operated on for the open wound that still plagued him, and since then he has been unable to work. Years after his failed execution Manuel Antonio

Maldonado, exiled in Belgium, still felt guilt because his brother had been killed. Nightmares and thoughts of suicide tormented him six years after the event (65). Blanca Esther Valderas was the only execution victim who had any substantial political experience, having been appointed mayor by Salvador Allende to a new commune in Entre Lagos. She was arrested with her husband, forced to abandon her children, and taken to the execution site by a group of men wearing vampire masks. Even when the couple was forced to kneel, she felt no fear for herself, only for her husband, because she had committed no crime.

In her introduction to the "true stories" Eltit comments on the astonishment the survivors felt when the representatives of the state turned into the agents of extermination, whose hatred seemed incomprehensible, given that some of the executioners were known to them.: "They did not want to understand or, more accurately, they cannot understand the dimension of the social breakdown in which they were caught. . . . There does not exist for them an imaginary that includes these practices of power." Eltit concludes, "The narratives of these witnesses show how much the tragedy brought about by the 1973 coup is definitively revealed to be *irreparable*. I mean there is no possibility of a juridical or a financial reparation that might cover much less objectify the multiple and complex dimension of the human debacle exercised during the seventeen years of military control of the country" (14).

The dead, in these stories, cannot be reduced to numbers. They are comrades, relatives, brothers. In some cases the survivor performs a farewell rite for one of the dead or records the last words of a dying comrade, restoring, at these moments, the person that the executioners had sought to reduce to garbage. Eltit describes this as a restitution, "a leap, a break in the chain of devalorization [*des-valor*] in which their lives were consumed." Commenting on the fact that many of them recorded the last words of dying comrades, she argues that this "restores them to the sphere of lost humanity; despite the horror, it makes them live and makes them die with a decency that had been scanted" (20).

Surviving an execution separates lives into a "before" and a long and cruel sequel in which the very notion of "closure" is a mockery. Perhaps what these stories best clarify is the poverty of reparations when compared to the destruction of the lives of those who must go on living.

Los que están muertos eran todos héroes, los que están vivos es porque colaboraron.

—Ana Longoni, *Traiciones*

SEVEN | Tortured Souls

In the confined spaces of the detention cells in Chile and Argentina, members of the military were gods with absolute power over the captives. Testimonies written many years after the events by women who collaborated with the torturers not only tell us about the long-term effects of torture but also reveal the military's fascination with the tortured woman. By far the most detailed of these accounts is *El infierno* by the Chilean Luz Arce, who, after working for the Allende government and subsequently being captured and tortured by Pinochet's secret police, finally collaborated. Since the transition to democracy, Arce has, like the Ancient Mariner, told her story over and over again. She gave her account to the Chilean Comisión de Verdad y Reconciliación (Truth and Reconciliation Commission), reiterated parts of it in dozens of hearings, and published it as *El infierno* in 1993, and recently she went over the facts again in an interview with Michael Lazzara.[1] She has come to occupy a twilight zone of contention in postdictatorship Chile: for some she is a symbol of treachery, for others a symbol of reconciliation. The title of the English translation of her book, *The Inferno: A Story of Terror and Survival in Chile*, suggests a triumphant outcome. In *Después del infierno* (*After the Inferno*), Michael Lazzara interviews Luz Arce, now in her sixties and decades removed from the events, and finds that she adheres stubbornly to her premise — that those who have not been tortured cannot understand her ordeal, much less judge her.[2] Variously described as an autobiography or a testimonio, it can be read as a confession, and indeed, she cites St. Augustine. But it is a confession with lacunae, a confession in which a powerful account of torture can blind the reader to more problematic aspects of the story: in particular, her silence around events that happened after 1989 and were thus not covered by the amnesty granted to the military for their violations of human rights during the Pinochet regime. Arce has claimed to know nothing about crimes of the more recent period. Two prominent Chilean critics, Diamela Eltit and Nelly Richard, have dismantled her carefully constructed narrative edifice.[3] In this chapter, I shall examine torture as it affects women's personalities and as an effective form of pacification.

Arce's testimony is a grim account of what it means to be broken by torture. The book records her militancy during the last year of the Allende regime, her capture by the DINA (the Chilean military intelligence), her decision to collaborate after extreme torture, and her eventual incorporation into army intelligence as an officer. During the Concertación (the period of coalition government that followed the Pinochet regime), she underwent a religious conversion that made it possible for her to "verbalize," as she puts it — to bear witness and come to some sort of terms with the past. In 1990, when she appeared before the Commission of Truth and Reconciliation, which was meant to heal the wounds after years of repression, she played an important role by describing the workings of the secret service and naming members of the DINA who had participated in torture and killing, even though those names, because of the mandate of the commission, could not be published in the official report.[4] The naming and the description of the torturers in *El infierno* in 1993 and in *Mi verdad: Mas allá del horror; Yo acuso* (*My Truth: Beyond Horror; I Accuse*), the testimonio of her fellow collaborator, La Flaca Alejandra,[5] are declarations of some significance, but they hardly dented the cloud of amnesia that affected Chile then and may still loom over the present. A third collaborator, Carola, went on working for the secret service until she was pensioned off and has made no effort to justify her decision. In the language of the DINA officers, the three collaborators were a *paquete* (package), a description that says a great deal about their less-than-human status. All of them gave up the names of militants, several of whom were caught and killed as a result of their collaboration. Although their accounts can be described as testimonios, they are different from those of subalterns in that the authors write their own versions of the story of being broken by torture, reassembled by the military, and restored to public life.[6] They undercut heroic narratives of resistance, represent selective memory as truth, and show the dark underside of liberal individualism. Torture becomes the alibi, that which justifies all that follows, and the dramatic motive of their story.

In *The Body in Pain*, Elaine Scarry argued that pain produces a split between one's own reality and that of others. Pain cannot be shared, and pain resists language by actively destroying it. It is thus rarely represented in literature. In Scarry's words, the goal of the torturer is "to make the one, the body, emphatically and crushingly *present* by destroying it, and to make the other, the voice, *absent* by destroying it."[7] It is in part this combination that makes torture, like any experience of great physical pain, mimetic of death. Yet in her account Luz Arce attempts to discursively reconstruct a process of extinction of discursivity. Scarry asserts that under torture, "world, self, and voice are lost, or nearly lost, through the intense pain of torture and not through the confession as is wrongly suggested by its connotations of betrayal" (35). Arce seems to acknowledge this process when she realizes that none of her tactics for resisting torture can be effective. It is as if her voice is absolutely useless — as if she does not exist, is not a person. For Scarry, you cannot commit an act of betrayal when the self has been destroyed and when the comfort and familiarity of everyday objects (the room, the shower, the oven) have been transformed into implements of terror. In the Southern Cone, the *parrilla*, the barbecue grill on which families prepared festive meals, became a place of excruciating pain where electroshock was applied to the sexual organs and the mouth, the places of pleasure. The detained entered a parallel universe that transformed every familiar object as well as the body into a pain that erased all thoughts. But although Arce describes this disintegration of self, she is also able to compose, in retrospect, a detailed verbal account of losing her ability to speak or think over the pain.

Scarry argues that while, "for the tortured, the body and its pain are overwhelmingly present" (46), the torturer's body remains distant, unaffected. Her argument overlooks rape, a form of torture usually but not always committed against women. Rape causes extreme mental as well as physical pain. The torturer's body, far from being unaffected, becomes an implement of aggression like the fist or the boot. Arce's account leaves us in no doubt that rape not only was a form of torture but also subjected her, despite her struggles, to the torturer's will. Nor was its purpose primarily to extract information; rather, it was intended to reduce her to a state of abjection while allowing the torturer to enjoy power. Early on in her detention, under an assumed name and identity, in Calle Londres 38 (a torture center run by the DINA), she is raped by a group of men who act in silence, as if speaking would establish the possibility of dialogue with the prisoner.

> Without saying anything at all they threw me on a mattress and they raped me. Several men. At first I tried to resist. I tried to keep them from taking off my clothes, and I kicked blindly. Later on the floor, and with the weight of those individuals on top of me, their putrid breath, I ached inside as if they had broken me, with a pain in my whole body. I am crying. Don't have any strength anymore. I only sense that I am something thrown down there that is being used; that if I resist it's like a stimulus, and that if I remain still, if I drift mentally to other places, it seems to be less of any incentive for them. I am a dismembered doll. Two men hold my legs while they touch me. My mouth is gagged with a dirty rag that keeps going down my throat, making me nauseous, first one, then another, then another. I am a single huge mass of growing nausea. I am overcome and I vomit. I can't expel the vomit that hits the gag and comes back in. It drowns me, more vomit. I can't breathe. Something warm overwhelms and suffocates me. I am just beginning to learn how to die. (38)

How can this testimony be assessed? It was written years after a devastating event that Arce describes with lucidity and in the present tense. It is a plausible reconstruction that aptly conveys her ability to deploy a tactical resistance. Even though she writes, "I am just beginning to learn how to die," it is her ability to weigh up her situation apparently while it is happening that is striking. Arce describes herself as a "dismembered doll," that is, an entity without will or physical capacity, and unable to speak because her mouth is gagged by a dirty rag. Although she tries to expel what disgusts her by vomiting, she cannot help reabsorbing the vomit because the disgust cannot be ejected and becomes a part of her.

In her book on disgust, Winfried Menninghaus describes it as the presence of an intruder, an unexpected sensation, something that is not desired. As such, it is the opposite of desire: "Everything seems at risk in the experience of disgust. It is a state of alarm and emergency, an acute crisis of self-preservation in the face of an unassimilable otherness, a convulsive struggle, in which what is in question, is, quite literally, whether 'to be or not to be.'"[8] Unlike disgust toward the abject other, however — the socially inferior or the ethnically different — Arce's disgust is provoked by the triumphant male. And who were those triumphant males? Foot soldiers for whom the female was at best a receptacle into which to channel their lust, their anger, their hostility. She was hardly a person as far as they were concerned.

Tortured repeatedly on the *parrilla* (grill), hung naked from the ceiling so that her feet did not touch the floor, her mouth damaged to such an extent that it was painful to speak, she was raped and beaten; she suffered hunger and verbal and sexual abuse. Briefly transferred to the military camp Tejas Verdes, she was soon returned to the detention center on Calle Londres, where during an interrogation she heard a gunshot. Because she was blindfolded, she never knew the source of the bullet that lodged in her foot. Treated in the Military Hospital, she was released only to be arrested again. This time she would be detained until the end of the military regime, for the most part in the secret prisons of the DINA (Directory of National Intelligence), which had been officially set up in June 1974.

The account of the hours of torture, the filth of the detention centers, and the constant harassment, written almost twenty years after the event, time and time again rehearses the story of defilement, abjection, and revival. Immersed in filth, sickened by the odors — the scent of the torturers, the smell of excrement when there was no bathroom available, the pollution that occurs when the rare pleasure of a shower is nullified by the presence of the tormentors — she turns disgust into a form of self-assertion and, as Menninghaus maintains, the opposite of desire. In the military hospital where she is treated for her wounded foot, a male nurse who takes her to the shower immediately attempts to rape her: "He pushed my head under water moments before he ejaculated. More water entered my mouth and nostrils as I fought him. I felt nauseous like each time I was sexually assaulted, and I ended up vomiting. . . . I remember the sergeant's disfigured face through the water, and the feeling of suffocation. But above all the impotence, pain, the desire to disappear, to not exist, to be nobody" (59). She has entered a different zone, one where the face of the other has become disfigured, no longer recognizably human. When she is again in the hospital, the same sergeant takes her to bathe and presses her down in the tub, and when she tries to resist he puts a hose in her mouth.

> Water started filling my stomach. I swallowed it and felt like vomiting. I was suffocating. Suddenly he took me out of the water, held me and started to kiss my thighs. I tried to breathe, to speak, to reason but I couldn't. I wanted him to take away that disgusting mouth that was slithering all over my body and sliding between my legs like a sickening slug. . . . His damned tongue felt so cold, or was I the one who was cold? (69)

She tries to fight him off, pleads with him. "Again that face and he started touching me once more, searching for my clitoris with his hands. I want you to feel pleasure, did you hear? he shouted as he hit me" (69). The scene dramatizes the contradictory demands of the rapist who knows he is inflicting pain but wants the woman to feel pleasure and thus confirm his mastery over her body. He bites her vulva, and blood stains the water. It is only when she begins to weep, thus acknowledging his mastery, that he finally ejaculates.

This vivid evocation of the mastery of the rapist and the pollution felt by the victim contradicts Scarry's description of the torturer whose body is held aloof from the torture scene, for here the torturer's body has become the instrument of torture. Not only does the touch induce intense disgust; the torturer's pleasure is precisely what revolts her. By describing his mouth (and by association his penis) as a sickening slug, she diminishes his mastery even though she is incapacitated. "I tried to breathe, to speak, to reason but I couldn't." Disgust replaces reason. The episode is a powerful account of the rapist's frustration and her helplessness, and as such it becomes a form of justification for her capitulation. She has been taken over by the male body. This will be her story.

In an attempt to smuggle messages out of the detention center, she persuades a young soldier, Rodolfo, to help her. It cost him dearly: he was killed, and Arce herself was beaten by an officer named Gerardo Urrich, who vented his hatred on her: "Whores, whores, that's what communist women are, and the sons of bitches are all faggots. I hate you, you know. I hate you! Now you're going to see fascism in action" (79). Kicking her, he tries to make her say the military are fascists. "Say you wanted to kill us! Say you hate us!" Urrich's hysteria suggests that he has difficulty turning a supine woman into the enemy. This is a frustrating war, one in which he wants to show himself to be superior to the whores and faggots but needs her to acknowledge the fact. This is the torturer's desire to be recognized as the victor, the superior. And though death usually resolved this struggle, the torturers had to be assured of their superiority even as they transgressed every human norm.

After repeated torture sessions, after listening to her friends screaming in pain, she makes her first concession by raising her finger and giving her true name, Luz Arce. This is one of several crucial moments in the story, for voicing her true name is also the acknowledgment of the power of the torturers over her, their ability to extract truth and the first stage of a prolonged struggle. Yet, as she tells it, she was finally broken not by the pain but by being made to face her brother, who had also been brutally tortured. "It's my brother! A Nooooo spewed from the depths of my soul, and it was as if I had eaten glass and my entrails were being torn, ripped to shreds. . . . Everything seemed to vanish. I stopped hearing, thinking, being. Everything seemed to fall apart" (91). This is her lowest point, when a certain social self, defined in relation to family, disintegrates without possibility of recovery; here she reaches the point of no return. It is the moment when brother and sister decide to collaborate:

> I felt like they had ripped from me more than just bits of my skin, but also bits of my soul. I felt that they had taken away any possibility to re-

main who I was. I can't explain it clearly. I didn't just feel full of pain and unease. I was beyond desperation. It was as if every scourge and disease had taken possession of me. The feeling of being lost often emerged with me. My nightmares attacked me even when I was awake. I think all that horror was driving me insane. (106)

The metaphor of broken glass marks the turning point when Arce's former self is "ripped to shreds" and she begins a new life. Whether the incident happened as she described cannot be verified. Her brother makes only a brief appearance in the story, as if he were an actor needed for only one scene. In this way she is able to narrate an event so devastating that she becomes another person, a transformation that is witnessed and ratified by her sibling.

In a study of the use of torture in Chile, Hernán Vidal describes it as "a primordial assault against the human being understood as bios, that is to say, life trained in the uses, securities and wellbeing of civilization, that attacks the most fundamental postures — to stand erect with dignity, to be capable of seeing the surrounding contingencies, to synchronise the peristaltic internal rhythms of the body through discipline, timetables, external calendars of hygiene in order to maintain bodily hygiene and the dignity that is associated with it."[9] Vidal draws on Agamben's distinction between bios (the socialized person) and zoe (bare life), the latter exemplified by the Muselmann, the remnant of a human being in the Nazi concentration camps, a person who had lost all human dignity, a person who could not bear witness. But although Luz Arce suffers the utmost degradation, she never loses her ability to describe what is happening to her.

The bodily disciplines associated with civilized life, this civilized armor, can no longer be sustained in the detention centers.[10] Not only is the prisoner naked, defenseless, and exposed, but now all those formerly private activities — pissing, shitting, and menstruation — are performed in front of onlookers. When, after being drugged, Luz Arce pleads to go to the bathroom because she is bleeding, she wonders, "Are they watching me?" (121). Voices command her to "put the cotton pad between your legs. Turn around and walk." Even after offering to collaborate, she goes on suffering every form of verbal and corporal degradation.

She is derided as a *puta* (whore), and even when she is addressed as Lucecita, the diminutive expresses a condescension that displays the speaker's confidence in his own metaphorical stature.

Arce's ability to describe her degradation throws into relief the comparative poverty of La Flaca Alejandra's narrative, which is blunt and without the detail that makes Arce's account so compelling. But both narratives falter at the moment they are confronted with the consequences of treachery. This occurs when members of the Central Committee of the MIR (Movimiento de Izquierda Revolucionaria) are captured and are tortured in the same detention center, several of them having been fingered by La Flaca Alejandra during street patrols. The MIR was the most important target for the DINA and for Pinochet himself. It was the most active of the clandestine movements and had attracted middle- and upper-middle-class youth. The MIR had organized security around the president during the last days of the Allende regime and had tried to persuade him to take military action against the growing right-wing opposition. The capture of Miguel Enríquez, the charismatic leader, became an obsession among the DINA officers, and their implacable interrogation of Luz Arce and La Flaca Alejandra represents only part of a vast operation of information gathering. Hernán Vidal points out that thanks to several collaborators the DINA would have pieced together information on the militants they tortured, including their physical and psychological characteristics, their daily habits, personal relations, and so on, therefore they had an advantage from the beginning. Most of the tortured prisoners, he claims, talked in some form or other.[11] In a later version of the events, Arce reveals that a receipt from a laundromat was what led the DINA to the safe house.[12]

As Vidal argues, torture was successful: it helped produce the information that allowed the DINA to locate Miguel Enríquez in the safe house and kill him in a shoot-out. His partner, Carmen Castillo, pregnant with his child, was in the house at the same time but survived the encounter and was given asylum in France, where she published her account, *Un dia de octubre en Santiago*, in 1982. It was a moment of supreme triumph for both Pinochet and the secret service. An efficient information machine operating by means of torture and using La Flaca Alejandra to recognize militants on the street had led to the capture of most of the leading MIR members, including Lumi Videla Moya and her husband, Sergio Pérez, both of them members of the Central Committee. Held in the same detention center as Luz Arce and La Flaca Alejandra, they were savagely tortured. The torturers promised Sergio when he was already moribund that he would be given medical attention in return for revealing the location of Enríquez's safe house, and it may have been this information that led to the siege and to the death of the leader. For Luz Arce and La Flaca Alejandra, the atrocious deaths of Lumi and Sergio would constitute a major crisis. La Flaca Alejandra tried to commit suicide after the death of Miguel Enríquez and her encounter with her former comrade, Lumi Videla, in prison was a moment of deep personal grief, a point of no return. She knew that the MIR had condemned her to death as a traitor, so liberation would have put her at risk. She was forced to live, under the protection of the DINA with the self-disgust brought on by her collaboration. Indeed, perhaps more than Arce, this former militant with the MIR found it difficult to repair her broken life.

Arce, who, although she had never belonged to the MIR, also knew Lumi, shared a cell with her from which they could hear Lumi's husband, Sergio, being tortured and in such pain that he begged the torturers to kill him. She comments, "There are no words to describe or soften [*paliar*] what happened to Sergio, her [Lumi's] pain and my impotence" (163). The key word here is "impotence," for no action was possible, and for once she was at a loss for words. Although she describes Lumi as more than a friend, "my sister who lives in me" (158), she must have known how ambiguous she appeared to the captured militant, who tried unsuccessfully to outwit the DINA by feigning collaboration. One of Lumi's last gestures when she realized that she would be killed was to give her leather jacket to Arce, who evidently sought some kind of absolution from a woman destined for martyrdom. As a warning, Lumi's naked corpse would be thrown over the wall of the Italian embassy, where some people had taken refuge. Arce learns Lumi has been killed when she see guards playing dice for her clothes. Romo, the torturer who professed a long-standing admiration for Lumi dating from the time that she had been a student activist, described her capture laconically. When she resisted, "El Troglo was forced to sock her on the head with the pistol and we threw her, bleeding into the truck but she was nothing, she was a strip of hairy leather. And that was what was left of Lumi, as a bundle [*bulto*]."[13]

Luz Arce and La Flaca Alejandra were left with two options — death or their full assumption of their identity as traitors — and having chosen this latter option, it only remained for them to seek out whatever advantages they could from their situation. Confronted with this devastating account of degradation and abjection, the reader may overlook the fact that both authors seek vindication through the publication of their stories. They argue that in those circumstances the reader would behave in exactly the same way. Just as the torturer wants to extract truth from pain, that pain is now the guarantee of the writers' truth and the justification for their subsequent actions. After a psychological crisis that followed the defeat of Pinochet and the inauguration of the government of the Concertación, Arce undergoes a religious conversion. Tutored by Dominicans, she is reconciled to the Church and learns to verbalize her experience. The introduction to *The Inferno*, written by a Father José Luis de Miguel, underscores that pain can be a form of redemption. He writes, "Only the crucified, the tortured, can make the cross redemptive and liberating" (xvi). He describes the book as a confession that also seeks "conversion, catharsis, reconciliation and the triumph of truth, the naked truth even when the truth hurts or proves embarrassing or dangerous, not least to the one who lived it and writes it" (xv). But that "naked truth," it turns out, is selective, leaving many questions unanswered. Was she present in torture sessions, as some allege? Were her denunciations of militants more numerous than she claims? Was the seduction of power so compelling that she aspired to integrate herself into the military?[14] Certainly she astutely courted the protection of powerful males, most significantly that of the second in command of the Villa Grimaldi secret prison, Rolf Wenderoth, without whose help she would likely have been killed. Through Wenderoth she came into contact with the head of the DINA, Manuel Contreras, later charged along with Pedro Espinoza Bravo with masterminding the assassination of Orlando Letelier in Washington. It was Contreras who, while dancing with her, told her she was the prettiest of the prisoners and who arranged her move from Villa Grimaldi to an apartment she shared with La Flaca Alejandra and the third but silent collaborator, Carola (María Alicia

Uribe). She confessed that she "bought her life minute by minute" by a constant process of placating and calculating the effects of her actions. Thanks to this form of capitulation and absorption into the system, she became a valued officer consulted as an expert on the Left. Ever an eager student (when working for Allende, she had instructed herself in Marxism), in her DINA years she compiled a Marxist dictionary for her captors and studied at the National Intelligence School (as did Marcia Alejandra), taking courses in counterintelligence, Marxism, international relations, marksmanship, and cryptography; she later taught there as well. The notion of advancement through education, a tenet of the welfare state, served her through the Allende regime, through the military dictatorship and through the Concertación. She must have been invaluable to the secret service, for she not only worked for them as an analyst but was allowed to use arms and carry a gun. When her name was mentioned by families of the disappeared who were demonstrating, she again tried to hedge her bets by resigning from the DINA, but the resignation was refused.[15] After the discredited DINA had been reorganized as the National Information Center (CNI), she was sent to Uruguay on a spy mission, an episode that she describes in a particularly murky fashion, stating that she cannot reveal aspects of the mission related to national security. The allusion to "national security" shows how rapidly an institution that served during "the state of exception" could be normalized with "the return to democracy." Her unrivaled knowledge of the inside workings of the DINA and the fate of many of the disappeared made her a valuable if controversial source of information when investigations into torture were initiated. Arce was indeed demolished, swallowed, digested, processed, and transformed by the DINA but was smart enough to transform her demolition into a testimonio that she hoped would exonerate her. *Verbalizar* became a form of self-restitution, facilitated by her religious conversion and the practice of written confession initiated by St. Augustine.

Hernán Vidal has argued that the childhood abuse Luz Arce suffered at the hands of a neighbor and her relationship with her father taught her to seek protection from males.[16] She was somehow "able to negotiate a rationalist distancing from her corporal materiality that permitted her to turn her body into a strategic and tactical instrument to resist torture and penetrate the bureaucratic apparatus of the DINA/CNI."[17] Certainly, according to her own account, she had a capacity for cool analysis as when she recognizes the brutal machismo of the officers, the fact that they "tend to express their paternalism in a wide variety of ways that range from changing your name to even acting like a kind of father who gave your life" (138). Vidal traces her detached attitude to sex to a traumatic experience in her childhood and quotes a passage from *The Inferno* in which she stated, "Sex is just another form of communication, something I can choose to practice or not. Then I made up or adopted a saying as my own, 'I'll give myself but I won't sell myself'" (247).[18] The distinction between "giving" and "selling" is intended to stress that she had regained some freedom. She focuses her attention at any given stage in her detention on tactical questions. Her capacity for exploiting a situation to her advantage was demonstrated when news of a combat with the MIR was transmitted to Manuel Contreras, the head of the DINA, while he was dining with her and the other collaborators. He needed to make a hasty exist and, in the absence of his bodyguard, Luz Arce offered to escort him. As a mark of his gratitude, he gave the female collaborators permission to bear arms. Seeking the protection of powerful males was a strategy that worked for her. Francisco Ferrer Lima, the commander in charge of the Ollagüe detention center, almost certainly saved her from death, and she had a steady relationship with Rolf Wenderoth Pozo, second in command of Terranova (Villa Grimaldi), the most notorious of the DINA detention centers. She herself explained that such relationships had little to do with sex or affection: "I sought the presence of someone who would chase away the ghosts and fears" (247). Despite her abject condition, as she makes the transition from abused prisoner to DINA employee, she preserves an illusion of free choice, an illusion that she defends at all costs. It was the protection of the higher officials that saved her from the brutal machismo of the guards, and for her part, she encouraged the paternalism of the older officers even when she recognized their responsibility for "assassination, torture and robbery" (213).

What was the attraction of these women whom the higher-ranked officers may not have seen in the most degraded circumstances, naked, filthy, and speechless, but whose protectors they became after the women had been beaten into submission? Is it that the tortured and subdued woman reflected their omnipotence? Perhaps their own wives seemed unexciting compared to the subdued militant, a role that Arce now assumed as she transformed herself into a docile employee.

Vidal focuses on her capacity for long-term rational decisions by citing an episode that took place during the New Year's celebrations of 1974–75, which turned into an orgy. In the absence of the commanding officers, drunken guards began to rape the prisoners. Luz Arce was sexually abused by an officer in his office, but because he was drunk, she was able to knock him unconscious with a knuckle duster in an office where guns were stored. For a moment she thought of using the guns in order to escape, but on reflection she realized that without a viable alternative to the military dictatorship, it would be a futile act of individual rebellion. When she reported the breach of discipline to the commanders, she did not tell them that she had been raped because she knew that the standard response to charges of sexual harassment is "You asked for it." Describing this episode before the Rettig Commission, she gave a stirring account of her initiative that had led to the dismissal of several of the underlings and the transfer of the officer who had abused her, an account that also left no doubt as to her importance to the organization as a rehabilitated subversive. The irony is that she acts as if the DINA were any other office whose employees could complain against unfair treatment. Perhaps the most revealing incident, however, was her second encounter with Major Urrich, who had beaten her and abused her as a Marxist whore. Urrich was injured in a shoot-out and spent time in the hospital. On his return to Villa Grimaldi he sought out Luz Arce just to tell her, "I survived, just to kill all of you" (367). But the story has an epilogue. Now a trusted employee, Luz Arce is given a pistol and sent out on a mission in a car driven by the same Urrich, who after his initial astonishment asks her to cover for him. On their return to Villa Grimaldi, Major Wenderoth "put his hand on my shoulder and said, 'I believe you've made another friend.' He was never a friend, of course, but he was no longer my enemy" (370). This revealing episode appears at the end of the book, just before her final reflection on "the iron fist," in which she affirms that "the only way to exorcise that inferno and set the stage for a genuine reconciliation is by recovering memory, as sad as it may be" (372). The problem is that reconciliation becomes another word for acquiescence to the torturer's world, for it is clear that her virtuoso narrative of torture acts as a cover for this other story of "reconciliation," which is, in reality, capitulation. In the 2002–7 interviews, when it was all past history, she was more forthcoming in describing the activities of Wenderoth and others and in implicating La Flaca Alejandra and Carola in street arrests.[19]

Although many capitulated under torture, Arce's self-incrimination as a *traidora* (traitor) turned out to be a clever move. She did not deny giving names, but claimed that she did not give information about leading militants, only those of minor actors, although this itself raises many questions, since it suggests that she had a certain power over who was to live and who to die. She may also have tortured or been present at torture sessions. Michael Lazzara prefaces his interview by citing the deposition of Maria Cecilia Bottai Monreal, who was detained between 1975 and 1976 in different detention centers and who claimed that her mother and sister, detained with her, had been tortured by Romo and Luz Arce.[20]

The critic Nelly Richard and the writer Diamela Eltit point out that it is not her capitulation after torture that is the problem but the fact that she and the other "traitors" went on working for the secret service for over a decade after the resignation of Pinochet and the election of the government of the Concertación, a period about which she gives little information in order not to incriminate herself. In particular, she gives no information on the fate of the disappeared, of whom she denies any knowledge. This is the stumbling block in her narrative, for it was disappearance that became a major scandal after the end of the Pinochet regime, when the discovery of mass graves began to reveal the extent of the extrajudicial executions. Only the vigilance and persistence of the relatives of the disappeared exposed the grim underside and the terrorist tactics of the DINA, for which Luz Arce and La Flaca Alejandra and Carola assiduously worked. On one occasion described in her late interviews she was told that two detainees were killed and thrown off a cliff.[21] It is precisely the question "What did they know and not tell?" that divides critics based in the United States from those in Chile. Vidal sees her testimonio as a monumental work in three respects: as a literary text, "because it represents up to the present, the highest expression of its genre; from an existential point of view, because it reveals a human being in whose existence there intertwined and reflected in an exemplary manner all the contradictions of a crucial historical period for the Chilean community; with regard to social sensibility, expresses and participates in the exploration of new ethical forms of conceiving of Chilean history."[22] He sees her narrative as a text that contributes to a cultural politics of human rights based on Kantian principles. One can agree that it tells us a great deal about the secret prisons, but whether she is a "sacrificial figure necessary for the community to see itself as it really is" is more doubtful. As Diamela Eltit and Nelly Richard have argued, these confessions are implicated in the dubious policies of reconciliation and mystification decreed by the Concertación, the coalition of parties that took power in 1990 after organizing the "no" vote against Pinochet's election. For twenty years, Chile was governed by the Concertación, and before Pinochet's arrest in London, the official story was that the 1973 coup had saved the country from chaos and that this justified the dictatorship. In her book on the politics of memory, Nelly Richard sums up the period of the Concertación as one of consensus, memory (that is to say, permitted memory), and the market. She finds that there is something "morally perturbing" in the unverifiability of the confessions of Luz Arce and Alejandra Merino: "The two autobiographical narratives of M. A. Merino and L. Arce also produce that moral disturbance that comes from the unauthenticated condition of what has been confessed. But what is singular about these publications is that the effect of this disturbance is symbolically controlled by the religious guarantee (God, the Church) that is called on to authenticate the sincerity of the repentance" (107). The prologue to *The Inferno* written by the priest José Luis de Miguel "exemplifies Christian forgiveness" and anticipates our own forgiveness as readers.[23] The problem for Richard is that "reconciliation" becomes another word for capitulation to the cynical cover-up of the Concertación.

Eltit argued in one of several essays she wrote on *El Infierno* and *Mi Verdad* that all autobiography is a writing of memory and as such cannot be read literally as a truth. Rather, it should be read as a dramatization of the I, as a biographical production in which the I activated in the text is particularly fictional. I am not referring to the traditional opposition between truth and lie but rather what I want to emphasize is that this genre seems to correspond to the task of the construction of another place, a different place in which it is possible to read the option, the fiction of "I" that is being constructed.... Parodying this gesture would be something like, "I when I write do not write but submerge myself in the 'real' reality of myself, and for that reason it is truth, and the institutional status of the book called autobiographical, which is institutional writing, legitimizes it."[24]

In other words, these texts are overdetermined by the institutional recognition of autobiography as nonfictional and therefore as truth.

What makes these texts significant is their place in a narrative of reconciliation that depended on overlooking the crimes committed by the military. The amnesty decreed by Pinochet before he left the government and the limitations placed on the Rettig Truth and Reconciliation Commission and on the Valech report on torture, which could not name the perpetrators, foreclosed a thorough examination of the past.[25] That is why it is not so much the collaboration that perturbs Eltit (many confessed under torture) but the gaps in the collaborators' accounts and "the difference between what they chose to tell in their confessions and what they professed not to know, namely the fate of the disappeared. This not knowing saves them from any legal measure, frees them from a judicial sentence and allows them through publication to break out of their silence."[26] The flexibility of these women is the very quality neoliberalism encourages. "If it was the ambition of the women to become officers of the DINA and to form part of the military contingent the evident problem is much more radical and also simple: It is the absolute seduction of power."[27] In an interview with Lazzara, Luz Arce complains that Eltit's reading is always from outside. "She can't do a reading from the inside because she did not have my experience."[28] In other words, the actual experience of rape and torture trump all other considerations. Torture is an alibi for her actions as a collaborator, and the bureaucracy of terror served as a sort of apprenticeship that would give her entry first into the reorganized society of the dictatorship when the DINA was replaced by the CNI (Centro Nacional de Informaciones) and then into the murky waters of the Concertación, with its limits on what could and could not be acknowledged.

It is instructive to read *The Inferno* and *After the Inferno* alongside *Ese infierno (That Inferno)*, a collective account of Argentine women captives who survived the notorious secret prison of the ESMA (School of Naval Mechanics) in Buenos Aires and collaborated with their captors.[29] It took twenty years for the women to record their experience in which they described their nakedness, the sexual harassments, and their relations with officers (32).

The conversations make clear that being broken was a durable state that changed their very characters. The women describe their experience as one of death that left them permanently damaged. They comment on their loss of spontaneity (65), a loss of ideals and enthusiasm and the self-questioning "Who am I?," their uncertainty about whether or not they were to be killed. They recall details of the torture sessions, the screams of companions being tortured, and the daily pain of having their legs cuffed and having to wear a hood. But these particular women were destined for recovery, for a provisional freedom that eventually allowed them to live at home while continuing to work for the ESMA. One of their recurrent questions is why a hundred or so of them survived when thousands died.

It was their relations with their captors that tells us about the torturers who, grotesque as it may seem, desired them. These women were selected for recuperation because they were young, educated, and middle class and a type of woman the naval officers and ranks seldom met. They were invited out to dine, to go dancing, and were expected to look good and behave in a feminine manner. One woman named Cristina was "adopted" by an officer who invited her to a dinner and sang her a song in German, and she sang at the same event. "El Tigre" (one of the most feared torturers) gave a prisoner named Miriam a silver bracelet for her birthday. Some were taken on supervised trips. On one occasion, a woman named Adriana traveled to Mexico, where she was made to pose as the partner of one of the agents.

What this tells us is that the military, knowing that they had the sovereign power to decide on who should live and who should die, exercised that power by allowing some women to live. These women were a small minority who escaped death because they fulfilled a need, perhaps by providing relief from the grim murk of the prison. The ESMA building is surprisingly small, and in its three stories were packed prisoners, guards (known as "greens" [los verdes] and "pedros"), the drowned and the saved. In this space, those who were destined to be recuperated were forced into a gruesome charade, acting as clerks and employees, working in offices, photocopying, making summaries of the news, translating and acting as escorts. Despite these privileges, they could not avoid hearing the screams of those being tortured, the coming and going of shackled and hooded captives who were being taken up and down the stairs for interrogation or out of the door from which there was no return. They lived in fear of being sent upstairs to the *capucha*, where prisoners were kept chained to their beds before being "disappeared" (179).

In the introduction to their collective testimony, the philosopher León Rozitchner asks, "How does one justify the privilege of preserving one's own life when so many lives were lost? To experience regret for being alive is the cruellest way of all to annul life. It is difficult to feel oneself a person elected by destiny to survive when those who chose were the torturers and the assassins of their own relatives and comrades."[30] There are other uncomfortable questions as well. Was the painful choice of death or betrayal offered to women more than to men? Jacobo Timerman, who early on in the military regime was imprisoned and tortured by the military, speaks of the sense of omnipotence that the torturers felt, the security that came from impunity. That feeling of omnipotence must have been enhanced by the women prisoners to whom they gave their protection in exchange for sex.

Perhaps what is most important about these texts is that they chart the moral ambiguities created by the military regimes and the way fear became embedded in social life to such an extent that it would be effective long after the return to democracy. Edelberto Torres Rivas summarizes the effect as the punishment of society "in order to defend 'itself' from 'itself.' . . . The search for order via the use of violence left society even more disorganized than before, paralysed cultural life for a significant period, undermined confidence at the interpersonal level, and left entire societies in a continuing state of fear."[31] Or, as Nelly Richard asks, "Through what deep [*rebuscados*] mechanisms, through what secret cracks, and blatant stumbling can there erupt the memory of a frustrated past, whose bitterness and resentments go on disrupting sub-terraneously the expeditious rhythm of this banal self-congratulatory present."[32] One such disruption was the unanticipated problem of the disappeared, of those whom the military had attempted to bury and forget and whose unanticipated political force I examine in the next chapter.

EIGHT | The Ghostly Arts

"Disappearance," writes Edelberto Torres Rivas, "is even more cruel than public assassination, since it raises the perception of danger by placing it in an imaginary world, unsure but probable, created by the possibility that the disappeared person is alive. While one suspects that the disappeared person may be dead, nobody knows the truth. Doubt, prolonged over time, is a highly productive way of sowing fear."[1]

Arrested in their homes or on the street, carried off in unmarked cars to an unknown destination, most of the disappeared would never be seen alive again. Appeals to the police or the military received no answer except perhaps the suggestion that the missing individual had run away with a lover. For the military, disappearance was a way of ridding themselves of opponents without having to go through legal channels, such as a trial. It was practiced on a large scale in Argentina and Chile but also in Brazil, Uruguay, Peru, and Colombia. In the 1960s it also happened to young activists in Mexico; there it took the obstinate courage of Rosario Ybarra de Piedra, whose son disappeared in 1973, to found Eureka and to bring disappearance to public attention in that country.[2]

For parents and relatives, the disappearance of a son or daughter, a father or spouse, meant months and years of agonizing loss. This was a

Peruvian peasants hold up messages about the disappeared. Photograph by Ernesto Jiménez.

triple deprivation — of a body, of mourning, and of a burial — and it was aggravated in the countries of the Southern Cone in the years following the dictatorship by amnesties that shielded the military.[3] In Chile, in the wake of the dictatorship, a revisionist history depicted the army as having saved the country from chaos.[4] In Brazil, the aftermath of disappearance did not give rise to collective protest as in Argentina and Chile, and grieving was a private affair.[5] In Uruguay, the Ley de Caducidad (Expiry Law) absolved the military and police from crimes committed during the military regime and successfully prevented any thorough investigation of the crimes of the military. It was finally repealed in 2011.[6] In Argentina, after an initial inquiry that gave rise to the *Informe de la Comisión Nacional sobre la Desaparición de Personas: Nunca más* (*The Report of the National Commission on the Disappearance of People: Never Again*

[1984]), a "full stop" was ordered, and the inquiry into the crimes of the military government was stalled for decades before being resumed.

For the military regimes, transparency was not an option. Killings had to be concealed to avoid international attention, and elaborate deceptions were staged. In this gruesome theater, the bodies of executed victims were sometimes displayed as if they had been killed in a battle with the armed forces. Many of the disappeared were executed or thrown from planes while drugged. Pregnant women prisoners who gave birth in the clandestine centers were executed and their babies handed over to supporters of the regime so that they would not be "contaminated," making the very life story of these children a colossal lie.

Powerful movements — in Argentina, the Mothers of the Plaza de Mayo, and the Grandmothers and Children of the Disappeared; in Chile, the Agrupación de los Familiares de los Desaparecidos (Association of the Family of the Disappeared)[7] — had their origins in the fruitless enquiries over the fate of relatives, although the ramifications in these countries were quite different. In Argentina beginning in 1977, when fourteen mothers paraded silently in the historic Plaza de Mayo and eventually drew other mothers and grandmothers and the children of the disappeared to organize, they attracted international attention from human rights movements and came to symbolize a new kind of female empowerment.[8] With redemocratization, the Mothers split into two sections: the group led by Hebe de Bonafini went on demanding histrionically that the disappeared be returned with life, while the other group, the Línea Fundadora (Founders), recognizing that the disappeared had been killed, demanded restitution.

There are considerable political implications in the two positions. To make the counterfactual demand that the disappeared be returned "with life" infuses the utopian into the political. The politics of the Founders, on the other hand, adheres to the practical and the possible — the identification of victims, the insistence on justice. The Grandmothers of the Plaza de Mayo, founded in 1977, set about tracing babies of mothers who had given birth in the detention centers. Many of these babies were given for adoption, often to military families. The discovery of this practice was the topic of a widely distributed 1985 film, *La historia oficial* (*The Official Story*), directed by Luis Puenzo.[9] Hijos is the name of the

Argentine association of the children of the disappeared, which has become a political force for identifying former killers.[10]

In the absence of information, thousands of stories circulated under the radar, and for the most part they were stories of loss told by families and sometimes by survivors. Marguerite Feitlowitz, who interviewed dozens of victims of the Argentine terror, talks of "the eruption of the past into the present."[11] But although testimony and memoir are the genres in which stories of atrocity are usually narrated, the disappeared cannot testify, and we can only imagine their agony from the accounts of survivors. In the absence of their narratives, photographs, films, and art installations are ghostly hauntings. The silence of the disappeared is absolute.

Disappearance was a form of cruelty that affected families for whom there could be no closure and whose agony turned into public scandal as the Mothers of the Disappeared in Argentina and the Families of the Disappeared in Chile began their vigils in public places (the Plaza de Mayo in Argentina, the Chamber of Deputies in Santiago) whose historic associations lent pointed significance to the absence of justice. As evidence of an existence, the mothers and family members carried snapshots taken at birthday parties, at events such as graduation or birthdays, taken on holiday or on outings with friends — photographs that had once been intended as fortuitous records for the perusal of family and friends but now became icons of the disappeared. They were often reminders of happy times, since these are the ones we tend to photograph. In their very normality they defied the ferocity of an end that could only be surmised and they put on display an intolerable connection between the normal and the abnormal, the innocuous and the criminal.[12] The silence of the demonstrating mothers and the silence of the disappeared were met by the silence of the authorities, all of which converged on the silence of the photograph.

Protests against disappearance were not confined to the Southern Cone. Photographs of the disappeared were also carried in Colombia after the Trujillo massacre.[13] The frontispiece of *Yuyanapaq: To Remember*, the collection of photographs of the civil war published by the Peruvian Truth and Reconciliation Commission, shows a rough hand holding a tiny photograph like those pasted on identity cards or passports, a

pathetic reminder of an identity reduced to this single memento.[14] Snapshots were affixed to the crosses erected by the mothers of the girls assassinated in Ciudad Juárez. Unlike the families of those disappeared in
the Southern Cone, many of these women had seen the mangled bodies
of their daughters, but the photographs of unfinished lives foreground
the unfinished business of bringing the perpetrators to justice.

Roland Barthes believed that photographs are linked to early theater, in which actors played the role of the dead, for "however lifelike we
make it (and this frenzy to be lifelike can only be our mythic denial of
an apprehension of death), photography is a kind of primitive theater, a
kind of Tableau Vivant, a figuration of the motionless and made-up face
beneath which we see the dead."[15] Perhaps that is why the photographs
of the disappeared, displayed as evidence, have come to seem uncanny.
The demand of the families that they be returned "with life," the an-
swered call "present" in response to the name of a disappeared person
during a roll call, is a haunting that underscores the extreme pathos of
their absence, the simultaneous and impossible meeting of hope and despair. Moreover, the photographs themselves grow old, as Nelly Richard,
writing of Chile, pointed out: "The families must incessantly reproduce
the social appearance of the memory of this disappearance, that is so
fragile in its threatened narrative that it must struggle against oblivion
and forgetting."[16] Although the faces in the photographs remain young,
the technology has advanced. Richard contrasts the touched-up, technologically sophisticated color photographs of General Pinochet held
by the women supporters who welcomed him on his return from detention in London in 1989, wearing T-shirts that said "Yo amo a Pinochet"
("I love Pinochet"), with the archaic-looking snapshots of the disappeared daughters and sons displayed by family members, snapshots that
seemed anachronistic because they were taken before the use of more
advanced technologies and were often photocopied. By contrast, the
cosmetically enhanced images of Pinochet were an apt metaphor for the
cosmetically enhanced appearance of national reconciliation displayed
by the coalition government. Richard suggests that the photographs
of the disappeared, frozen in time, inadvertently introduced an unwel-
come reminder of the past into the glamour of the market economy:
"The families of the victims know the difficulty of maintaining alive

and relevant (applicable), the memory of the past when all the consumer society's rituals are set to distract and take away the meaning and force of concentration."[17]

This unanticipated gap between the technological sophistication of the present and the not-so-distant past — a past that was supposed to have been buried — was bridged by the tenuous strands of memory, a faculty that has come under some suspicion. Indeed, Susan Sontag asserts flatly there is no such thing as collective memory and suggests that

> perhaps too much value is assigned to memory, not enough to thinking. Remembering is an ethical act, has ethical value in and of itself. Memory is, achingly, the only relation we have with the dead. . . . But history gives contradictory signals about the value of remembering in the much longer span of a collective history. There is simply too much injustice in the world. And too much remembering (of ancient grievances: Serbs, Irish) embitters. To make peace is to forget. To reconcile, it is necessary that memory be faulty and limited.[18]

True, she is writing of war photographs, but her downgrading of the memory of ancient grievances (Bosnian Serbs? the Irish?) suggests that the privilege of the metropolis is to ignore what does not directly afflict them, a dangerous assumption given the media curtain that prevents "us" in the First World from recognizing our responsibility. And this is not to mention the ancient grievances of slavery, of the Indian wars, of Chinese coolies and Japanese citizens — one could go on. Sontag does not appreciate that ancient grievances also account for the narratives of defeat and repression of those whom collective memory is often the only access to their submerged history. How could the remnants of the Salvadorian indigenous whom I mention in chapter 5 make sense of their impoverished present if there were no transmitted memories of the 1932 massacre? How else could the disappeared continue to haunt Argentina and Chile, Colombia and Peru, decades after they were killed?

The involuntary memories of the disappeared, through the mechanical reproduction of photography, becomes deliberative memory. Benjamin's beautiful comparison of remembrance and forgetting with Penelope's web best expresses its workings.

And is not this work of spontaneous recollection, in which remembrance is the woof and forgetting the warp, a counterpart to Penelope's work rather than its likeness? For here the day unravels what the night has woven. When we awake each morning, we hold in our hands, usually weakly and loosely, but a few fringes of the tapestry of a lived life, as loomed for us by forgetting. However with our purposeful activity and, even more, our purposive remembering each day unravels the web and the ornaments of forgetting.[19]

Remembering in this sense is a form of work, not simply a spontaneous occurrence.

Andreas Huyssen considers the present memory boom as a response to "the capitalist culture with its continuing frenetic pace, its television politics of quick oblivion, and its dissolution of public space in ever more channels of instant entertainment [that] is inherently amnesiac." Thus "our obsessions with memory functions as a reaction formation against the accelerating technical processes that are transforming our *Lebenswelt* (lifeworld) in quite distinct ways."[20] In Latin America, particularly in Chile and Brazil, these transformations occurred precisely at a moment of severe repression, when memory became the only resource for the families of the disappeared, the photograph the only trace, as well as later, when the coalition government that followed the dictatorship effectively nourished a public culture of amnesia. Official history was challenged by what the filmmaker Patricio Guzmán termed "obstinate memory."[21] Ironically, then, disappearance, designed to obliterate an existence, became one sure way of keeping the memory alive, since for the families there was no possible closure as long as there was no body. That is why the photographs of the disappeared came to haunt the military in Argentina, Chile, Uruguay, and Brazil, even though for many years they were protected by amnesty laws, for these photos exposed the official lie that hundreds of (mainly young) people had simply vanished.

This humble and democratic art, available to anyone with a camera, has been the target of important critics, from Susan Sontag to Siegfried Kracauer, who stated that "the flood of photos sweeps away the dams of memory. The blizzard of photographs betrays an indifference toward what the things mean."[22] Writing during the Weimar Republic, there were reasons for skepticism of mass-produced images. Sontag is certain that war photographs cannot instruct us in the true reality of war: "We don't get it. We truly can't imagine what it was like. We can't imagine how dreadful, how terrifying war is; and how normal it becomes. Can't understand, can't imagine what every soldier, and every journalist and aid worker and independent observer who has put in time under fire, and had the luck to elude death that struck down others nearby, stubbornly feels. And they are right" (125–26). But surely people do not mistake photographs for experience. Documenting cruelty does not mean reproducing its initial impact; and photographs, as Susan Linfield claims, play an important role in "robbing us of the alibi of ignorance."[23] For Barthes, "painting can feign reality without having seen it. Discourse combines signs, which have referents, of course, but these referents can be and are most often 'chimeras.' Contrary to these imitations, in photography I can never deny that the thing has been there. There is a superimposition here: of reality and of the past" (76).

"Disappearing" thousands of executed victims, erasing them from existence, was, for the military governments of the Southern Cone, simply a disposal problem. Given that their project required fighting "everything contrary to western and Christian ideology,"[24] the large number of deaths that this involved and the need to conceal the extent of the slaughter from the prying eyes of international observers forced the military to hide the extrajudicial deaths from the public eye. The audience for this massive masquerade was both international and national. The goal was to create an atmosphere of normality, and all kinds of atrocities were perpetrated behind this facade. General Videla, president of Argentina from 1976 to 1981, in an interview on US television, presented the official explanation, which blamed disappearance on the victims and minimized the responsibility of the military:

> They have disappeared in order to live clandestinely and to dedicate themselves to subversion; they have disappeared because the subversive organizations have eliminated them as traitors to the cause; they have disappeared because in a shootout with fire and explosions the corpse was mutilated beyond identification; and I accept that some persons might have disappeared owing to excesses committed by the repression.

That is our responsibility and we have taken steps that it not be repeated: the other factors are beyond our control.[25]

In a television speech reproduced in the film *Disappearance* (discussed further below), he impatiently says that "disappearance simply means that the person is not there." *Nunca más*, based on thousands of testimonies and published by the National Commission on the Disappearance of Persons in 1984, charged that "with the technique of disappearance and its consequences, all ethical principles that the great religions and the most lofty philosophies enacted during millennia of suffering and calamities were trodden down and barbarously ignored."[26]

What the military did not anticipate was that the disappeared would return to haunt them. In these societies of masquerades, the counterfactual demand by the Mothers of the Plaza de Mayo in Argentina and the Families of the Disappeared in Chile that the disappeared be returned with life exposed the prevarications of the military by taking the lie as literal truth, creating a new form of opposition, one that relied on this ghostly pretense. With the passage of time, this demand appealed "not to immediate political action but rather to a ritual or even redemptive dimension."[27] This spirituality was not always channeled by the Church, although in Chile, where the Association of the Families of the Disappeared, founded in 1974, received Church support, demonstrations of family members who chained themselves to the railings of the National Congress (which had been closed since the coup) and to the cathedral underscored both the lay and the religious aspects of disappearance. The demonstrations placed the government in a dilemma, since by coming down on the protestors they would show their authoritarian hand to the world, while if they ignored them, they risked undermining their carefully constructed wall of silence.[28] The families created a rift in the very center of sovereign power between their demonstration of the integrity of the family (which the military rhetorically protected) and the pretense that these people had no existence. The photographs then acquired a significance that could not have been anticipated at the moment when they were taken, for they demanded, in Levinas's fashion, a response by displaying the photographed face. Of course, Levinas is not referring simply to a photograph but to a face that in its mortality "calls for me, begs for me, as if the invisible death that must be faced by the Other, pure otherness, separated, in some way, from any whole, were my business."[29] Nevertheless, in a ghostly fashion, the photographed faces of the disappeared appeal to the living from a place that the living cannot occupy. Nelly Richard finds photographs of the Chilean disappeared profoundly disturbing. Quoting Pierre Bourdieu on the function of photography in funeral rites "to recall that they had been alive and that they are dead and buried," she asks "how to interpret the dual ghostliness [*fantasmalidad*] of the bodies and the destinies of the bodies and the destinies of these victims of 'presumed deaths' that materially lack the traces of a proof of truth to confirm the objective outcome of the dilemma of life-death."[30] The families confronted injustice by showing a face as a visible accusation "of the scandalous anonymity that still protects the executioners" (67).

That the disappeared were dead was not immediately obvious to the families. It took unanticipated revelations for that truth to be brought home. In Chile, it was the discovery of bodies of executed prisoners who had been thrown into abandoned furnaces in Lonquén, a discovery that confirmed suspicions of mass executions and clandestine burial grounds and undermined the hope that disappeared detainees might still be alive. Supported by the Vicariato, an office of the Catholic Church, the members of the Coalition of Families of Disappeared Prisoners made a pilgrimage to the site. For the Catholic Church, the Lonquén discovery meant "redirecting the energy of the mourners from the hope that their loved ones be restored with life to an emphasis on suffering as the basis for a just society."[31] Members of the Communist Party, on the other hand, adopted the secular comfort of a poem by Neruda, with its promise that the martyred would be "with us" in the final struggle.[32] But this is only the beginning of a story for which there is no neat conclusion. In snuffing out lives in secret, the military governments let loose the ghosts that haunt them in the present.

The Condemned

Some of the prisoners in the ESMA detention center in Buenos Aires were photographed before being executed. The photographs smuggled out by Víctor Basterra, a former detainee who still worked there after

his release, show the faces of young people who know they have no future. These photographs became the life work of Marcelo Brodsky. In
his books *Nexo* and *Memory under Construction*, he underscores the fact
that memory is not necessarily spontaneous but demands a conscious
effort, especially when there are gaps between the moment of disappearance and one's ultimate acknowledgment of the deaths. What especially
engages him is the period of suffering between life and death. In *Nexo*
(*Connection*), described as a photo essay, photographs of moldering files
of habeas corpus proceedings, "each one presented in the hope of finding a son, a father or a brother alive," are the visible traces of the legality that has been abandoned.[33] The yellowing documents shelved in
storerooms are now the "buried books" of the disappeared, the record
of "steps taken to no avail, proceedings that have ended without providing a answer and that now have come to rest stored on the shelves." A
series of photographs shows the damaged books buried by their owners during the military regime and the fragment of a video by Eduardo
Feller (2001) titled *The Wretched of the Earth*. Accompanying the photographs, some of which were displayed in an installation at the Buenos
Aires Book Fair in 2000, is a text that includes the statement "We, the
generation that lived through the dictatorship, burned our own books, a
part of our identity."[34] The dusty title of Frantz Fanon's *The Wretched of
the Earth* (reproduced from Feller's video) is a reminder of an unfinished
project of emancipation. Whereas the buried book of a Haitian judge
I discussed in the first chapter survived to tell the story of a massacre,
these buried books refer to a truncated culture that had, in the 1960s,
aspired to liberate the "wretched of the earth," the very class of people
who are once again victims, the "wasted lives" of neoliberal expenditure.
The exhumed books testify to the profound cultural shift between the
1960s and the present, between the world the disappeared inhabited and
what it has now become.

The tipping point for Brodsky, who for some years lived in exile in
Spain, was the disappearance of his older brother, Fernando, whose activities before his capture in 1979 are summarized in his secret dossier;
they amounted to distributing leaflets, taking part in shooting practice,
joining small political parties, and attending political meetings and
study groups. Brodsky's first attempt to represent Fernando's disappear-

ance, an installation ironically titled *Buena memoria* (*Good Memory*), highlighted the fact that a "good memory" makes it impossible to forget a bad event. The installation exhibited a blown-up photograph of the 1967 first-year class at the Colegio Nacional, with notes and crosses over the faces of those who had disappeared, had been killed, or had gone into exile. The installation closed with a photograph of the churning sea into which the bodies of many detainees were thrown.[35] Over the years, Brodsky constantly came back to the many meanings and frustrations of memory. In his book, *Nexo*, he shows images of trees planted in the Tucumán Memory Park by relatives of the disappeared. On these trees the relatives attached notes and photographs, and as these weathered, they "deteriorated, implying a kind of second disappearance for those who would have been remembered."[36] What this tells us is that memory is not a holdall that can be drawn on as needed but constantly has to be reconstructed from fragments and fortuitous remains. Memory of atrocity is not simply available but is constituted post hoc with the aim not only of clarifying the fate of the disappeared but of documenting a crime. And it is always fragile.

Memory under Construction, an anthology of essays and photographs, was published as a contribution to the debate over the conversion of the ESMA (Navy Mechanical School) detention center into a memory museum. This came about in 2004 when, under President Néstor Kirchner, it was designated a space for memory and for the promotion and defense of human rights. It is one of the many "places of memory" in the Southern Cone. The ESMA museum now includes a memory archive (*archivo de la memoria*), a cultural center (Centro Cultural Haroldo Conti, named after the disappeared writer), and a center organized by the Mothers of the Plaza de Mayo. For me, a present-day visitor, it was hard to imagine that such a small space could accommodate so much nefarious activity — offices for registering new inmates and making false identity cards for officers, torture chambers, a place where pregnant women gave birth, accommodations for the navy personnel, and, on the third floor, the *capucha*, where the prisoners were kept cuffed to their mattresses and where the loot from the raids on suspects houses and apartments was kept.[37]

Searching archives for evidence of his brother's fate, Brodsky was presented with the secret intelligence report showing one photograph of Fernando taken soon after his arrest and a second, taken after torture, that was among those smuggled out of the detention center by Víctor Basterra. In this later photograph, he is wearing an undershirt, his hair is unkempt, and there are deep bags under his eyes. In *Memory under Construction*, published in 2005, this photograph is reproduced as the first of a series showing detainees, several of whom are still listed as disappeared. These photographs offer a stark contrast to the photographs carried in demonstrations, for they make visible the extinction of hope. The eyes gazing fixedly at the camera express weariness and resignation, as if they already know their fate, and the dark rings show the effects of torture and sleeplessness. One of the most moving photos is of a middle-aged woman wearing a pinafore dress and a flowered blouse that she had probably made herself. She is the kind of lower-middle-class woman one might meet in the marketplace or the grocery store except that she has shackles around her ankles. Her name is given as Ida Adad. What could she (or the others) have done to merit brutal extermination? The photograph of Fernando is reproduced a second time, alongside Brodsky's essay "The Undershirt," but this time it is shown photocopied on a torn page being held by two fingers. The yellowed paper marks the long interval between the time of the photograph and the present. In his essay Brodsky describes "a minimal undershirt wrinkled, covering an adolescent body after a torture session."[38]

After nearly thirty years, there is no "getting over" this particular loss. This is the truth that photography reveals to us in the portraits of the forever young. Nor does the disappearance that disrupts the lives of the wives, husbands, children, parents, and grandparents end with the disinterment of bodies and the identification of remains. The ESMA photographs show us the faces of those who have been deprived of all youthful élan, who have forgotten the time of optimism and plans for the future. They tell us about fear. In *Regarding the Pain of Others*, Sontag was reacting against what she sees as the exaggerated claims of photography's power to represent a violent event. But these photographs are terrible because what they capture is not the event but a foregone conclusion. In other words, we read death in their faces. Andreas Huyssen argues that contemporary installations such as those of Brodsky transgress the limits between installation, photograph, monument, and memory and address the spectator not only as an individual but also as a member of a community confronting the task of commemoration.[39] They also confront us with the terrible truth that ours is an age of excavation and exhumation as we seek lost generations.

This was brought home in the documentary film *The Disappeared*, in which the son of parents murdered by the military and given for adoption to a working-class family by an officer discovers his true identity. Far from being a happy ending, it is the introduction to a belated mourning in which he finds not a mother but a cadaver that he must now rebury.[40]

The Real of the Desert

The title of Catalina Parra's video installation *Fosa*, filmed in 2004 in the Atacama Desert in northern Chile, is the unequivocal reminder that the desert was a tomb, a graveyard, the sepulcher of several hundred of those "disappeared" by the military during the Pinochet regime. In this brief video the spectator confronts, not Slavoj Žižek's "desert of the real," but the real of a desert on which rain never falls, where nothing grows, in parts of which there has been no rain for four hundred years and where the few human traces are of nomadic tribes and the disinterred bones of the recent dead. A wind blows incessantly over this barren landscape, and the only other sound is of a mechanical shovel excavating and filling sacks with desert soil in a simulation of production. The only human presence is the shovel's operator. The video reminds the viewer that victims of the Pinochet government were not only buried in the desert but also exhumed by electric shovels; their bodies were then reburied elsewhere or thrown into the ocean, leaving only fragments. Because exhumation in the installation is a mechanical task whose product is dirt, it speaks to the reduction of a human being to matter. At the same time the sacks of dirt are strangely humanoid, recalling the *imbunche* of Chilean folklore, which Parra described in reference to a 1987 exhibition as "the person who has all the body orifices sewn shut, all the holes blocked so that the evil spirits can't get out of his body, so it's a kind of censoring of release."[41] Compressed in those sack figures is the hidden history of men and women who were killed and buried in the desert so that they would then be forgotten, as if the national amnesia decreed by the Pinochet regime and the coalition government that followed it could forever guard the secret of their deaths. The Monument to the Disappeared, visible as a patch on the horizon, refers us to this other history, the history that involved the suppression of dissidence, the extermination of the opposition, and a government dedicated to reinventing the nation as a neoliberal paradise. The distant monument is the visible sign of the burial of utopian promise that would be replaced by regimes that wanted no reminder of the past. In much of her previous work, especially in her collages, Parra deployed irony and ambiguity, using newspaper headlines, posters, and her own comments. In *Fosa*, the spectator is put to work as he or she processes a rich array of meanings and the multiple strands that link extraction, excavation, exhumation, exposure, and exploitation, while the grating noise of the machine provides dissonance. But what is most striking about the video is the reiteration of the reduction of the human, restored only as simulacrum by a machine activated by a worker who has become part of its mechanism. This is the desert of the real.

Patricio Guzmán's film *Nostalgia for the Light*, also shot in the Atacama Desert, sutures two seemingly incompatible temporalities — that of present-day Chile, where citizens still search for remains, and that of the universe. Human time shrinks before the eons of the time of the universe, visible in the brilliant star-studded sky and measured by the astronomers who work the immense telescopes. Their gyrations are the opening images to the film. The desert is first shown as uninhabited and uninhabitable, although gradually the human trace becomes visible — the rock drawings of ancient travelers; the mining camp that had once housed exploited workers and later Pinochet's prisoners. It is the task of the filmmaker to give both dimensions their due. When a survivor of the Chacabuco concentration camp describes the prisoners studying the night sky, the film makes explicit the connections that link the short life spans of the human and the *longue durée* of the universe.

In the desert we see some distant figures, who turn out to be women still searching for the remains of their husbands, brothers, and sons. One of them has found part of skull, a foot in a sneaker that had belonged to her young brother. Her photograph shows an adolescent, whose bones now reveal that he was executed by two bullet shots. It is hard for her to

Catalina Parra, *Fosa*. Courtesy of the artist.

understand the fury of the executioner. Another woman who gives her age as seventy searches for her husband's remains. She has been searching for many years and will go on searching for fragments. What the film wants us to know is that there is a spirituality that is expressed not only in religious speech but also in devotion to the dead.

A young woman working as an astrologer is the daughter of disappeared parents. Brought up by grandparents and now herself a mother, she knows her parents can never be returned alive and that, measured against the time of the universe, human lives are minuscule, although life itself, if we think beyond the individual, does not end. The indestructible calcium in our bones belongs to the immense time of the universe. It is comfort of a sort, but not enough to overcome the incurable melancholy discussed in chapter 1 and the cruelty that cannot be understood or explained. Guzmán measures, against the eons of universal time, memories of his childhood and the ephemeral lives of those who had been obliterated. It is the brevity of the latter that gives the film its pathos.

Partial View

Photographs of the disappeared are the nexus that connect people to a past that they cannot know and that cannot be relived. Atrocities, on the other hand, are not photographed; their results — the strewn bodies, the exhumed corpses — are excavated as evidence, but it is hard to restore their humanity. It is also possible that we have, as Susan Linfield argues, lost "the capacity to respond to photographs, especially those of political violence, as citizens who seek to learn something useful from them and connect to others through them."[42] The president of the Peruvian Truth Commission, Salomón Lerner Febres, described the photographs of the internal armed conflict in Peru (1980–2000) that the Truth Commission collected, displayed, and published with the title *Yuyanapaq: Para recordar* (*Yuyanapaq: To Remember*) as a prolongation of the truth "that we undertook to recuperate when we allied ourselves with memory along with justice."[43] But the "truth" is difficult to extract from these photographs. They do display, over and over again, the faces of hardship, the stubborn enigma of death, and the desolate aftermath of war. The frontispiece shows rough hands holding a photograph of a middle-aged man, one of the disappeared. The tiny photograph, the size of a postage stamp, transmits the pathos of the loss of an unrecorded life, a life of labor, now reduced to this insignificant record.

But the book also mirrors the dissensions that still linger in Peru. While the army and police in the photographs are described as "forces of order," the prisoners are labeled "subversives," and the photographs often show the Shining Path and the MRTA in a bizarre or exotic light. In one photograph, a group of accused terrorists in vivid black-and-white-striped prison outfits wait outside a gate through which an army detachment is preparing to march. The photograph establishes a clear distinction between the upright beefy soldiers in camouflage and the "terrorists," three of whom are crouching and hiding their faces. One of the young men is standing up and looking at the camera. He cannot be more than fifteen years old. Although there is no doubt that the Shining Path were responsible for atrocities, the photograph cannot tell us whether these individuals were guilty. Rather, it relies on the contrast between the force of order and the disorder of the prisoners, who are

Women witnessing exhumation of male villagers. Photograph by Ernesto Jiménez.

made to appear not only abject but exotic and foreign. In another photo-graph, a group of Huamanga women sit under a placard announcing that they are constructing "a Latin America without disappeared." Echoing the Argentine Mothers of the Plaza de Mayo, their placard reads, "They took them away alive and alive we want them," the mantra of the families of the disappeared all over Latin America. Poorly dressed, hands folded on their laps, the women are portraits of grim determination. But there is a deep vacuum where information should be. From the spatial and temporal distance of the viewer, questions — for instance, were their men killed as "subversives"? and what makes people become "subver-sives" in the first place? — have no answer. Many critics have written of the deep discontent especially among young people who, after years of university, found they had no prospects and embraced the change that the Shining Path promised, but there is little indication in *Yuyanapaq* that the gross inequalities of Peruvian society could have had anything to do with the uprising. In the photograph of Ernesto Jiménez, on the other hand, the three indigenous women standing before the exhumed and decaying bodies are clearly in shock. One woman turns away, one

woman kneels, and a third stands with her hands raised. These anonymous female mourners are the modern Antigones, whose dead have been
buried outside the walls of the *civis*. The area is barren, a no-man's-land.
If the figures shown against the rocky barren background have a story to
tell, the photograph can only tell us part of it. Who were the men who are
now bodies? What was their crime? I turn the pages of *Yuyanapaq* and
encounter the photograph of a girl's body being thrown onto the bed of
a truck. The caption tells us that she is a political activist, but we cannot know how she met her death. Her body is soiled, her battered face
unrecognizable, and her shirt has been pulled up to uncover her young
breasts, but there is nothing erotic in the soiled and scratched torso, and
nobody is looking. The men removing the body are concentrating on the
task, and the other people in the photograph do not seem particularly
interested, as if the event were no more out of the ordinary than the
daily garbage collection. In the background, groups of men seem to be
gossiping. The bodies are clearly being disposed of as rubbish, but we
can never know what drew the teenager to rebel and fight or how she
met her death. In another haunting photograph, a solitary girl in black
is shown vigorously sweeping an enclosed patio surrounded by a brick
wall and a covered walkway. Arched walls, reminiscent of a convent,
frame the patio as if were a stage, so her activity (sweeping up scraps of
paper) appears exaggeratedly vigorous, even desperate. The caption tells
us that she is thirteen years old and is in an orphanage for war victims,
having witnessed the assassination of her parents. But that story cannot
be photographed. What we see is a muted desperation enclosed within
the walls of the orphanage, like a metaphor for a life enclosed in grief and
hardship. Viewing these photographs, I cannot quite accept Sontag's assertion that "the illustrative function of photographs leaves opinions,
prejudices, fantasies, misinformation untouched."[44]

The photojournalist Susan Meiselas, who was in Nicaragua and El
Salvador during the civil wars, understands the ambiguous role of the
photographer as witness to conflicts that are not immediately understandable. She asks, "What does it mean to be doing this? . . . For whom
am I doing this work?"[45] Some of her photographs — those of the
skeletal bodies of the Salvadorian villagers killed in El Mozote by the
army — provided evidence of the massacre that I discussed in chapter 4.

Mother and child in coffin, El Salvador. Photograph by Susan Meiselas, courtesy Magnum Photos.

But Meiselas is keenly aware not only of the responsibility of the photographer but also of spectatorship, especially when the spectator belongs to a different culture. A 1983 photograph of the funeral of a mother and child killed during a clash between the military and the insurgents in El Salvador shows a coffin in the foreground in which lie the two bodies, clothed in white. The open coffin is surrounded by a group of men, evidently peasants, who stand in contemplation, and behind them are women and children, their faces exhibiting stunned grief. One of the men in the forefront has his hands spread in what seems to be a gesture of despair and impotence. Outside the frame are the distant spectators, ourselves, temporarily and spatially removed from the event. It is as if the photograph is telling us that we cannot be part of it.

These photos force us to think of spectatorship and of the difference between presence and temporal and spatial distance from an event. This is explicit in Meiselas's photograph of a group of young boys crowded in front of a small patio and staring at a bloodstain on the floor. The bloodstain, we learn from the blurb, is the visible trace of a young man shot while distributing leaflets. Kept back by a small hedge, these poorly

Young boys near the blood of a student slain while distributing leaflets,
San Salvador. Photograph by Susan Meiselas, courtesy Magnum Photos.

dressed spectators on the threshold of adulthood express the avid curiosity of those drawn to the scene of the crime. And we, in turn, are
drawn to it because to some degree we too want sensation, a show of violence that we can safely watch. The photograph forces us to confront our
own distance from the event, about which we can learn nothing from the
photograph. What the photo does tell us is something else, something
about the fascination with violence that draws in spectators both near
and distant.[46]

In 2004, Meiselas returned to Nicaragua, where she had formerly photographed the uprising against Somoza in 1978 and 1979 that culminated
in the victory of the Sandinistas. This time she shot a video in the very
places where she had shot the episodes of war. The juxtaposition of past
and present is at once an aide-mémoire through which the present re-
members or relives the past and a comment on the present, showing how
mobile history is, how it is constantly reiterated and reformulated. As
Diana Taylor writes, "The staging of the photographs . . . forms part of
a living and ever-shifting repertoire of cultural imaginings. Reinserting
them where they were taken twenty-five years after the fact allows people

to participate in the production and reproduction of knowledge of that past by 'being there' now, being a part of the transmission.”[47] While this is true, there is a poignancy that is disconcerting, for the photographs record the banality of the present in its everydayness, as it blankets and obliterates the fervor of revolution and the intoxication of war.

The book of an exhibition of Meiselas's photographs, appropriately named *In History*, has a tiny snapshot of a young man at the top of the cover and, at the bottom, a photograph of folded hands. At first sight, it could be taken for a photo of a disappeared person, but the back cover tells a different story. It is the snapshot of the young man attached to the black dress of a woman, possibly his mother. The snapshot is not of a disappeared person but of a Peshmerga martyr, someone who voluntarily gave his life for a cause and is remembered for it. It is a sharp reminder that our postmodernity is shadowed by martyrdom as well as disappearance, that our lives lived in safety may have a flip side in lives voluntarily or involuntarily sacrificed.

NINE | Apocalypse Now

In a review of *The Last Narco* published in the *London Review of Books*, the reviewer Ben Ehrenreich summed up Mexico's 2010 death count as follows:

> There have been more than 2000 killings in Juárez so far this year. On 24 August, 12 people were killed in violence allegedly related to organized crime; more than a quarter of that day's national total (if you don't count the 72 Central and South American migrants found dead in the northeastern state of Tamaulipas, executed en masse by their kidnappers). Nationwide, in a single three-week period, the mayor of the Tamaulipas town of Santiago was found dead, his body showing signs of torture (six police officers including the mayor's bodyguard were subsequently arrested); four decapitated corpses were hung from a bridge in Cuernavaca; 27 unidentified men said to be members of a cartel known as the Zetas were killed in a shoot-out with the army in Ciudad Mier, also in Tamaulipas; eight "presumed sicarios," or hit men, were killed in a 13-hour gun battle with the army in northern Veracruz; eight people died after Molotov cocktails were thrown into a bar in Cancun; soldiers at a checkpoint in the northern city of Monterrey opened fire on a carload

of civilians, killing a 52-year old man and his teenage son and injuring five others; two headless and limbless corpses were found outside a children's museum in the capital of the south-eastern state of Guerrero; and another mayor was assassinated when gunmen interrupted a meeting in the town hall of El Naranjo, San Luis Potosí. Hundreds have died less spectacularly.[1]

But in 2011, if anything it got worse. In April, bodies of Central Americans attempting to cross into the United States were found buried in three grave sites in Tamaulipas; seven young men were found tortured and killed in Cuernavaca, one of them the son of the poet Javier Sicilia. In Veracruz, in November three trucks filled with bodies were left close to the site of Guadalajara's famed book fair just before it opened. In Mexico, 11,890 people were assassinated in 2011. And in 2012, Jonathan Littell added to the chorus of doom with a devastating report on "the seamy side of Ciudad Juárez" to which he gave the title "Lost in the Void."

The more than fifty thousand who have died during President Calderón's "war on drugs" are the casualties of a war in which neither women nor children are exempt and in which journalists have paid a heavy price. The head of Milo Vela (Miguel Angel López Velasco), who was killed with his wife and son in his home, was thrown into the street bearing the message "This is a present for journalists. More heads are going to roll and Milo Vela knows it well."[2] The United Nations named Mexico "the most dangerous country in the world for the exercise of journalism."[3]

The fabric of Mexico, the ideologies and practices that had propelled the nation during the decades following its revolution, are in crisis. A showcase for neoliberal policies pasted onto a corrupt society in which institutions were already compromised and offered collusion rather than resistance to the drug trade, it is now the showcase for disaster. The army, sent in by President Calderón to wage war against the drug cartels, has not only failed to curb the traffic but has become yet another abusive power. Violence has increased since the army's intervention, and members of the armed forces commit rape and murder.[4] Most commentators attribute the violence to a complex of factors, among which two stand out: first, the insertion of the drug trafficking into an already corrupt state, and second, the poverty caused by the collapse of the agrarian economy as a result of the North American Free Trade Agreement (NAFTA) and the flooding of the market with cheap US corn, which has in turn created a pool of unemployed who are ready and able to work for the cartels. Half of the Mexican states and about nine hundred municipalities are controlled by drug cartels whose activities are not confined to drug smuggling but have now diversified and engage in extortion, protection rackets, illegal immigration, kidnapping, oil theft, and pirated goods.[5] For Charles Bowden the dire situation in which a pretense of normality obfuscates the everyday violence "is the fruit of living without history. This is the result of amnesia in television, radio, and print. This is the sweet drug that comes from fantasy. The authorities are real. The police enforce the laws. The courts function. There is a consensus here to believe the unbelievable, to insist that things are normal — the government is in charge."[6] Based on years of reporting from Ciudad Juárez, he notes the "rhythm of casual violence in that city that marks a new era beyond our imagination."

> Violence courses through Juárez like a ceaseless wind, and we insist it is a battle between cartels, or between the state and the drug world, or between the army and the forces of darkness. But consider this possibility: Violence is now woven into the very fabric of the community and has no single cause and no single motive and no on-off button. Violence is not a part of life, now it is life.[7]

But why isolate Ciudad Juárez, or Mexico as a whole? In many countries of Central America and parts of Latin America, the positive aspects of globalization — the transnational alliances of social groups, the multiplication of cultural styles, the forging of new urban identities, the resources of technology, and unprecedented mobility — have erected a glossy facade on societies, but beneath this facade, cruelty formerly exercised by military governments is now exercised by powerful gangs responsible for a culture of fear and intimidation. The apocalyptic fantasies encouraged by crime sprees were given an ironic cast in Brazil when, in a fake interview that quickly spread through the Internet, the imprisoned capo Marcola, head of the PCC (Primer Comando de la Capital), supposedly declared that only an enlightened dictator could bring about reforms: "And it would cost billions of dollars and imply a deep psychosocial transformation in the political structure of the country. It's impossible. There is no solution." This is a view not only expressed in fake interviews but also voiced by scholars, politicians, and ordinary people. In an interview by Héctor Pavón in the Argentine newspaper *El Clarín*, the sociologist Rosanna Reguillo says, "I speak from a realistic pessimism, a huge concern for what is happening in Mexico."[8]

Juárez: Mirror of the Future?

Women are the losers in the antistate. It was first of all the rape, murder, and mutilation of women in Ciudad Juárez that drew international attention to the US-Mexican border, and although the atrocities committed by the drug cartels have eclipsed the murder of women in the news, these crimes have not stopped. On the contrary, impunity is blatant: in 2010, for example, when Sergio Rafael Barraza Bocanegra killed his wife Rubi Marisol in Ciudad Juárez, he was released by three judges, clearly signaling that he had powerful protection. This was violently confirmed when Rubi's mother, Marisela Escobedo, protesting his release in front of the State Congress building, was shot to death. A short time later Josefina Susana Ortiz Reyes, a woman well known for her activism on behalf of the murdered women of Ciudad Juárez, was shot and killed, along with four members of her family. On a protest march following the murder of Marisela, many of the demonstrators covered their faces for fear of reprisals. What is all the more extraordinary is that while Ciudad Juárez and the state of Chihuahua have all the scaffolding of government — state assembly, governor, judges, and police — it is a colossal trompe l'oeil.[9]

The rape and assassination of women in Ciudad Juárez, many of them young workers in the maquiladoras, are not only scandalous indictments of the justice system but also evidence of a widespread contemporary phenomenon variously termed feminicide and femicide.[10] The proliferation of documentary and feature films, *narcocorridos*, novels, poetry, and expository writing, and support groups is, however, in inverse proportion to clarification of the crimes, which scandalized because of the brutality of the deaths, the torture and mutilation of bodies, and the impunity of the perpetrators, who have been protected by government silence. The UN Human Rights Commission representative in Mexico,

Amerigo Incalcaterra, was forced to resign in May 2008 because he had criticized the unpunished attacks on journalists and indigenous peoples and the unpunished assassinations of women.[11]

The troubles on its northern border escalated when Mexico became a source of cheap labor and quick fortunes from drug trafficking after the Colombian cartels increasingly channeled drugs through Mexico. On the border with the United States, a fluid population of workers in the border industries, would-be emigrants to the United States, and drug traffickers who controlled the area through intimidation and bribery was integrated into a raucous regional culture that challenged the hegemony of the nation-state. During prohibition, Ciudad Juárez had attracted US citizens. It became a city of dance halls and nightclubs playing jittery *norteño* music and a place where cowboy swagger proclaimed male superiority. In the 1970s, assembly plants began to spring up, avoiding high US wages and taking advantage of the pool of young women workers, many of them drawn from other regions of Mexico. As this growing population spread into the barren regions north and south of the city, developers provided rudimentary roads, water, electricity, and bus services. The journalist Sergio González Rodríguez, whose book *Huesos en el desierto* (*Bones in the Desert*) was one of the first to analyze the killings of women and trace impunity to the highest level of government, wrote of the spectral impression of a city surrounded by desert.[12] He described the city as a backyard (*un traspatio*), a term that became the title of a feature film written and directed by Sabina Berman.[13] *Traspatio* suggests a whole history of what it means to be a backyard, a place for obsolete things — for rejects, discards, and for enterprises that can be run more cheaply south of the border. González Rodríguez comments on the juxtaposition of efficient industry and unplanned proliferation: "sporadic greenery, irregular asphalt, dirt streets that alternate with the efficiency of machines, telecommunications, modern services, vanguard industry. A prosthesis of concrete, high technology, rubbish in the urban wastelands adorned with plastic, potholes, oxide and rags."[14] This conjunction of arid desert, tortured corpses, and sophisticated foreign-owned factories is a stark revelation of how economic development brought enterprises that employed young women workers who had to cross the desert wasteland to get home, thus facilitating criminal savagery. The desert where murdered girls' bodies were dumped after being cruelly raped, tortured, and killed was a space laden with symbolism of freedom from the law, unplanned development and rubbish dumps.[15] He suggests a comparison between the assembly plant and the concentration camp, which Agamben regarded as the "biopolitical paradigm of the modern."[16]

The girls were not only murdered but killed with the utmost cruelty, sacrificed for the perverse pleasure of the male. In a case described by González Rodríguez, "the aggressor takes her head while he bites the earlobe and then with a great force dislocates the neck, probably by placing a knee on the shoulder blade (on the thoracic vertebra) and twisting the neck suddenly as in other cases."[17] Describing the dislocated neck and vertebrae of an unidentified body, tagged as case 233, he writes, "The neck and vertebrae had been dislocated," so the examiner "had to accept the possibility that, while raping the victim, the aggressor ended by dislocating her neck when he attained orgasm and enjoyed her convulsions at the moment of death."[18] This damage inflicted on another human being suggests not only sadistic enjoyment but also extreme rage against the female. According to Diana Washington Valdez, a journalist from El Paso, forensic experts believed that breaking the victim's neck enhanced sexual pleasure: "Breaking the neck at a certain point of the vertebrae generates a convulsion that certain attackers deliberately seek."[19] But the pleasure is also, as Ileana Rodríguez suggests, *Lustmord*, or death pleasure.[20]

The opening and closing shots of the film *Bajo Juárez* and many scenes in Lourdes Portillo's documentary *Señorita Extraviada* (one of the first to attract international attention to the murders) linger on the rocky and dusty terrain.[21] The *lotes* or divisions where many of the bodies were dumped, aptly named Lomas de Poleo (Windy Heights) and Lote Bravo (Savage Lot), were bleak graveyards that linked the unplanned growth of the city to the women's deaths. The maquiladoras had attracted women from all over Mexico, providing enough jobs to attract a pool of young women, many of whom lived in shanty towns on the outskirts of the city. One of the recurrent images in the film *Señorita Extraviada* is of shoes: new shoes in shoe stores, dusty sneakers found near the bodies, shoes dangling on the windows of a taxi driver's car. The shoes have multiple meanings — cowboy boots epitomize the regional culture, sneakers speak of the long walks home, and fashionable shoes in a store designate the consumer culture to which the girls aspired. The shoe also figures in the documentary *Bajo Juárez: La ciudad devorando a sus hijas* (*Bajo Juárez: The City Devouring Its Daughters*), by Alejandra Sánchez and José Antonio Cordero.[22] That film interweaves two contrasting stories: that of a girl from Veracruz who emigrates to Ciudad Juárez and is happy to find a job in a maquiladora, and that of Lila Alejandra, murdered in 2001, juxtaposing both the lure of the city and its deadly embrace. Clips from a video made during Lila Alejandra's *quinceañera* (the celebration of a girl's fifteenth birthday that in many Latin American countries marks her entry into adult life) contrast starkly with the shots of graves and scraps of clothing, the evidence of a solitary ending. Her *quinceañera*, which was videotaped at a moment when the future must have been full of promise, shows a proud girl on the verge of womanhood, a girl who became a loving single mother. Her own mother, Norma Peralta, a schoolteacher, was left as the lone caretaker of Lila Alejandra's two children and has become one of the persistent voices of the families of the disappeared, cofounder in 2001 of Nuestras Hijas de Regreso a Casa, which has generated an extraordinary response.[23] In 2011 she survived an assassination attempt. Over the course of the film, the viewer learns that Lila had been forced into a car and brutally tortured, possibly for days, before being killed. *Bajo Juárez* goes beyond scenes of mourning and speculation about the murders to explore the political and cultural impact of the deaths, the international repercussions, and the impunity of the perpetrators, as well as the increasing militancy of the families, who took their protest to the gates of the presidential residence, then occupied by President Fox. By demanding that the girls be restored with life and erecting crosses inscribed with the names, the association of families of the murdered women fused the secular with religious iconography. The crosses are meant to redeem the brutalized bodies, to restore a sense of the sacred, yet the very wording of the organization's name, Nuestras Hijas de Regreso a Casa (May Our Girls Return Home), speaks of a threshold that cannot be crossed, a state of perpetual mourning without reprieve. On their webpage they write,

It is complicated for us to express in words the deep [*desgarradora*] pain of knowing that our young daughters were assassinated in such circumstances, and the immense suffering that does not go away and we cannot stop crying every time that we think of them and look at their personal effects and their photos and our suffering increases as we imagine how the final moments of our daughters assassinated by torture must have been.[24]

Despite the arrest of an Egyptian named Sharif Sharif, who would die in jail; despite the round-up of a gang known as The Rebels and some bus drivers, all of whom were at various times accused of the crimes; and despite the arrival of a US expert in serial killings, there has been no clarification, leading the families, journalists, and experts to the same conclusions — that the killings were a symptom of deep-rooted misogyny and that the perpetrators were untouchable and beyond the rule of law.

When, in 2001, the cruelly tortured bodies of Claudia González, Esmeralda Herrera, and Laura Berenice Ramos were found with those of five other women on a waste ground known as the "cotton field," the International Court of Justice sentenced Mexico to investigate and to apologize to the victims' families, erect a memorial, offer reparation, and create a database of the disappeared.[25] But the killings did not stop. By 2012, when González Rodríguez published *The Femicide Machine*, Ciudad Juárez had become "a more dangerous and desolate place ... with 116,000 abandoned dwellings, 80,000 small businesses shuttered, 10,000 orphaned children, and 200,000 families exiled."[26]

For Rita Laura Segato, the crimes are expressions of a zeitgeist that we have not acknowledged: "The humble deaths of Juárez ... awaken us and leads us to a more lucid reading of the changes that the world is experiencing in our time, as it becomes every moment more inhospitable and terrifying."[27] Segato's essay, first published in the feminist journal, *Debate Feminista*, stated bluntly that Ciudad Juárez "demonstrates the direct relation that exists between capital and death, between accumulation and unregulated concentration and the sacrifice of poor, mestiza women, devoured where the monetary and symbolic economies, the control of resources and the power of death are

articulated."[28] On the basis of her visit to the city in 2004, she lists a series of sinister coincidences — the failure of the television system as she
was about to begin her talk and a body left at the place of another victim
whose mother she had interviewed.[29] Sabina Berman was also harassed
when she went on location to make her film *Traspatio*. Segato, who had
previously interviewed a number of imprisoned rapists in Brazil, maintained that the killers were not mentally unbalanced. They acted as a
group that shared the deep symbolic structures that "organize our acts
and fantasies and make them intelligible" (81). The Juárez killings were
performances of sovereignty that required the psychological and moral
defeat of the other and an exhibition of the power of death that required
an audience. These were expressive crimes: that is, the bodies constituted a language that expressed the power of the *fratres* over life and
death and consolidated them as a group. All who witnessed the event
were accomplices whose silence was guaranteed. The torture, mutilation, and rape of lower-class mestiza women not only demonstrated and
confirmed male domination but also publicized the power of the perpetrators to society at large. Segato argues that the formation of masculine
subjectivity requires repeated confirmation. Acknowledging misogyny
as a factor, she argues that these crimes are committed to assert masculinity before an audience of peers. Assassinations are a group activity
that inscribe a language of absolute power on the bodies of victims who
are generic, belonging to a particular class of persons — that is to say,
young, long-haired, mestiza working women. She points out that the
killings must have involved powerful men because they required considerable resources — transport for the kidnappers, places where the girls
were kept captive, and sites where the bodies could be stored before they
were dumped. One thinks of the Marquis de Sade, whose lordly mis-
treatment of poor women, some of them prostitutes, also focused on
a particular type rather than individuals and also deployed considerable resources. But the Marquis de Sade acted alone, whereas the Juárez
perpetrators are anonymous people with the power to maintain their
anonymity. They may be agents of the law, prominent citizens, corrupt
officials, or high-level criminals. Furthermore, they control the territory.
Indeed, one of the most striking of Segato's conclusions is that, in the
age of neoliberalism, "micro-fascisms" have come to exercise totalitarian

control over certain regions "in a regressive conjunction between post-modernity and feudalism, where the female body is once again icon and annex of territorial domain."[30] The inhabitants of these territories identify with a regional culture that consolidates their sense of difference from the rest of the nation. Border culture has long idealized the macho and the outlaw, reinforcing a sense of male omnipotence. In singling out women workers, some of whom were immigrants to the city, the killers took advantage of the terrain, the dusty deserted roads leading to poorly lit streets on which women walking home were a convenient prey of the bitter and resentful male. And then there is the silence. Nobody has confessed to witnessing these lurid ceremonies and the communal performance of terror. Not surprisingly, attempts to translate these crimes to the big screen by pitching them as crime dramas are unconvincing. *Bordertown*, which featured Jennifer López as a fearless reporter, is an example of the inadequacy of a plot device that requires a single heroine and villain to tell a story where the murderers and victims are a multitude.

In an impassioned analysis, Ileana Rodríguez links the murder of Juárez women to the assembly plants that drew them in as cheap labor from the provinces without offering them security once they left the plant. "*Maquilas* produce migrations, demographic saturation, urban restructuring, reordering of gender relations, sociocultural segregations and overall disorder,"[31] Rodríguez writes, charging that the murders also reveal the weak foundations of liberal democracy: "Crime and violence have disrupted liberalism's goals and exposed the flip side of nation, state, and human rights." Her book *Liberalism at Its Limits* describes liberalism as a totalizing philosophy that was fashioned in Europe and claims to be universal yet is inapplicable to what she terms "creole societies," that is, societies in which civil society does not include all citizens, in which some sectors do not count. She astutely points out that "cultural analysts interrogate the nature of the state by denouncing its indifference to *feminicidio*, yet they simultaneously demand that justice be served to the bereaved families of these women and that protection be given to all the nation's citizens. Thus, while they rebuff the state, they hold it accountable to the well-being of the community" (178). This situation is further complicated by the fact that in Mexico, political society is harnessed to criminal society; the political establishment "partakes in [the criminal world] and is the beneficiary of all kinds of labor — legal (maquila) and illegal (traffic — of drugs, organs and pleasure)" (160). What remains unexplained is the fury and sadism of the killers, who are not necessarily members of drug gangs but could be "respectable" members of society. Like the civilians who, during the Colombian civil wars, murdered at night and during the day acted as normal citizens, the Juárez killers must mask their nocturnal savagery and a deep-rooted misogyny that requires the cruel extermination of working-class women. For, as Lagarde y de los Ríos tells it, the women's deaths were horrendous: "Some were beaten to death, others were strangled, decapitated, hung, stabbed, and shot; some were mutilated and bound. For some, their remains were placed in a sack, a suitcase, or a box, put in concrete, dismembered, burnt, or stretched."[32] The degree of cruelty recalls the massive genocides of the 1980s, and many scholars have remarked on the links between the militarized societies of the 1980s and 1990s and present-day atrocities. The dirty wars turned the degradation of women into a routine occurrence. The men who committed crimes under army orders were released into societies that did nothing to protect women and had a history of domestic violence and marital infidelity. Added to this is the erotic thrill experienced not only by the participants but also spectators, including distant spectators like ourselves.

The feminicides in Juárez, although the most publicized, are not unique. The Spanish newspaper El País, reporting on a meeting in Madrid titled Iberoamérica Frente al Feminicidio: El Fin de la Impunidad (Iberoamérica Confronting Feminicide: The End of Impunity), organized by Casamérica, gave some startling statistics: In El Salvador, where violence against women increased by 197 percent during the last decade, there were 477 murders between January and October of 2010. In Guatemala 5,300 were killed between 2001 and 2010, and in Honduras during the same period 1,464 women were killed, 44 percent being young women between fifteen and twenty-nine years old.[33] There is no telling how many of these deaths could be attributed to "domestic violence." Nevertheless, it is clear that societies now combine intense surveillance in some sectors (for instance, the gated communities of the rich) with protection rackets run by drug cartels, while at the lower levels there is no protection at all.

One could argue, with Charles Bowden, that northern Mexico is indeed "the laboratory of the future" and that the murder of women was a foretaste of what was to come in other Mexican states and in Guatemala and Brazil. The brutality of war has been succeeded by a "peace" that guarantees impunity. During Guatemala's civil war, rape was perpetrated in one in every six killings.[34] The Federación Internacional de Derechos Humanos (International Federation of Human Rights) stated that "persons who learned from the lived experience of the war — be it because they were victimizers or because as children or adolescents they witnessed these events as normal — reproduce the violence of the past, and once again brutalize women."[35]

Rosa Linda Fregoso and Cynthia Bejarano argue that the murder of women is not simply a form of homicide: "Unlike most cases of women's murders, men are not killed *because* they are men or as a result of their vulnerability as members of a subordinate gender, nor are men subjected to gender-specific forms of degradation and violation, such as rape and sexual torture, prior to their murder."[36] What few could have foreseen was that the conditions for such degradation were created when the neoliberal state relinquished responsibility for the protection of its neediest citizens. What some have termed "savage capitalism" keeps its eye on profit, not on people.

The Headless Man

What links the assassination of women to drug killings is that both are expressive crimes that publicize the ideology and power of rogue groups. While the killing of women confirms grotesque forms of masculinity, beheadings are acts of sovereignty in the shadow state of drug cartels that now control many areas of Mexico, especially the states along the border, but also Guerrero, Tamaulipas, Michoacán, and Tabasco. There are gang-controlled areas in Guatemala, El Salvador, and Honduras. "Gang control" means the demonstration of power through extreme acts of cruelty — in other words, an extreme cult of masculinity. La Familia in Michoacán adopted the self-help books of John Eldredge as instructional manuals on becoming a man. A boy has a lot to learn in his

journey toward manhood, and he learns it through the active intervention of the father and the fellowship of men.[37] Since masculinity comes
from God the Father, it follows that the goal of masculinity is to be powerful and dangerous, a force to be reckoned with. A man must have the
heart of the Warrior. Eldredge, of course, never advocates criminal activity for his Warriors, but the subordination of women implied in his
doctrine and the endorsement of the wild at heart made it such a plausible training manual that La Familia paid to have his works distributed in
rural schools. They created a parallel state in Michoacán, where poppy
and marijuana are cash crops, and they became the largest supplier of
amphetamines to the United States. Their masculine ethos was backed
up by a religiosity that sanctioned violence. Its creed was succinctly
stated in a message that accompanied six severed heads thrown into
the Luz y Sombra nightclub in Uruapan: "The Family does not kill for
money. It does not kill women. It does not kill the innocent. Everyone
should know that those die who ought to die: this is divine justice."[38]
The executioners describe themselves as God's enforcers. Evil has now
become good; to kill is a divine right.

Beheadings are forceful messages, forms of publicity that demonstrate
that there is only one head — the head of the gang. The documentary
film *Sicario*, in which a former enforcer for a cartel describes in luxurious
detail the torture and killing of those who cheat the organization, makes
it clear that enforcers are machines without a will of their own.[39]

In his book *El hombre sin cabeza*, González Rodríguez reviews mytho-
logical and historical beheadings, from the head of Medusa to Judith's
decapitation of Holofernes and various regicides, including the execution of Louis XVI and the postmortem beheading of Padre Hidalgo,
whose head the Spaniards paraded around the country. But the present-day beheadings are dark promises, signaling the return of the god
Pan, whose demise marked the end of the pagan world, which has now
returned with a vengeance, such that there is no resistance to the spread
of pornography, slavery, killings of organized crime, enforced prostitution, the abuse of children, serial killings, mutilations, and beheadings.
The dark forebodings that overshadow discussions of the feminicides
are augmented by the headless bodies that carry messages of violence
and retribution to the population.

Beheadings are associated with vengeance and sacrifice, and they even became avant-garde when Georges Bataille named his journal *Acéphale*. Although González Rodríguez cites Bataille to the effect that man "encountered beyond himself not God, that is the prohibition of crime but a being who ignores prohibition" (117), he is reluctant to claim that the contemporary beheadings are anything more than "vulgar crimes" that began to proliferate as recently as 2006 and were a summons to "implant barbarism, extreme aggressiveness [by] depositing headless bodies and severed heads, and by mutilating and quartering" (59). Beheadings were practiced by the Maras, the deadly Salvadorian gang, and the practice may have been introduced by the *kaibiles*, whose atrocities passed into Mexico after the end of the Guatemalan civil war. González Rodríguez describes beheading as an "act of fundamentalist fury" and argues that the beheader "wants to make clear to the rest his absolute contempt for order and norms of any type." He thus assumes the role of "messenger of the dark side of humanity, sees himself as the restorer of the kingdom of death and the vast savagery that imposes destruction and imposes a negative meaning on the world" (60). Like the decapitation of Louis XVI, the modern beheading initiates terror. The beheaders are men for whom killing is both métier and religion. The symbolic importance attached to the head as the place of sovereignty, of thought and identity, makes its severance profoundly significant. Heads are placed on parked cars or in refrigerators. Most of them carry messages: "Esto es lo que les pasa a las personas que se hacen pasar por Z, estafadores, secuestradores y ratas" (This is what happens to people who pass for Z [Zetas], cheats, kidnappers, and rats), or, in another case, "Siguen escarbando y revolviendo el agua, hijos de la chingada madre y verán como le va ir" (Go on, muddying the water, sons of bitches, and you'll see what happens to you). The ultimate insult is a pig's head placed on a headless body as a sign of reversion to "bestiality." Publicity is important to the cartels. In an era of sophisticated advertisement, they evoke another era: their statements involve bodies hanging from bridges, warnings issued on crudely painted blankets that are hung from overpasses. But the symbolic significance of beheading goes right to the issue of sovereignty, making it a dramatic statement of the mutilation of the sovereign state.

These headless societies are dominated by fear: they are societies in which advanced science and technology coexist with the most primitive implements — the sword, the scythe, the machete, the tourniquet, the knife.[40] The religious beliefs of the cartels are, like their implements, throwbacks to another era. The Zetas worship La Santa Muerte (Holy Death), represented as a robed skeleton carrying a scythe. She is a symbol of negativity, a grinning death's head that presides over the dark reality lived by the underclasses in a nation that tries to ignore them: eternal death instead of eternal life. Religion, which formerly helped shore up society, providing it with a moral code more powerful than civic codes, has not so much disappeared as gone over to the dark side. Most of the original thirty-six members of Los Zetas have been killed, a fact that confirms their trivialization of life. "La vida no vale nada" ("Life Is Worth Nothing") was once a popular song and could certainly be a motto for the cartels. In the past, saints were exemplary: they embodied suffering, abnegation, charity, sacrifice. But the saints of the underworld have nothing to do with virtue. Take Juan Soldado, for instance. This soldier who was accused of raping and killing eight-year-old Olga Camacho in Tijuana in 1938 and was sentenced to die according to the *ley de fuga*[41] has became a patron saint along the western portion of the US-Mexico border. The innocent victim is forgotten, while the presumed guilty (Juan Soldado confessed to the crime) is awarded sainthood.[42]

In an interview with González Rodríguez, a beheader for the Zetas described how he acquired his skills, recalling the torturers I mentioned in chapter 5, who prided themselves on doing a good job. Beheadings are carried out systematically by Los Zetas, a paramilitary group that was originally the enforcement militia for the Gulf Cartel and is now an independent organization. It engages not only in drug trafficking but also in illegal immigration and the protection racket, in operations that extend from Tabasco and along the Gulf Coast into Arizona. The Zetas control part of the Petén in Guatemala, and a corridor through Central America leading south to the cocaine fields of Colombia and Venezuela. "Controlling an area" means waging turf wars for territorial control on an ever-changing map of criminal activity.

The beheader had been recruited when looking for work, by members of the Zeta organization who trained him and enrolled him in the cult of Saint Death. He describes a beheading as a skill that involves cutting the neck of a victim after his execution so that a large amount of blood is released, making the head easier to transport.

> First I drink four or five tequilas before doing it. When the moment arrives, with or without witnesses from the group and when the body is still warm, I turn it face down and propping it on a stool or a chair I let the machete fall, always using both hands in order to have the strength and so as the blow doesn't spring back from the vertebral column. Afterward I wrap the head in a towel or in the dead man's clothes so that all the blood comes out, because they taught me that the neck veins are full of blood. At the time I think, don't let them do this to me. But this one was looking for it. Let it turn out well so that they see I do my job so they don't take it away from me. (148–49)

He then collects a little of the victim's blood to take to the private ceremony that takes place after the beheading, during which he prays before the altar of Saint Death. What religion sanctifies is this absolute indifference to the life of another. Like La Familia, the Zetas require supernatural sanction, and they have a rich tradition of folk culture and its celebration of *calaveras* (skeletons) on which to draw.

Many of the killers who work for the cartels are in their teens. Given the deterioration of the education system and the lack of work, killing for the cartel gives boys a sense of empowerment, especially as they earn good money. They are careless of life and lacking in empathy, and their often primitive methods are deployed in a postmodern world of up-to-date technologies. Think, for instance, of the young members of Mara Salvatrucha, which started among Salvadorian immigrants in Los Angeles, spread to El Salvador, has been active in Honduras and in several US cities, and has garnered an international following through the Internet.[43] In northern Mexico, macho defiance has its expression in *narcocorridos*, boasting songs that celebrate famous drug lords, warn their enemies, and praise the drug.[44] It is little wonder that apocalyptic fears take hold as they did at the end of the nineteenth century, but this time with the added terror of a reversal of progress. Sergio González Rodríguez's *El hombre sin cabeza* ends with a description of Pozo Meléndez, also known as La Boca del Diablo (the Devil's Mouth). It is an opening in the earth, three meters long, whose depth is legendary: "If you throw a stone there, you hear it bounce off the walls over and over again until the fall is lost in the unknown." The drug traffickers use Pozo Meléndez to disappear the bodies of their enemies, just as before them, during the French occupation of Mexico, a French detachment had been sent to their deaths there, and, at the beginning of the 1900s, a group of rebels disappeared along with their horses. Many left-wing guerrillas reportedly met the same end, one by one, decades ago. González Rodríguez describes the Devil's Mouth as "the exact figure of a primordial force that is devouring everything in its path: the ideal destiny for the man without a head. The crevice" (181–82).

Apocalyptic forebodings (predicted by some for the year 2012) are in vogue. Carlos Monsiváis made fun of them in his book *Apocalipstick*, noting the fusion of dark prognostication with the cosmetic glamour of the media. Although this is by no means the first time that the end of civilization has been announced, it now signals a widespread disillusion with civil society. Ideas of progress and reform, promises of a better life and a more just society, had seemed like the foreseeable outcome of industrial progress but now have no purchase. It is not surprising, then, that the combination of superstition, cold-blooded death, and the illegal economies in which drugs and emigrants travel northward along clandestine routes have inspired not only a great deal of pulp fiction, films, and ballads but also two powerful and very different denunciations: Charles Bowden's *Murder City* and Roberto Bolaño's *2666* both offer powerful warnings of the end of civilization and also of the mad dash to its death.

Murder City

Both Bowden and Bolaño depict Ciudad Juárez as a premonitory sign of what is to come. For Bowden, it is the advanced post of irrational violence. Bolaño's novel opens with a quotation from Baudelaire as its epigraph: "Un oasis de horror en medio de un desierto de aburrimiento" (An oasis of horror in a desert of boredom).

Bowden's *Murder City* is more like a haunting than conventional reporting. He is haunted by the fate of Miss Sinaloa, a beauty queen with white skin who, for a while, was housed in an asylum in the desert, run by a radio evangelist. The exact facts of her case constantly shift in his account. In one version

> Miss Sinaloa is a beauty who comes to party in Juárez and is raped. Miss Sinaloa is a beauty who comes to party in Juárez and consumes enormous amounts of cocaine and whiskey and becomes crazy, so *loca* that the people call the police and the cops come and take Miss Sinaloa away and they rape her for days and then dump her at the crazy place in the desert. She has long hair and is beautiful, and a doctor examines her and there is no question about the rapes. She has bruises on her arms and legs and ribs. She is now almost a native of the city. (15)

Miss Sinaloa, beauty defiled, has contributed to her own defilement, but unlike the consumers north of the border, she is punished, and her experience makes her "almost a native of the city." Bowden argues that the focus on the dark women workers of the maquiladoras distracts attention from the ubiquity of the violence and from cases like that of Miss Sinaloa. What he observes in Ciudad Juárez is "a new way of life, one beyond our imagination and the code words we use to protect ourselves from life and violence. . . . And the violence has not an apparent and simple source. It is like the dust in the air, part of life itself" (22).

Refusing to put all the blame for the chaos on drug gangs, Bowden writes that "forces are unleashed on the land with names like poverty, fix, murder, and despair, and our tools cannot master these forces." By putting all the blame on the drug trade, we lose sight of a greater phenomenon: the everyday violence that marks the loss of the value of life. Miss Sinaloa and El Pastor, a born-again Christian who runs an asylum for the damaged, are the iconic figures of desolation, the drowned and the saved. Miss Sinaloa is the proof that neither whiteness nor beauty is sacred. White Mexico is as susceptible to drugs and violence as the rest of the continent. The Pastor is a savior who cannot promise an end to the madness, only an asylum for the refugees of the drug wars.

In Bowden's telling, Ciudad Juárez is the scene of a huge con that goes by the name "the war on drugs," in which the United States is complicit. He describes the Mexican people as "road kill" in the war in a country with no functioning justice system: "Into this fray, American policy experts charge with drones, agents, counterinsurgency tacticians, and various traveling salesmen for judicial rights. No one talks about raising wages in the American-owned factories and no one talks about the vicious war on drugs that imprisons Americans, kills Mexicans and terrorizes American addicts. No one says that our answers to poverty and drugs and migration have been failures and have, in fact, increased the problem" (238).

"Killing," Bowden writes, "is not deviance, it is a logical career decision for thousands floundering in a failing economy and a failing state" (74). Bowden interviewed a killer who had been trained in an FBI school, where he was "taught how to detect drugs, guns and stolen vehicles" (133). As a member of the state police, this killer was part of a kidnapping racket before the death of the drug boss Amado Carrillo in 1997, which inaugurated a new chapter of violence. At that point, he "acquired his skill set: strangulation, killing with a knife, killing with a gun, car-to-car barrages, torture, kidnapping, and simply disappearing people and burying them in holes" (134). Nonetheless, he was only a small cog in the machine: "Now he watches the city disassemble itself. The cars vanish into junkyards to be sold for scrap. The stores are all robbed. Everyone tries to extort money from everyone else" (138). The style is melodramatic, as fits the crimes. But Bowden himself seems fatalistic. It is as if an evil wind has blown over the city, as if he is the lone rider putting himself in danger, wandering around the perilous city, interviewing assassins. He talks not of an apocalypse but of a new and deadly form of everyday life.

The book is dedicated to Armando Rodríguez, "gunned down on November 13, 2008, after filing 907 stories on the murders of that calendar year. Like the rest of us, he was a dead man walking. His last story appeared hours after he was killed." The book is an illustration of what has happened to journalism when reporting is no longer possible. There can no longer be a fourth estate.

From the Local to the Global

Roberto Bolaño's novel *2666* stages Ciudad Juárez as an incident in a global breakdown. As if it were a premonition, his earlier novel, *Los detectives salvajes* (*The Savage Detectives*), had run aground in the desert of northern Mexico, where the journey of the poet protagonists comes to an abrupt and violent end. But that was before he met Sergio González Rodríguez and read about the murder of women workers. In an interview in *Playboy* magazine, when asked about his idea of heaven and hell, he named Ciudad Juárez as his idea of hell — "our curse and our mirror, the restless mirror of our frustrations and our infamous interpretation of freedom and our desires."[45] It reveals Bolaño as the moralist of nihilism who would find in Ciudad Juárez, ironically renamed Santa Teresa in the novel, its ultimate expression. Here there are no limits, no taboos, and the senselessness of life and death is revealed in all its cruel banality. If the aridity of the landscape drew him to the Sonoran Desert in the first place, his meeting with Sergio González Rodríguez on the occasion of the publication of *Huesos en el desierto* in Spain may well have changed the course of the novel. Indeed, he later acknowledged that "González Rodríguez's technical help in the writing of my novel (*2666*) has been substantial." He described *Huesos en el desierto* as "not only an imperfect photograph — how could it be anything else? — of evil and corruption" but also one that "transforms itself into a metaphor of Mexico's past and of the uncertain future of all of us."[46]

In Bolaño's earlier writing, it was the fate of Latin America that had sent young people into exile, had forced them to become wanderers. In short stories and in his novel *Los detectives salvajes*, his characters belong to a generation born in the 1950s, a generation that was exterminated or scattered by violent events such as Pinochet's 1973 coup. In a speech he gave on receiving the Rómulo Gallegos Prize in Caracas, he described everything he had written as a farewell letter or letters to a fallen generation. "We were stupid and generous as are young people who give everything and do not ask for anything in return . . . and now, of these young people nothing remains; those who did not die in Bolivia, died in Argentina or Peru and those who survived went to die in Chile or Mexico and those who were not killed there were killed afterwards in Nicaragua, in Colombia, in El Salvador. All Latin America is sown with the bones of these young and forgotten youths."[47] What died with this lost generation — in Mexico, with the dead of Tlatelolco, with the disappeared in the Southern Cone — was the revolutionary ideal of a more just and generous society that, in his writing, is shared only by small groups of poets, poetry signifying for him an ideal and a lost cause. It was not left-wing politics per se that he mourns, but the idealism that had been so brutally crushed. His entire oeuvre can be read as an elegy for those ideals. In one of his poems, "Los pasos de Parra" ("Parra's Footprints"), he writes,

> But we know that all
> Our affairs
> Are finite (happy, yes, fierce)
> The revolution is called Atlántida
> And is fierce and infinite
> But it doesn't do any good.
> Start walking, then, Latinamericans
> walk and walk
> Searching for the missing footprints
> Of lost poets
> In the motionless mud
> to lose ourselves in nothingness
> Or in the rose of nothingness
> There where are heard the footsteps
> of Parra
> And the dreams of generations
> Sacrificed beneath the wheel
> And not historied.[48]

It is hard to imagine a more complete manifesto of nihilism than this revolution named after a lost city in a doomed attempt to salvage the utopian, and all that which is not "historied," that is, not figured in the historical narrative.

In 2666 it is not only the fate of a generation that gives urgency to his prose but the global immensity of crime. The novel is a vast encyclopedia in five sections: part of the second book, most of the third, and the entire fourth are set in Ciudad Juárez (known here as Santa Teresa), with all the allusions to asceticism and piety that the name Teresa implies, whether it reminds us of Santa Teresa de Ávila or of Thérèse de Lisieux. Like Jonathan Littell, who in his monumental novel *The Kindly Ones* takes on evil and cruelty in a world in which the political and the civic have deteriorated into crime, Bolaño ventures into the necropolis, although without Littell's cynicism. Although 2666 was supposedly finished at the time of Bolaño's death, I suspect that there was no possible "conclusion" to the novel.[49]

The epigraph of 2666 suggests that freedom and the quest for pleasure without the restraint of an ethics lead to boredom or worse. As is well known, 666 is the Mark of the Beast, the sign of the Apocalypse. Critics often quote from the novel *Amuleto*, in which the narrator, crossing Avenida Guerrero in Mexico City, is reminded "not of a cemetery of 1974, nor one of 1968 but rather a cemetery of 2666, a cemetery forgotten between the dead or newly born eyelid, the dispassionate wateriness of an eye that from wishing to forget something finally forgets everything."[50] The comparison is so bizarre as to stop the reader in his or her tracks. It is a vision neither of the present nor of the past but of the suspended time of the dead or of time as perceived by the newborn, who as yet has no notion of time. It suggests not only an end to memory but a radical amnesia, the suspension of consciousness. Once we strip humanity of transcendental destiny, once the utopian has been discredited, once we take away the ethical imperatives of either religious belief or humanism, there is nothing to rein in our infamous desires. What freedom has brought about is self-destruction through the quest for pleasure that leads to boredom or worse.

The unsolved murder of women in Ciudad Juárez became a symptom of the destruction of the human, in which terrible events are related as episodes in a search, in this case the search by a group of poets seeking the elusive writer Benno von Archimboldi, the pseudonym of a German named Hans Reiter, author of cryptic novels that few read. The search is inaugurated in the first chapter of the novel, when four poets — three men (Espinoza, Pelletier, and Morini) and one woman (Liz Norton) — attempt to discover his whereabouts. The violence of our time is already suggested when two of them, Espinoza and Pelletier, rough up a Pakistani taxi driver for no particular reason. Their search eventually runs aground in Santa Teresa. Only in the final section of the novel does the reader discover that Archimboldi, born Hans Reiter, was a soldier in the German army that invaded Russia and was a witness to the massive state crimes of the Soviet and Nazi regimes in the

1930s and 1940s. The novel is a monumental act of mourning not only for the generation born in the 1950s but for the Holocaust dead, for the Russian dead, and for the young women born in the 1970s and 1980s. In this light, the Sonoran Desert comes to epitomize "the oasis of horror in a desert of boredom." Commenting on the epigraph, Bolaño once stated, "There is no more lucid diagnosis for the illness of modern man. To escape boredom, to escape deadlock, all we have at hand, though not so close at hand, because even here an effort is required, is horror, or in other words, evil."[51] Modern life is anesthetized to such a degree that only evil provides a stimulus, and even that is only achieved with effort.

Bolaño's novel is a meditation on crime, human nature, knowledge, and futility. It is packed with apparently random disquisitions drawing the reader gradually into the abyss that the novel approaches gradually, almost reluctantly, by way of the four picaresque poets. The second section draws the reader gradually toward Ciudad Juárez as it follows the wanderings of Almalfitano, a Chilean exile living in Spain, whose wife, Lola, leaves him to camp out in a cemetery, from which she visits a mad poet confined in the Mondragón asylum. She then goes to France, only returning to tell Amalfitano that she has been diagnosed with AIDS. With their daughter Rosa, he emigrates from Spain to Mexico, where he teaches in Santa Teresa University, which "was like a cemetery that suddenly begins to think, in vain. It was also like an empty dance club" (185). His life in Santa Teresa is lived without any hope or desire, without even the slender pretext of the search that animates the poets. He embodies a loss of faith in any rational order. Discovering a geometry book written by a poet, a book that he does not remember buying, he imitates a Duchamp art action and hangs it on the washing line "just to see how it survives the assault of nature, to see how it survives the desert climate" (191). The book is the expression of order, reason, and conclusions that are notably lacking in everyday life. The dream of rationality is now exposed to the elements, as if neither abstract knowledge nor logic has any place in a society that is both cruel and aimless. By the time night falls, the hanging book has the shape of a coffin.

The murder of women at this point in the novel is no more than a sinister message carried by the *mal viento* (the evil wind of popular superstition):

At that same hour, the Santa Teresa police found the body of another teenage girl, half buried in a vacant lot in one of the neighborhoods on the edge of the city, and a strong wind from the west, hurled itself against the slope of the mountains to the east, raising dust and a litter of newspaper and cardboard on its way through Santa Teresa moving the clothes that Rosa had hung up in the backyard, as if the wind, young and energetic in its brief life, were trying on Amalfitano's shirts and pants and slipping into his daughter's underpants and reading a few pages of the *Testamento Geométrico* to see whether there was anything to it that might be of use, anything that might explain the strange landscape of streets and houses through which it was galloping or that would explain it to itself as wind. (202–3)

The passage exemplifies the compression of the prose and its packed layers of allusions. The evil wind not only brings a message of death but also penetrates the clothes of the living with incestuous desire and is beyond all rational control. Perhaps the passage also mischievously refers us to the natural catastrophes of García Márquez's novels, suggesting an acid revision of the Colombian writer's rosier view of Latin America. On a car trip, Amalfitano falls asleep and dreams of prehistoric rocks out of which there emerges a mirror, "the sad American mirror of wealth and poverty and constant useless metamorphosis, the mirror that sails and whose sails are pain" (206). He is a man who trusts nothing and for whom everything disintegrates into a nightmare of disillusion.

The third section of the novel, dedicated to Fate, a black journalist who specializes in the lost causes of the US black population, is a roundabout journey through black history and the global catastrophe of slavery. Fate works for a Harlem paper, interviewing Afro-American rebels like the last communist, and Barry Seaman, one of the founders of the Black Power movement. He goes to hear Seaman preach in a Chicago church a sermon that is a strange mixture of reminiscences of the other founder of the Panthers, Marius Newell, followed by ruminations on money and on utility and even a recipe for cooking Brussels sprouts. Seaman's reminiscences and advice seem to represent the unclassifiable knowledge that accumulates over a lifetime, including all kinds of unpacked items that may be meaningless to others. Later, while Fate is sleeping and dreaming in his Chicago hotel room in front of a television set, the channel shows a program on the deaths in Ciudad Juárez and the illegal immigration into Arizona. It is as if Fate is surrounded by information that he either does not hear or cannot decipher, like the abandoned sneaker he sees in the park, whose proleptic insertion into the story is a premonition of the abandoned sneakers of the murdered women left in the Sonoran Desert. The apparently random detour before Fate arrives in Santa Teresa offers a wealth of information that he is incapable of understanding, for instance, the conversation he overhears in a restaurant when he is en route to Santa Teresa, between a young man and a certain Kessler (a thinly disguised reference to the FBI agent Ressler called in to advise the Juárez police). Kessler is interested in the difference between crimes that make the news and mass crimes — such as slavery or the Paris Commune — in which the deaths of thousands are a matter of indifference because they belong to the outcasts of society, those who don't count. It is yet another premonition.

At the boxing match in Santa Teresa that he has been sent to cover, Fate meets the group that will induct him into the hectic life of drink, drugs, and women and bring him into contact with Rosa Amalfitano, whose lover, Chucho Flores, has introduced her to cocaine. This is "the desert of boredom" of the novel's epigraph and the bridge that eventually leads to the murders, to the cocaine culture, and to Archimboldi, whose nephew, Klaus, is accused of the crimes and whose imprisonment will eventually bring the elusive writer to Santa Teresa. Fate's good deed is to rescue Rosa Amalfitano, with the collusion of her father, and take her to the Tucson airport as a privileged escapee who eludes the terror that is implacably narrated in "The Part of the Crimes." It is left to Guadalupe Roncal, a reporter whom Fate had met in Santa Teresa, to interview Reiter, the supposed assassin. And it is she who issues the enigmatic and much quoted sentence "Nadie presta atención a estos asesinatos, pero en ellos se esconde el secreto del mundo" (No one pays attention to these killings, but the secret of the world is hidden in them) (439).

The accumulation of descriptions of the murdered women in the fourth part of the novel goes beyond documentation and becomes an implacable litany of evil. It exceeds any testimony, thanks to the repetition of the forensic details, the detailed descriptions of the remains, the punctilious data of a calendar of crimes month by month that includes not only the feminicides but also other crimes, domestic violence, the rape of women and boys by police, and the revenge killings of drug traffickers in a city where impunity reigns. Like Bowden, Bolaño recognizes that the killing of women is one aspect of an entire culture and that waste disposal is its purpose. That is why he has the FBI agent, Kessler, taken to the Chile dump, "the biggest illegal dump in Santa Teresa, bigger than the city dump where waste was disposed of not only by the maquiladora trucks but also by garbage trucks contracted by the city and some private garbage trucks and pick-ups, subcontracted or working in areas that public services didn't cover" (602). What this meticulous catalogue tells us is that garbage dumping that had formerly been regulated by local authorities was now shared with all kinds of uncontrolled private operations in an illegal enterprise. On his way there, Kessler passes through shanty towns covered in dust inhabited by people who seem to belong to another dimension. He cannot roll down the car window because, as one of the police tells him, "The smell, it smells like death. It stinks" (603).

Dozens of stories, some of them violent, surround the discovery of the crimes — a love affair between a policeman and a psychiatrist, the crimes of an iconoclast, the disappearance of Kelly, an upper-class woman, a narco killing. While some police investigate the crimes, others rape prostitutes in the jails and turn a blind eye to the contract killers who castrate and kill young gang members in the prison. Referring to an exceptional month when almost no women were killed, Bolaño writes, "There were fights. There were drug deals and arrests. There were parties and long hot nights. There were trucks loaded with cocaine crossing the desert. There were Cesna planes flying low over the desert like the spirits of Catholic Indians ready to slit everyone's throats" (519). "Catholic" is used here in the sense, perhaps, of "general" or "universal," as opposed to the particular and therefore impartially threatening. The marauding Indian that had threatened civilization is now replaced by another kind of Apache, the marauding planes of the drug traffickers. The fusion of everyday life with deadly criminal activity makes the police records of the women's deaths not only atrocious but ominous.

Most of the gruesome discoveries are narrated in the language of the police report:

> On November 16, the body of another woman was found on the back lot of the Kusai maquiladora, in Colonia, San Bartolomé. The cause of death, according to the forensic report, was asphyxia due to strangulation. She was completely naked and her clothes were five yards away, hidden in the bushes. Actually, not all of her clothes were found, just a pair of black leggings and red panties. Two days later, she was identified by her parents as Rosario Marquina, nineteen, who disappeared on November 12 while she was out dancing at Salón Montana on Avenida Carranza, not far from Colonia Veracruz where they lived. It just so happened that both the victim and her parents worked at the Kusai maquiladora. According to the medical examiners, the victim was raped several times before death. (603–4)

Another report registers the discovery of the body of a girl of about sixteen.

> She had been stabbed only once, in the abdomen, a stab so deep that the blade had literally pierced her through. But her death, according to the medical examiner, was caused by strangulation and a fracture of the hyoid bone. From the place where the body was found there was a view of a succession of low hills and scattered white and yellow houses with low roofs, and a few industrial sheds where the maquiladoras stored their reserve parts, and paths off the highway that melted away like dreams, without rhyme or reason. (503)

Bolaño's description of the setting —"paths off the highway that melted away like dreams, without rhyme or reason"— implies that there is no goal or purpose. The girl's death is as gratuitous as the haphazard features of the landscape.

Bolaño parodies the language of the police reports, whose pedestrian prose aspires to be "scientific" and professional but in fact forces the reader to imagine what the dry prose tries to cover. Discovering the scarcely identifiable remains of a woman, the inspector "found a pair of pants, threadbare from exposure. As if the killers had removed the victim's pants before tossing her in the bushes. Or as if they had brought her up there naked, with her pants in a bag, and later discarded the pants a few yards from the body. The truth is, none of it made any sense" (595). And this "none of it made any sense" becomes the leitmotif of the entire episode. When the body of a thirteen-year-old girl whose "right breast had been severed and the nipple of her left breast had been bitten off" is found, what surprises the reporters most is that no one has claimed or acknowledged the body. "As if the girl had come to Santa Teresa alone and lived there invisibly until her murderer or murderers took notice of her and killed her" (466–67): a body, that of a ten-year-old, who was evidently not an inhabitant of Santa Teresa, suggests the mystery of her presence and her loneliness. There is no community to protect her. "Her physical description was sent by fax to police stations round the country. The investigation was handled by Inspector Angel Fernández and the case was soon closed" (501). It is as if the anonymity and isolation of this particular victim was an added dimension to the cruelty of the crime, exhibiting as it did the total insignificance of a life. The body of the unknown woman was added to the collection of bodies used by medical students at the University of Santa Teresa. The body has no name, no home, no nationality. There is nothing to mark the woman's passage through the world. What Bolaño has recorded is the end of the human as such and the ferocity of misogyny that underwrites it.

In the course of the novel, a certain Yolanda Palacio, head of the Department of Sexual Crime, reveals that more than two thousand women are raped every year in Santa Teresa; she does not even estimate the number of rapes that go unreported. Half of them are committed against minors. The very culture is misogynist, an everyday misogyny reinforced in conversation, attitudes, and jokes. A policeman named González, breakfasting with his colleagues, entertains them with a litany of misogynist jokes (552–53). He tells one joke after another, mostly to illustrate female stupidity: The perfect woman is half a meter tall, big ears, flat head, toothless and very ugly. Why? "*Pues* two feet tall so she comes right up to your waist. Big ears so you can steer her, a flat head so you have a place to set your beer, no teeth so she can't bite your dick and hideously ugly so no bastard steals her away" (552). More than a joke, it is the expression of what absolute control of a woman would imply — namely, her lack of any human traits. Reeling off joke after joke, González declares that God is "machista" because he made man the superior being, which causes the inspector to wonder, "Who's the first to *think them up*" (553). Nevertheless, he offers some macho wisdom of his own: "A woman's path lies from the kitchen to the bedroom, with a beating along the way" (553). Or "Women are like laws, they were made to be broken" (553). After the last joke, "a great blanket of laughter arose over the long room, as if death were being tossed in it. Not all of the cops laughed, of course" (553). The jokes are a social ritual binding some of the men together and thus an apparently harmless version of the misogyny of the band of brothers. Others kept silent, "hunched over in contemplation of essential questions, which doesn't get you anywhere. Numb with sleep, in other words with their backs turned to the laughter that invited a different kind of sleep" (553). The voicing of misogyny is the dominant note in this episode, and one that the silent minority cannot challenge. In this section of the novel, "home" does not have the connotations of comfort and family affection; rather, it is the nightmarish scene of male domination: a "home" is where two of the girls' bodies are found, and a "home" was where Rosa Amalfitano sniffed cocaine.

Among the reports of the discovery of bodies, one case is narrated in a different key. An officer of the judicial police,[52] Juan de Dios Martínez investigates the case of two schoolgirls snatched on their way to school. Two siblings who were with them reported it to neighbors, who tried to contact the father and mother, both of whom were at work in an assembly plant. The managers refused to allow the mother to be contacted during work hours, and her coins ran out before the father could get to the phone. The neighbor then experiences "what it was like to be in purgatory, a long helpless wait, a wait that begins and ends in neglect, a very Latin American experience, as it happened, and all too familiar, something once you thought about it you realized you experienced daily, minus the despair, minus the shadow of death sweeping over the neighborhood like a flock of vultures and casting a pall, upsetting all routines, leaving everything overturned" (528). There is something else that is familiar here, namely Bolaño's obsession with something very "Latin American": the helplessness of the average citizen.

Tracking a make of car that was exclusively owned by the city's rich kids, the officer Juan de Dios Martínez and Lino Rivera enter a house and discover the naked body of Herminia on a bed and, in the shower, the corpse of her sister, Estefanía. Although there were signs of strangulation on the neck, she had been killed by a bullet after being beaten. She may also have been hung up by the neck and subjected to mock strangulation. Both girls had been raped as well as tortured. Herminia had suffered four heart attacks. The murders are so extreme that they leave the police inarticulate (527–34).

The body of a young girl found near the grounds of a secondary school is impaled on a stake (intentionally or not, it recalls the Guatemalan massacres). The painful death and the fact that the killing was near a schoolyard, in a place associated with youth and childhood, pointed to an atrocity for which there were no limits. "They dumped her on the ground and then they shoved a stake up her ass, what do you think of that? Brutal, *mano*," said José Márquez. "'But she was dead by then, wasn't she?' 'That's right, she was already dead,' said Juan de Dios Martínez" (496). The police in this novel are not all villains, but, like everyone, they are confronted with something that passes their understanding.

Among the police reports is an interview (attributed to Sergio González Rodríguez) with a Mexican woman politician and a congressional representative who relates the disappearance of her childhood friend Kelly. She organized parties, and this job took her into the dangerous territory of drugs and prostitution. Investigating the disappearance with the help of a lawyer, the woman follows clues that point to the involvement of high-ranking politicians and industrialists and orgiastic scenes in isolated ranches that are somehow connected to the disappearance. This is modern crime, like the shooting of a snuff film that Bolaño also describes and that is to be distinguished from what Bolaño terms "folkloric" crimes, involving people who "started off celebrating and ended up killing each other, uncinematic deaths, deaths from the realm of folklore, not modernity: deaths that didn't scare anybody" (540). Kelly's disappearance, the snuff film shot on an Argentine ranch, are clearly "modern" despite the latter's rustic surroundings. The folkloric is exemplified by the life story of the police recruit Olegario Cura Expósito, nicknamed Lalo Cura (*la locura*, i.e., madness), the descendant of a line of single mothers, all named Maria Expósito (Foundling).

All of these women, after being raped, had given birth to daughters, who in turn were raped and then bore more daughters. The male child, Lalo, was not only an exception to this chain of rape and oppression but also the last of the line. The folkloric rapes, unlike those of the maquiladora women, did not require the death of the woman, and the birth of a child ensured the continuity of the family (554–58). What this distinction between modern and folkloric crimes tells us is that the former are incidents in a modernity that is the rogue version of civilization.

Among the many *petites histoires* that make up "The Part of the Crimes" is the life story of a healer and seer, Florita, who is invited onto a television program where she "sees" bodies and enables their discovery. Florita is the link between the folkloric and the modern, while the iconoclast who mutilates statues in the churches belongs to the folkloric. What constitutes everyday knowledge, Bolaño suggests, is a chaotic mixture of superstition, cults, passion, folklore, organized religion, and local patriotism, none of which can account for the mutilated bodies. Bolaño was often laconic or cynical in his public statements, but there is no doubt that he was deeply affected by the murders, which must have confirmed his dark view that modernity is twisted. More than documentation, *2666* is a violent revelation of what the Argentine philosopher Enrique Dussel has termed the destruction of humanity, as well as a massive question mark posed for readers.[53]

Charles Bowden, who wrote the text for *Juárez: The Laboratory of our Future*, which reproduced and celebrated the courage of local photographers and journalists, describes the city as the conjunction of exploitative industry, crime, and neglect whose premonitory significance North Americans ignore. He describes a photograph of the mummified head of a murdered girl as "screaming and screaming and screaming" (69). For both authors, the murders signal the end of an era that could still believe in the amelioration of society. Rogue males expressing power by means of cruel acts make us question whether the deep structures of gender formation can be altered and whether such an alteration would require systemic change in both our economy and our culture. Mexico represents, in exaggerated form, a hostility toward women that, despite feminism, despite the partial acquisition of women's rights, is deeply embedded. We are not talking of the werewolf here, of man becoming wolf, but of extreme forms of masculinity that are endorsed by society itself. The term "machismo" was coined in Mexico. When Hank Rhon, a Tijuanan personality, boasts that his favorite drink is tequila laced with the penises of tigers, lions, and dogs, he is speaking to an audience he knows will celebrate the boast. There is an unleashed quality about contemporary machismo that has burst forth exactly at the moment when more women are acquiring power.

For Bolaño, the battle was lost long before, during the 1930s and 1940s, when atrocity was routinized in the Russian and German empires, taking on modern rather than folkloric forms. Interned in a prison camp after the German defeat, Reiter listens to the confessions of Sammer, an Eichmann-like atrocity merchant for whom the extermination of Greek Jews was an administrative problem. Sammer is found strangled, possibly killed by Reiter himself, who shortly afterward is freed and settles in Cologne, where he begins to write his obscure and difficult novels published by a wealthy and eccentric Hamburg publisher named Bubis. Archimboldi's novels are never described or quoted, so the reader can know nothing about them except that they are obscure and difficult. Years later, the author travels to Mexico, having learned that his nephew Hans is in prison charged with rape and murder. There he reunites with his sister, Lotte, who is on the same mission. The novel does not end so much as peter out. A note from the editor, Ignacio Echeverría, informs the reader of the author's note that the narrator is Arturo Belano, "and this is all friends. Everything I have done, everything I have lived. If I had the strength, I would cry. Arturo Belano says farewell." What he has done is deliver a devastating judgment of the "desert of boredom" that needs an "oasis of horror" in which pleasure and cruelty are inseparable.

Can anything be salvaged from apocalyptic devastation? In the last section of 2666, the reader once again encounters the theme of the buried book. During the German advance, Hans Reiter, the future Archimboldi, is wounded and receives the Iron Cross. Sent to Kostekino, an abandoned village, once inhabited by Jews, he finds the papers of Boris Abramovich Ansky hidden behind the stove, an artifice that allows Reiter to follow the story of the Soviet persecution of writers and the extermination of the Jews. He carries the manuscript under his uniform during the long war and the retreat, but is unable to save it. It is irretrievably damaged when Reiter swims down a river to escape the Russian advance, and it will henceforth exist only in Reiter's memory.

In my first chapter, I wrote of the book buried in the Dominican Republic after the massacre and rediscovered in a mutilated form; in chapter 7 I mention the photographs of once-buried books that have become the repositories of lost causes. But in *2666*, the once-hidden book survives only in the transient memory of a writer.

AFTERWORD | Hypocrite Modernity

Cruelty on the massive scale described in these pages is not a spontaneous and individual act, committed by deviants. It requires sanction
from the state or from the rogue organization, as well as a process of
dehumanization. It is often directed not toward an equal but toward a
helpless and hated enemy: a peasant, a child, a pregnant woman, or a
member of an indigenous group, each of whom transgresses the ideal
masculinity that kills the mother and exalts the father. But while cruelty
clearly is a transgression of "the inherent dignity and of the equal and
unalienable rights of all members of the human family," listed in the 1948
Declaration of Human Rights as "the foundation of freedom, justice and
peace in the world," it cannot be explained as a throwback to some prior
state of humanity. Not only has cruelty been instrumental in the coop-
tation of the nation-state by private interests and the softening up of civil
society through a regime of fear; it is also a scar on liberal society.

The cruelties narrated in the first eight chapters of this book are
events of a recent past that continue to infiltrate the present, although
in many countries a temporal distance between cruel events and their
public acknowledgment minimizes their impact. To cite one instance:
the massacre of sixteen political prisoners, four of them women, at the

Trelew Naval Base in 1972 is only now, in 2012, being publicly acknowledged and judged. Time lapse also accounts for the fact that Pinochet's
supporters are also once again giving public demonstrations of support
for his legacy.

For some, the past atrocities were so extreme as to exceed the scope of
politics. Horacio González chose the ceremony marking the conversion
of the ESMA detention center in Buenos Aires into a museum to reflect
on the crimes against humanity committed there:

> If violence always affects that which is human, in this case the excess
> includes a beyond the threshold. In effect, the use of techniques of the
> state, secret and bodily slavery, the complete abjuration of the juridical,
> the deprivation of names, the expropriation of notions of space and time,
> the usurpation of identities, and the absolute humiliation still within the
> calculated mechanisms of death all lie beyond the pale of the word poli-
> tics even when that word has always had its charge of violence.[1]

Violence is not only beyond politics, but also beyond representation:
"the memory of horror resists representation." For González, emptiness
and absence are figures for the incommensurable, the unspeakable, the
impossibility of communication (45).

But the problem with making the crimes unspeakable is that they
become mystical, outside the bounds of political action. On the other
hand, the "reconciliation" proposed by Truth Commissions is difficult
to put into effect when lasting prejudices and divisions remain in place
and sectors of the population are still subjected to discrimination. The
Peruvian report on truth and reconciliation concluded that reconciliation must be based on the positive recognition of Peru as a multiethnic,
pluricultural, and multilingual country: "This recognition is the basis
for overcoming the practice of discrimination that underlies the multiple disagreements in our republican history."[2] But how can this be
done when there is no structural change to remove gross inequalities? I
concur with Robert Meister when he argues that "unlike earlier versions
of human rights that sought to hasten the advance of human equality,
today's commitment to human rights often seeks to postpone large-scale
redistribution. It is generally more defensive than utopian, standing for
the avoidance of evil rather than any vision of the good."[3] Meister de-

scribes the protagonists of human rights discourse as Perpetrators, Victims, and Beneficiaries, arguing that the latter reap the benefits, while the victims are shortchanged as long as their societies maintain unjust social systems. The figures for Latin America support his argument: Guatemala, El Salvador, and Honduras, in which homicide rates are extremely high, are not only the most unequal in America but are also nations where a high percentage of crimes go unpunished. In Meister's view, "transitional justice" and human rights discourse in the twenty-first century "is a continuation, by more benign means, of the counter-revolutionary project of the twentieth — to assure the beneficiaries of past oppression will largely be permitted to keep the unjustly produced enrichment they presently enjoy" (31). But Meister also wants to allow a role for violence in the pursuit of social justice without considering the difficulties of controlling violence once it has become an instrument.

An equally tantalizing question that recurs in nearly every chapter of this book and is often ignored is the formation of subjectivities whose very identity requires violence. Military training is crucial in this respect: during the military regimes and the civil wars of the 1980s and 1990s, the military was prepared to "drain the sea" of guerrilla supporters, and in doing so they placed the enemy (man, woman, or child) outside the human. Inherited by the drug cartels in weak states, this brute masculinity has become a veritable death worship and has given rise to apocalyptic fears that immobilize significant political action.

This paralysis also afflicts distant readers like ourselves who can read about cruelty without it disturbing our everyday lives. The distant response to cruelty is examined by Horacio Castellanos Moya in his novel *Insensatez* (*Senselessness*), in which he explores what happens when atrocity is *read* in postwar society by a protagonist obsessed with sex, money, and reputation. The Salvadorian narrator has been hired in Guatemala to edit the evidence, compiled by the Church, of survivors of atrocity that would be published, under the authority of Bishop Gerardi, with the title *Nunca más* (*Never Again*). Most Latin American readers would likely know that Bishop Gerardi was assassinated a day after *Nunca más* was officially released, a crime that was explored in Francisco Goldman's *The Art of Political Murder* and is recapitulated at the end of Castellanos Moya's novel, which measures the distance between

everyday life in the postwar present and the violent past. The Salvadorian editor reads the horrific testimonies of indigenous survivors, but at
first he is mainly struck by the "poetry" of translated indigenous speech.
In the intervals between reading about extreme cruelty, he finds himself
caught up in the passions of everyday life and propelled into all kinds of
absurd situations by his overactive imagination. Minor setbacks — the
failed seduction of Pilar, a Spanish girl involved in human rights activities; being attacked in a newspaper article by a rival; not being paid on
time — are the everyday events that enrage him to the point of imagin-
ing committing murder and violent acts. Attempting to seduce another
Spanish girl, Fatima, who is awaiting the arrival of her boyfriend, a Uruguayan army officer, he imagines the soldier's violent revenge as if it were
registered in the archive of atrocities he is reading. What happens to
this somewhat contemptible protagonist is that he becomes captured
by the past, and violence begins to dominate his fantasies to the point
that it affects his everyday life. When a certain woman passes him in
the corridors of the bishop's palace, he is reminded that she suffered extreme torture and mass rape at the hands of the military, "particularly
at the hands of Lieutenant Octavio Pérez, who henceforward he cannot
get out of his mind. Even when he attends a cocktail party, Lieutenant
Pérez seems to be lying in wait, ready to capture and interrogate him
[using] his most expeditious method of beating me up, then taking me
to his macabre abattoir" (118). The events recorded in the manuscript
he is reading colonize his imagination to such an extent that even when
sequestered in a secluded house where he is supposed to finish his edit-
ing without distraction, he begins to hallucinate until he is transformed
into Lieutenant Octavio Pérez himself, seizing a baby and swinging it
around under the horrified eyes of the parents. "His mind wandered of
its own free will like a journalist, around the village commons, where
the soldiers, machete in hand, chopped up the bound and kneeling residents" (127), and his hallucinations are so real that they make him flee
the compound, believing that he is pursued by a posse, and shouting
quotations from the document: "*Wounded, yes, is hard to be left, but dead
is ever peaceful.*" Fearing for his sanity, he abandons the project and escapes to Switzerland.

The novel is a graphic account of how reading about atrocity impresses itself on the imagination and makes it impossible for this ridiculous and deluded man to escape from the memory of it, even far from Guatemala. Drinking in a bar during the Swiss Carnival, he is haunted by the phrase "They were people just like us we were afraid of" (137). Like us, he imagines both the pain of the victims and the exhilaration of the torturers. But at the end of the novel, he goes about shouting, "We all know who the assassins are," now converted from a distant and indifferent spectator to participant, as if reading of the atrocities has the power to transform the picaro into a fully conscious and even a responsible human being who is now anxious to find out whether the report had been published under his suggested title, *We All Know Who the Assassins Are*, a phrase which is doubly ironic but which he repeats over and over again on his way back to his apartment, where he finds and reads his friend Toto's telegram: "Yesterday at noon the bishop presented the report in a bombastic ceremony in the cathedral; last night he was assassinated at the parish house; they smashed his head in with a brick. Everybody is fucked. Be grateful you left" (143). However profound the impression left on them by the testimonies, readers are still at a distance and free to be in some other place. And that is a huge problem that no scholar can evade.

NOTES

Notes to Introduction

1. Segato, "La escritura en el cuerpo de las mujeres asesinadas en Cd. Juárez," 98. Unless otherwise indicated, all translations from sources in Spanish are my own.
2. Freud, "Timely Reflections on War and Death," in *On Murder, Mourning and Melancholia*, 170.
3. Freud, "Why War?," in *On Murder, Mourning and Melancholia*, 221–22.
4. Freud, *Civilization and Its Discontents*, 81.
5. Derrida, "Psychoanalysis Searches the States of the Soul: The Impossible Beyond of a Sovereign Cruelty," in *Without Alibi*, 262–63.
6. Arendt, *The Origins of Totalitarianism*, 459.
7. Agamben, *Homo Sacer*, 171.
8. Mbembe, "Necropolitics," 11–40.
9. Mbembe, "Necropolitics," 26–27.
10. Dussel, *The Invention of the Americas*, 12.
11. Dussel, *The Invention of the Americas*, 48.
12. Taussig, *Shamanism, Colonialism and the Wild Man*, 28.
13. De las Casas, *A Short Account of the Destruction of the Indies*, 70.
14. Guatemala, Comisión de Esclarecimiento Histórico (CEH), *Guatemala: Memoria del Silencio*, 1:16–17.
15. For more on developmentalism, see Escobar, *Encountering Development*.
16. Timerman, *Prisoner without a Name*, 39.
17. Timerman, *Prisoner without a Name*, 39–40.
18. Foucault, *"Society Must Be Defended,"* 257.
19. On the indigenous rebellions in the Andes, see Flores Galindo, *Buscando un Inca*.
20. Sarmiento, *Facundo*, 45–46.
21. In a short autobiographical essay first given as a speech and then published as a preface to *Obras completas*, Neruda comments that "after 1820 (the Independence), the Chileans dedicated themselves to killing Indians with

the same enthusiasm as the Spanish invaders. Temuco (where Neruda was born) was the last heartbeat of Auracanía" (31).

22. Taussig, *Shamanism, Colonialism and the Wild Man*, 25; see also 27–28.

23. The story is included in Lida, *Letras hispánicas*, 301–30.

24. Fuentes "Chac Mool," *Cuentos sobrenaturales*, 9–24; Cortázar, "La noche boca arriba," in *Final del juego*, 171–79; Boullosa, *Llanto*; Paz, *Critique of the Pyramid*; Gustavo Sáinz, *Fantasmas aztecas*.

25. He used it in a lecture given at Barnard College on 17 October 2011.

26. Saldaña, *The Revolutionary Imagination*, 43.

27. See Schirmer, *The Guatemalan Military Project*.

28. Grandin, "The Instruction of a Great Catastrophe," par. 6.

29. Ubilluz, Vich, and Hibbett, *Contra el sueño de los justos*, 29–31.

30. Kokotovic, *The Colonial Divide in Peruvian Narrative*, 2.

31. Turits, *Foundations of Despotism*, 165.

32. The buried book underscores the contrast between the fate of the literary record and oral transmission.

33. Koonings and Kruijt, introduction to *Societies of Fear*, 7.

34. There is a difference between the mass hysteria of the massacre and the torture scene discussed in chaps. 2 and 7. See especially the discussion of the "war pack" in Canetti, *Crowds and Power*, 99–103.

35. Colombia, Grupo de Memoria Histórica de la Comisión Nacional de Reparación y Reconciliación, *Trujillo*, 14–20.

36. See Colombia, Grupo de Memoria Histórica de la Comisión Nacional de Reparación y Reconciliación, *El Salado*.

37. Colombia, Grupo de Memoria Histórica de la Comisión Nacional de Reparación y Reconciliación, *Trujillo*, 74–75.

38. Feitlowitz, *A Lexicon of Terror*, 8–11.

39. For an extended account of the training of Latin Americans in counterterrorism, see Gill, *The School of the Americas*.

40. Danner, *The Massacre at El Mozote*, 49.

41. Danner, *The Massacre at El Mozote*, 50.

42. Sofsky, *Violence*, 25.

43. Levi, *The Drowned and the Saved*, 105–6.

44. Levi, *The Drowned and the Saved*, 126.

45. Report of the Chilean National Commission on Truth and Reconciliation Chile, 140.

46. Lauria-Santiago, "The Culture and Politics of State Terror and Repression in El Salvador," in *When States Kill*, 100.

47. Hylton, *Evil Hour in Colombia*, 44–45.

48. Eldredge, *The Way of the Wild Heart*.

49. On the judicial arguments for rape as a form of torture, see Meyer, "Negotiating International Norms: The Inter-American Commission of Women and the Convention on Violence against Women," in *Gender Politics in Global Governance*, 58–71.

50. Theidon, *Entre prójimos*, 127–30.

51. See DuBois, *Torture and Truth*.

52. Scarry, *The Body in Pain*, 53–57.

53. *New York Times*, 12 May 2011.

54. Menjívar and Rodríguez, *When States Kill*, 18.

55. Rodríguez, *Liberalism at Its Limits*, 191–92.

56. Rodríguez, *Liberalism at Its Limits*, 170.

57. Segato, "La escritura en el cuerpo de las mujeres asesinadas en Cd. Juárez," 97.

58. See Verbitsky, *El vuelo*, and Guzmán, *Romo: Confesiones de un torturador*.

59. Uceda, *Muerte en el pentagonito*, 419–21.

60. Rozitchner, prologue to *That Inferno*, xx.

61. Actis et al., *That Inferno*.

62. Rodríguez, *Women, Guerrillas and Love*; Saldaña-Portillo, *The Revolutionary Imagination in the Americas and the Age of Development*.

63. Theweleit, *Male Fantasies*, 216.

64. See Calveiro, *Poder y desaparición*.

65. Segato, "La escritura en el cuerpo de las mujeres asesinadas en Cd. Juárez," 89–94.

66. González Rodríguez, *El hombre sin cabeza*, 59–60.

67. *El Diario*, 3 January 2011.

Notes to Chapter One

1. Mbembe, "Necropolitics," 21–22.

2. The *code noir* protected the Catholic religion, expelled the Jews, and prevented Protestants from "causing trouble."

3. P. de Vaissière, *La société et la vie créoles sous l'Ancien Régime*, was one of the sources for C. L. R. James, *The Black Jacobins: Toussaint l'Ouverture and the San Domingo Revolution*.

4. See Fischer, *Modernity Disavowed: Haiti and the Cultures of Slavery in the Age of Revolution*, esp. chap. 9.

5. See 1805 Constitution of Haiti promulgated by Emperor Jacques Dessalines, available on the web: www.webster.edu/~corbetre/haiti/history/earlyhaiti/1805-const.htm.

6. Fischer, *Modernity Disavowed*, 228–29.

7. See Alvarez, *In the Time of the Butterflies*; Vargas Llosa, *The Feast of the Goat*; Díaz, *The Brief Wondrous Life of Oscar Wao*.

8. Díaz, *The Brief Wondrous Life of Oscar Wao*, 225.

9. Turits, *Foundations of Despotism*, 162.

10. Turits, *Foundations of Despotism*, 165.

11. Cuello, *Documentos del Conflicto Dominico-Haitiano de 1937*, 315.

12. Cuello, *Documentos*, 45.

13. Quoted by Turits, *Foundations of Despotism*, 167.

14. Cuello, *Documentos*, 392.

15. "El sentido de una política," a speech given by Manuel Arturo Peña Batlle, quoted in Cuello, *Documentos*, 501.

16. Cuello, *Documentos*, 501.

17. Letter dated 18 December 1937, quoted in Cuello, *Documentos*, 292.

18. Cuello, *Documentos*, 293.

19. Cuello, *Documentos*, 304–12.

20. Cuello, *Documentos*, 308–9.

21. Cuello, *Documentos*, 503–6, esp. 505.

22. Turits, *Foundations of Despotism*, 171.

23. Turits, *Foundations of Despotism*, 172.

24. As alleged by Peña Batlle in his speech, quoted in Cuello, *Documentos*, 501.

25. Cuello, *Documentos*, 98.

26. Benjamin, "Theses on the Philosophy of History," in *Illuminations*, 255–66.

27. Freud, "Mourning and Melancholia," in *On Murder, Mourning and Melancholia*, 201–18. Idelber Avelar's *The Untimely Present* links postdictatorship mourning to allegory in literary writing and draws on Maria Torok and Nicolas Abraham, *The Shell and the Kernel: Renewals of Psychoanalysis*.

28. Eng and Kazanjian, "Introduction: Mourning Remains," in *Loss*, 3.

29. Philoctète, *Massacre River*.

30. Avelar, *The Untimely Present*, 2–3.

31. The title of Kiran Desai's novel *The Inheritance of Loss* reminds us that this is the inescapable experience of the formerly colonized.

Notes to Chapter Two

1. Foucault, *"Society Must Be Defended,"* 338.

2. Guatemala, Comisión para el Esclarecimiento Histórico (Commission on Historical Clarification (hereafter CEH), *Guatemala: Memoria del silencio*. See also the Recovery of Historical Memory Project: The Official Report of the Human Rights Office of the Archdiocese of Guatemala, *Guatemala: Nunca más*.

3. Díaz Polanco, *Indigenous Peoples in Latin America*, 56.

4. Ginés de Sepúlveda, "Tratado sobre las justas causas de la guerra contra los indios." On the colonial divide, see Kokotovic, *The Colonial Divide in Peruvian Narrative*.

5. Arguedas, "El horno viejo," in *Amor mundo y todos los cuentos*, 169–80.

6. In Bolivia, which now has a president of Aymara descent, there are pockets of extreme forms of discrimination and persecution of the indigenous, notably in Santa Cruz.

7. Echeverría, *Modernidad y blanquitud*, 60–69.

8. Grandin, *The Last Colonial Massacre*, 13.

9. Peru, Comisión de Verdad y Reconciliación (henceforward CVR), *Informe final*. Available online at www.derechos.org/nizkor/peru/libros/cv. The commission was set up during the interim presidency of Valentín Paniagua and was accepted by President Alejandro Toledo in 2001. It included anthropologists, engineers from the region of Ayacucho, lawyers, a Catholic priest, and a Protestant. Toledo added a retired general and two more Catholic dignitaries. The commission held public hearings at which victims spoke in Spanish, Quechua, or one of the Amazonian languages. There is a Quechua version of the report, *Hatun willakuy*. See also Montoya Rojas, "Power, Culture and Violence in the Andes," as well as Christine Hunefeldt and Misha Kokotovic, *Power, Culture and Violence in the Andes*. On page 19, they noted that the *Informe* did not include data on the disappeared.

10. CVR, "Prefacio," *Informe final*, available online at www.derechos.org/nizkor /peru/libros/cv/i/pre.html.

11. CEH, *Guatemala: Memoria del silencio*, 1:24–26.

12. Grandin, "The Instruction of Great Catastrophe: Truth Commissions, National History, and State Formation in Argentina, Chile and Guatemala," 46–67. That it was a genocide was argued by the Commission on Historical Clarification and also proved when Spain set up an investigative body. This was shown in the documentary film *Granito*, filmed by Pamela Yates, Paco de Onís, and Peter Kinoy.

13. Oficina de Derechos Humanos del Arzobispado de Guatemala, *Guatemala: Nunca más*. See also Jonas, *De centauros y palomas*. Two days after its presentation on 26 April, its principal organizer, Monseñor Juan Gerardi, was brutally assassinated. The search for the culprits is the subject of Francisco Goldman, *The Art of Political Murder*.

14. CEH, *Memoria del silencio*, 1:61–63.

15. CEH, *Memoria del silencio*, 1:93.

16. CEH, *Memoria del silencio*, 1:94.

17. Schirmer, *The Guatemalan Military Project*, 237–39.
18. For the impact of the guerrilla on the village of Acul, see Sanford, *Buried Secrets*.
19. CEH, *Guatemala: Memoria del silencio*, 1:184–5.
20. CEH, *Guatemala: Memoria del silencio*, 1:199.
21. CEH, *Guatemala: Memoria del silencio*, 1:200.
22. Schirmer, *The Guatemalan Military Project*, 45.
23. Schirmer, *The Guatemalan Military Project*, 81.
24. On "Indian Soldiers and Civil Patrols of Self Defense," see Schirmer, *The Guatemalan Military Project*, 81–83.
25. Schirmer, *The Guatemalan Military Project*, 114.
26. This language was also used in Argentina. See Taylor, "Military Males, 'Bad' Women, and a Dirty, Dirty War," in *Disappearing Acts*, 59–90.
27. The film *Granito* (2011), directed by Pamela Yates, has an interview with Rios Montt in which he stated that although he was the commander in chief, he didn't know what the army was doing on the ground. He has now been brought to trial for war crimes but continues defending himself on the grounds that he was not informed about atrocities.
28. Dussel, *1492: El encubrimiento del otro*, 209–10.
29. Jáuregui, *Canibalia*, 13–14.
30. CEH, *Guatemala: Memoria del silencio*, 2:38.
31. CEH, *Guatemala: Memoria del silencio*, 2:38.
32. Montejo, *Testimony*, 85.
33. Montejo, *Testimony*, 86.
34. Jáuregui, *Canibalia*, 15.
35. CEH, *Guatemala: Memoria del silencio*, 2:32, 4:183–89.
36. CEH, *Guatemala: Memoria del silencio*, 3:18.
37. CEH, *Guatemala: Memoria del silencio*, 7:163–68.
38. CEH, *Guatemala: Memoria del silencio*, 7:63–71.
39. CEH, *Guatemala: Memoria del silencio*, 7:147–52.
40. Yates revisits the scene in her film *Granito*.
41. Falla, *Massacres in the Jungle*.
42. Set up by an interim president, Valentín Paniagua, the Truth and Reconciliation Commission was not universally welcomed, particularly by the army.
43. CVR, preface to the *Informe final*.
44. Manrique, *El tiempo del miedo*, 25.
45. CVR, *Informe final*, section 7, 102.

46. Butler, *Precarious Life*, 33.

47. CVR, "Pueblos ajenos del Perú: Rostros y perfiles de la violencia," *Informe final*, section 3.1.

48. Vargas Llosa, "Sangre y Mugre en Uchuraccay," in *Contra viento y marea*, 3:1, 87, includes the commission's report, his own account of the incident, and correspondence with critics. The English version of his personal account was published in the *New York Times Magazine* on 31 July 1983 with the title "Inquest in the Andes."

49. Peru, *Yuyanapaq: Para recordar: Relato visual del conflicto armado interno en el Peru, 1980–2000*, 40–41.

50. Quoted in Pino, "Uchuraccay: Memoria y representación de la violencia política en los Andes," in Ponciano del Pino and Elizabeth Jelin, *Luchas locales*, 32.

51. Vargas Llosa, "Inquest in the Andes," 33.

52. Vargas Llosa, "Historia de una matanza," in *Contra viento y marea*, 3:178.

53. The official report is included in *Contra viento y marea*, 3:87–128.

54. Vargas Llosa, "Historia de una matanza," in *Contra viento y marea*, 3:186–87.

55. Vargas Llosa, "Inquest in the Andes," 50; "Historia de una matanza," in *Contra viento y marea*, 3:188.

56. Mayer, "Peru in Deep Trouble: Mario Vargas Llosa's 'Inquest in the Andes' Reexamined," 187. See also Kokotovic, *The Colonial Divide*, 169–73.

57. Vargas Llosa, "Inquest in the Andes," 50–51; "Historia de una matanza," in *Contra Viento y Marea*, 3:189–90.

58. Vargas Llosa, "Inquest in the Andes," 50–51 (my italics); "Historia de una matanza," in *Contra viento y marea*, 3:189–9.

59. Ubilluz, "El fantasma de la nación cercada," in *Contra el sueño de los justos*, 79–85.

60. Cornejo Polar, *Escribir en el aire*, 26. An English translation is due to be published by Duke University Press.

61. Theidon, "How We Learned to Kill Our Brother?," 544.

62. Theidon, "How We Learned to Kill Our Brother?," 544.

63. Ubilluz, "El fantasma de la nación cercada," in *Contra el sueño de los justos*, 30.

64. In an unpublished paper, "Murder or Suicide," I argue that Quechua upset the boom writers Cortázar and Vargas Llosa because they considered it outside the literary exchange of the European languages and therefore doomed to be provincial.

65. Theidon, "How We Learned to Kill Our Brother?," 548.

66. See Theidon and Peralta Quinteros, "Uchuraccay: La Política de la Muerte en el Perú."

67. Méndez Gastelumendi, "The Power of Naming, or the Construction of Ethnic and National Identities in Peru: Myth, History and the Iquichanos," in Past and Present, 127–59.

68. Theidon, "How We Learned to Kill Our Brother?," 553–54.

69. Theidon and Quinteros Peralta, "Uchuraccay: La política de la muerte en el Perú," 27–31.

70. Vich, El caníbal es el otro, 56–75.

71. See Weismantel, Cholas and pishtacos. See also Manrique, Tiempo del miedo, 287–303.

72. Ubilluz, "El fantasma de la nación cercada," in Contra el sueño de los justos, 36.

73. Fuentes, "Chac Mool," in Cuentos sobrenaturales, 9–24; Cortázar, "La noche boca arriba," in Final del juego, 181–96.

74. Quoted by Starn, "Maoism in the Andes," 44.

75. Vargas Llosa, La utopía arcaica, 9.

76. Popper, The Open Society and Its Enemies, 1:200–201.

77. For a sympathetic assessment of Vargas Llosa's attachment to the ideas of Popper, Isaiah Berlin, and Georges Bataille, see Kristal, Temptation of the Word.

78. Vargas Llosa, "Questions of Conquest: What Columbus Wrought, and What He Did Not," 45–53. For a discussion of this essay, see Kokotovic, The Colonial Divide in Peruvian Narrative, 174–78.

79. Kokotovic, The Colonial Divide in Peruvian Narrative, 176.

80. Díaz Polanco, Elogio de la diversidad, 157.

81. Vargas Llosa, foreword to Hernando de Soto, The Other Path.

82. Vich, El caníbal es el otro, 80–81.

83. Rodríguez, Liberalism at Its Limits, 20–35.

84. Ubilluz, Contra el sueño de los justos, 79.

Notes to Chapter Three

1. A full account of the capture and torture of the prisoner known as the "Gringa," as given by the torturer "El Brujo," is included in Silva Santisteban, El factor asco, 176–81. See also Peruvian Comisión de Verdad y Reconciliación (henceforward CVR), Informe final de la Comisión de Verdad y Reconciliación, 5:134.

2. On genocidal rape, see MacKinnon, "Rape, Genocide and Women's Human Rights," in Are Women Human?, 180–91.

3. Diken and Laustsen, "Becoming Abject: Rape as a Weapon of War," 111–28.

4. CVR, "Violencia y desigualdad de género," 8:46.

5. Guatemala, Oficina de Derechos Humanos del Arzobispado, *Guatemala: Nunca más.* "Los mecanismos de horror," 2:61.

6. Diken and Laustsen, "Becoming Abject," 113.

7. CVR, "Violencia y desigualdad de género," 8:2.1.

8. CVR, "Violencia sexual contra la mujer," 6:1.5, 276.

9. The reports from the Truth Commission on violence against women appeared in a separate volume with the title, *Abusaruwanku. Violación de mujeres: Silencio e impunidad.* The reference is to page 64.

10. The arguments for considering rape as a Crime Against Humanity are laid out in the Preliminary report submitted by the Special Rapporteur on Violence against Women: Its Causes and Consequences, Peruvian Commission on Human Rights, 50th sess., November 1994.

11. *Guatemala: Memoria del silencio,* 3:27.

12. *Guatemala: Memoria del silencio,* 3:26.

13. *Guatemala: Memoria del silencio,* 3:26.

14. *Guatemala: Memoria del silencio,* 3:249–50.

15. *Guatemala: Memoria del silencio,* 3:249–50.

16. An English translation of the commission's reasons for concluding that these amounted to a policy of genocide, titled "Acts of Genocide," is included in Grandin, Levinson, and Oglesby, *The Guatemalan Reader,* 387–94.

17. *Guatemala: Memoria del silencio,* 3:27.

18. *Guatemala: Memoria del silencio,* 3:28.

19. This particular incident was documented by the Office of Human Rights of the Archbishop of Guatemala, *Guatemala: Nunca más,* I, 1:211.

20. In *The Beast and the Sovereign* (1;90) Derrida places both the beast and the sovereign outside the law. What concerns him is how sovereign states constitute others as rogue or outside humanity.

21. *Guatemala: Memoria del silencio,* 3:29.

22. MacKinnon, *Are Women Human?,* 187.

23. *Guatemala: Memoria del silencio,* 3:34.

24. *Guatemala: Memoria del silencio,* 3:35.

25. *Guatemala: Memoria del silencio,* 3:67.

26. *Guatemala: Memoria del silencio,* 3:56.

27. *Guatemala: Memoria del silencio,* 3:31.

28. *Guatemala: Memoria del silencio,* 3:29.

29. *Guatemala: Memoria del silencio,* 3:37.

30. *Guatemala: Memoria del silencio,* 3:51.

31. González Izás, "Arbitrary Power and Sexual Violence," in *The Guatemala Reader*, 408.

32. Grandin, "The Instruction of Great Catastrophe: Truth Commissions, National History and State Formation in Argentina, Chile and Guatemala," 14.

33. Poole and Rénique, *Peru: Time of Fear* is a useful survey of the civil war. Apart from the Sendero Luminoso, another guerrilla group, the Movimiento Revolucionario Tupac Amaru (MRTA), was also active in the province of Huallanga. The Peruvian Truth Commission reported on rapes by Sendero and MRTA members that I discuss in chapter 6. See also Gorriti, *The Shining Path: A History of the Millenarian War in Peru*.

34. Peru, *Abusaruwanku*, 135–36. For a commentary on this incident that I discuss later in the chapter, see Vich, "Disparos y torturas: El discurso de la subalternidad," in *El caníbal es el otro*, 36–56.

35. Peru, *Abusaruwanku*, 128.

36. Peru, *Abusaruwanku*, 98.

37. Rodríguez, *Liberalism at Its Limits*, 191.

38. Peru, *Abusaruwanku*, 99.

39. Theidon, *Entre prójimos*, 121.

40. Peru, *Abusaruwanku*, 100.

41. CVR, 6:348.

42. Silva Santisteban, *El factor asco*, 53–67.

43. Peru, *Yuyanapaq: Para recordar*, 27.

44. Peru, *Abusaruwanku*, 101.

45. Peru, *Abusaruwanku*, 97.

46. Peru, *Abusaruwanku*, 120–21; Theidon, *Entre prójimos*, 122.

47. Peru, *Abusaruwanku*, 96.

48. Peru, *Abusaruwanku*, 147–53.

49. Theidon, *Entre prójimos*, 109.

50. CVR, 6:338–39.

51. *Guatemala: Memoria del silencio*, 3:21 .

52. Peru, *Abusaruwanku*, 101.

53. Theidon, *Entre prójimos*,109.

54. Theidon, *Entre prójimos*,127–28

55. Theidon, *Entre prójimos*, 123–27.

56. Theidon, *Entre prójimos*, 64–76.

57. Theidon, *Entre prójimos*, 50.

58. "Sinchi" is the name for the special forces.

59. Silva Santisteban, *El factor asco*, 77–87.

60. *La teta asustada* won a prize at the Berlin Film Festival. The "frightened breast" was suggested by Theidon's description in her book *Entre prójimos* of the indigenous women's embodiment of sentiments of fear.

61. MacKinnon, "Defining Rape Internationally: A Comment on *Akayesu*," in *Are Women Human?*, 237–46.

Notes to Chapter Four

1. Littell, *The Kindly Ones*, 589.
2. CEH, *Guatemala: Memoria del silencio*, 3:288.
3. Butler, *Precarious Life*, 28–29.
4. Agamben, *Homo Sacer*, 107.
5. See Milgram, *Obedience to Authority*.
6. García Rivas, *Memoria de un ex-torturador*, 67.
7. CEH, *Guatemala: Memoria del silencio*, 3:401–2.
8. CEH, *Guatemala: Memoria del silencio*, 4:183–91.
9. Žižek, *The Plague of Fantasies*, 7.
10. Schirmer, *The Guatemalan Military Project*, 115. On p. 116 she includes a sketch from an army document that shows how the reconstituted Indian might look when "modernized."
11. Taussig, *Shamanism, Colonialism and the Wild Man*, 171–72.
12. Taussig, *Shamanism, Colonialism and the Wild Man*, 134.
13. CEH, *Guatemala: Memoria del silencio*, 2:57.
14. CEH, *Guatemala: Memoria del silencio*, 2:57.
15. CEH, *Guatemala: Memoria del silencio*, 2:57.
16. CEH, *Guatemala: Memoria del silencio*, 2:61–62. The pits have now been excavated and some of the perpetrators have been brought to justice.
17. For the relation between the kaibiles and Los Zetas, see chapter 9.
18. CEH, *Guatemala: Memoria del silencio*, 2:57.
19. Silva Santisteban, *El factor asco*, 95–99.
20. See Gill, *The School of the Americas*.
21. Quoted by Menjívar and Rodríguez, introduction to *When States Kill*, 17.
22. Scarry, *The Body in Pain*, 29.
23. Scarry, *The Body in Pain*, 36.
24. Menjívar and Rodríguez, *When States Kill*, 3–4.
25. Rejali, *Torture and Democracy*, 4.
26. Timerman, *Prisoner without a Name*, 39.
27. Timerman, *Prisoner without a Name*, 39.
28. Schirmer, *The Guatemalan Military Project*, 285–89.

29. DuBois, *Torture and Truth*, 157.

30. Silva Santisteban, "Testimonio de 'El Brujo,'" in *El factor asco*, 176–81.

31. Rozitchner, "Introduction" to *That Inferno*, xx.

32. Quoted by Feitlowitz, *A Lexicon of Terror*, 193.

33. Astiz and other members of the so-called Grupo de Tareas of ESMA were finally tried and sentenced to life imprisonment in October 2011. In 2005 Scilingo was condemned to 660 years in jail; this sentence was later commuted to imprisonment until 2022.

34. Verbitsky, *El vuelo*, translated as *The Flight: Confessions of an Argentine Dirty Warrior.*

35. See Uceda, *Muerte en el pentagonito.*

36. Uceda, *Muerte en el pentagonito*, 86.

37. Silva Santisteban, *El factor asco*, 101.

38. Uceda, *Muerte en el pentagonito*, 86.

39. Uceda, *Muerte en el pentagonito*, 100–101.

40. Uceda, *Muerte en el pentagonito*, 93.

41. Uceda, *Muerte en el pentagonito*, 94.

42. In 2007 Fujimori was convicted and given a sentence of twenty-five years in prison.

43. Uceda, *Muerte en el pentagonito*, 334–35.

44. See García Rivas, *Memorias de un ex-torturador.*

45. *Tropa de Elite* (2007) was directed by José Padilha and adapted from the book by Luiz Eduardo Soares, André Batista, and Rodrigo Pimentel. It was published in English as *Elite Squad.*

46. Milgram, *Obedience to Authority*, 5.

47. Foucault is also a name that comes up in the book on which the film was based. In the film, the discussion of Foucault's theories in the university seems intended to underscore the gap between trendy theory and the reality of the favela.

48. *Cidade de Deus*, a film directed by Fernando Meirelles and released in 2002, was based on the book of the same name by Paulo Lins published in 1997. The book was translated as *City of God* by Alison Entrekin. It is the name for a district for rehabilitated favela dwellers on the outskirts of Rio, and the book was based on real incidents.

49. Arturo García Hernández and Emir Olivares Alonso, "Posible, anular a criminales 'sin hacer un solo disparo,'" *La Jornada*, 3 May 2012.

50. See Castellanos Moya, *El arma en el hombre.*

51. Lemebel, "Las orquídeas negras de Mariana Callejas" in *Perlas y cicatrices*, 14–16.

52. Lemebel, "Las orquídeas negras de Mariana Callejas," in *Perlas y cicatrices*, 15–16. The translation only approximates to Lemebel's baroque original.

53. The artist Catalina Parra made "El Imbunche" the theme of one of her installations during the dictatorship. See Rychen, "Stitching Together Reality."

54. Eugenio Ruiz-Tagle is the one whose tortured body was described by his mother before the Truth Commission.

55. Bataille, "De Sade's Sovereign Man," in *Eroticism*, 164–73.

56. Williams, "Sovereignty and Melancholic Paralysis in Roberto Bolaño," 125.

Notes to Chapter Five

1. Gorriti, *The Shining Path*, 29.

2. Gorriti discusses Marx's attitude toward sacrifice in *The French Civil War* and in Mao's thinking. See Gorriti, *The Shining Path*, 100.

3. Ernesto "Che" Guevara, *Episodes of the Cuban Revolutionary War*. Che's ideal of the guerrilla fighter is discussed by Saldaña-Portillo in *The Revolutionary Imagination in the Americas and the Age of Development*, 78–90, and Rodríguez, *Women, Guerrillas and Love: Understanding War in Central America*, 45. Rodríguez is discussing the book by Omar Cabezas, *Fire from the Mountains: The Making of a Sandinista*.

4. *Foco*, a focus point or spark, referred to the group of guerrilla fighters who would spark a more general uprising. The antecedent was Castro's camps in the Sierra Maestra in eastern Cuba. The strategy was described in Debray, *Guerrille du Che*, and Guevara, *Episodes of the Cuban Revolutionary War*.

5. The Sandinistas in Nicaragua are now again in power as are former members of the Salvadorian insurgency, although neither can be said to be implementing socialist policies.

6. The best known is Ingrid Betancourt, *Even Silence Has an End*. American captives in the same jungle prison — Marc Gonsalves, Keith Stansell, Tom Howes, and Gary Brozek — also published a memoir, *Out of Captivity: Surviving 1,967 Days of Captivity in the Colombian Jungle*. Gabriel García Márquez also contributed to this literature with *News of a Kidnapping*.

7. See Rodríguez, *Women, Guerrillas and Love*; Saldaña Portillo, *The Revolutionary Imagination*, 81–83.

8. Rodríguez, *Women, Guerrillas and Love*, xv.

9. Peru, *Abusaruwanku*, 61–93.

10. Piglia, "Ernesto Guevara: Rastros de lectura," in *El último lector*, 132.

11. Quoted by Jon Lee Anderson from his interview with Ciro Bastos. See Anderson, *Che: A Revolutionary Life*, 543.

12. One of the best sources for this incident is the biography of Che by Jon Lee Anderson. He interviewed Ciro Roberto Bustos and Héctor Jouvé. Anderson also has a detailed account of the recruitment of the core group in Cuba, particularly of Ciro Roberto Bustos's recruitment and training. Jouvé was caught, imprisoned, and tortured.

13. Anderson, *Che: A Revolutionary Life*, 546.

14. These crimes are listed in Jorge Lanata's novel, *Muertos de amor*, 58–59.

15. See Jouvé, "La guerrilla del Che en Salta, 40 años después," in *No matar*, 1:11–29.

16. Rozitchner, "Primero hay que saber vivir: Del vivirás materno al no matarás patriarcal," in *No matar*, 1:367–406.

17. Del Barco, *No matar*, reprinted as *No matarás* (*Thou Shalt Not Kill*) in the *Journal of Latin American Cultural Studies*, 115–18.

18. Piglia, "Ernesto Guevara," 132.

19. Lanata, *Muertos de amor*, 66–67.

20. Rozitchner, "Primero hay que saber vivir: Del vivirás materno al no matarás patriarcal," in *No matar*, 367–406.

21. Anderson, *Che: A Revolutionary Life*, 577–78.

22. Anderson, *Che: A Revolutionary Life*, 588.

23. Rozitchner, "Primero hay que saber vivir: Del vivirás materno al no matarás patriarcal," in *No matar*, 367–406.

24. Rozitchner, "Primero hay que saber vivir," in *No matar*, 375.

25. Rozitchner, "Primero hay que saber vivir," in *No matar*, 367–406.

26. Dove, "Memory between Politics and Ethics: Del Barco's Letter," 288.

27. Dalton, *Pobrecito poeta que era yo*.

28. Pedro Geoffrey Rivas's poem was published in 1936. It is available in the online collection, at www.artepoetica.net/pedro_geoffroy.htm.

29. Dalton, *Pobrecito poeta que era yo*, 155.

30. Dalton, *Pobrecito poeta que era yo*, 185.

31. Ehrenreich, "Diary: Who Killed Roque Dalton?," 43–43.

32. Bolaño originally gave this information in an interview with the Spanish journal *Lateral*. It is cited in an online essay by Guillermo Parra, "Poor Poetry — Roque Dalton and Roberto Bolaño" in *Venepoetics*, 22 May 2007. Available at venepoetics.blogspot.com/2007/03/poor-poets-roque-dalton-and-roberto.html.

33. Bolaño, quoted in Parra, "Poor Poetry."

34. Quoted by Zaid, "Colegas enemigos: Una lectura de la tragedia salvadoreña," in *De los libros al poder*, 157–211.

35. Zaid, "Colegas enemigos," 177–82. One of the documents was issued by

FARN (Las Fuerzas Armadas de la Resistencia Nacional), a breakaway group that attributed the death sentence to the appropriation of power within the organization by a clique.

36. Zaid, "Colegas enemigos," 177.

37. Zaid, "Colegas enemigos," 177–82.

38. Zaid, "Colegas enemigos," 184.

39. Zaid, "Colegas enemigos," 187.

40. Ehrenreich, "Diary," 43.

41. Ehrenreich, "Diary," 43. He also describes Villalobos's turn to the right after the end of the civil war.

42. Ehrenreich, "Diary," 43.

43. Lauria-Santiago, "The Culture and Politics of State Terror and Repression in El Salvador," in *When States Kill*, 85–114, n. 1.

44. Roncagliolo, *La cuarta espada: La historia de Abimael Guzmán y Sendero Luminoso*. See also Degregori, *El surgimiento de Sendero Luminoso: Ayacucho 1969–70*; Gorriti, *The Shining Path: A History of the Millenarian War in Peru*; and Manrique, *El tiempo del miedo: La violencia política en el Perú 1980–1996*.

45. The photograph is attributed to Cordon Press.

46. Peru, *Yuyanapaq: Para recordar*, 90.

47. Many scholars have commented on the extraordinary influx of students into higher educational institutions in the 1970s and 1980s, many of them from poor families. On women in the Sendero, see Kirk, *Grabado en piedras: Las mujeres del Sendero Luminoso*.

48. On the "hunt for heresies and penance" see Gorriti's description of the Military School in *The Shining Path*, 21–36.

49. Peru, Comisión de la Verdad (henceforth CVR), "Los orígenes de el Partido Comunista del Perú," in *Informe de la Comisión de la Verdad*, vol. 1.

50. Roncagliolo, *La cuarta espada*, 70.

51. Roncagliolo, *La cuarta espada*, 70. See also CVR, "Los actores armados," in *Informe final*, vol. 1.

52. Peru, *Yuyanapaq*, 3.

53. Starn, "Maoism in the Andes," 414.

54. *The Tempest*, ed. Burton Raffel (New Haven, CT: Yale University Press, 2006), act 2, scene 1, lines 132–38.

55. Starn, "Maoism in the Andes," 410.

56. Starn, "Maoism in the Andes," 410.

57. For the difference between Mariátegui and Guzmán's thinking, see Orin Starn, "Maoism in the Andes," 414.

58. Roncagliolo, *La cuarta espada*, 75. The contrast with Che as described by Ricardo Piglia in *El último lector* is striking.

59. The speech in English translation is included in Guzmán, "We Are the Initiators," in *The Peru Reader*, 310–15.

60. Guzmán, "We Are the Initiators," 314.

61. Guzmán, "We Are the Initiators," 313.

62. Guzmán, "We Are the Initiators," 313.

63. Starn, "Maoism in the Andes," 408.

64. Degregori, *Que difícil es ser Dios*,14.

65. Degregori, *El surgimiento de Sendero Luminoso*, 293.

66. Starn, "Maoism in the Andes," 409.

67. Quoted by Roncagliolo, *La cuarta espada*, 72.

68. Starn, "Maoism in the Andes," 410.

69. Degregori, *Que difícil es ser Dios*, 25.

70. Roncagliolo, *La cuarta espada*, 130–33.

71. Strong, *Shining Path*, 95.

72. Gorriti, *The Shining Path*, 84.

73. The poem is quoted by Kirk, *Grabado en piedra*, 12.

74. Uceda, *Muerte en el pentagonito*, 120.

75. Gorriti, "The Quota," in *The Peru Reader*, 322.

76. Hassan, "What Motivates Suicide Bombers?," *Daily Times*, 5 September 2009. Available online at www.dailytimes.com.pk/default.asp?page=2009 /09/05/story_5-9-2009_pg3_6.

77. Mbembe, "Necropolitics," 39. He also quotes Paul Gilroy's argument in *Black Atlantic* on the preference for death over servitude.

78. Gorriti, *The Shining Path*, 106.

79. Gorriti, *The Shining Path*, 105.

80. CVR, *Informe final*, 7:1, 67.

81. Vich, "Tiempos de guerra: Aproximaciones a la poética senderista," in *El caníbal es el otro*, 26–27. Vich also questions whether the author of the poems he discusses, Rosa Marinache, really existed or whether the writer is Guzmán himself. "Marinache" is quite similar to *marimacho*, a disrespectful term for lesbian.

82. Vich, "Tiempos de guerra," in *El caníbal es otro*, 27.

83. CVR, *Informe final*, 1:1.2.

84. Gorriti, "The Quota," in *The Peru Reader*, 323.

85. CVR, *Informe final*, 5:2.5, 74–76.

86. CVR, *Informe final*, 5:2.5, 76.

87. Gorriti, *The Shining Path*, 176–77.
88. CVR, *Informe final*, 6:1.
89. CVR, "Los pueblos indígenas: El caso de los Asháninka," *Informe final*, 5:2.8, 254.
90. CVR, *Informe final*, 5:267–69.
91. Guzmán, "Desarrollar la guerra popular sirviendo a la revolución mundial," in *Guerra popular en el Perú*, 220–32.
92. See Nicario, "Memories of a Cadre," in *The Peru Reader*, 332.
93. CVR, *Informe final*, 6:292.
94. Roncagliolo, *La cuarta espada*, 241.
95. See Kirk, *Grabado en piedra*.
96. Roncagliolo, *La cuarta espada*, 175. The film *Dancer Upstairs*, directed by John Malkovich and based on the book by Nicholas Shakespeare, doesn't manage to translate the episode successfully into cinema.
97. Roncagliolo, *La cuarta espada*, 164. On the mystery surrounding the death of his first wife, see Kirk, *Grabado en piedra*, 50–51.
98. Roncagliolo, *La cuarta espada*, 206.
99. Gorriti, *The Shining Path*, 369.
100. Gorriti, *The Shining Path*, 372.
101. For an account of the attacks on the prisons, see Strong, *Shining Path*, 151–56.
102. Roncagliolo, *La cuarta espada*, 241.

Notes to Chapter Six

1. Levi, *The Drowned and the Saved*, 84.
2. Eltit, prologue to Cherrie Zalaquett, *Sobrevivir a un fusilamiento*, 12.
3. Van Alphen, "Symptoms of Discursivity: Experience, Memory, and Trauma," in *Acts of Memory*, 26.
4. See Dalton, *Miguel Mármol*.
5. See Amaya, "Sólo me embrocaba a llorar," in *Luciérnagas en El Mozote*.
6. Levi, *The Drowned and the Saved*, 14.
7. See Amaya, "Sólo me embrocaba a llorar," in *Luciérnagas en El Mozote*.
8. Dalton's novel *Pobrecito poeta que era yo* narrates the trajectory of a group of friends, one of whom decides to become a militant; through this character Dalton tells the story of his own imprisonment and escape.
9. For a discussion of Lewis's claims and method, see Franco, *Plotting Women*, 159–74.
10. Beverley, "The Margin at the Center: On Testimonio," in *The Real Thing*, 23.

11. For a sensitive discussion of the relationship of Mármol with Dalton, see Barbara Harlow, "Testimonio and Survival," in *The Real Thing*, 70–83.

12. Lindo-Fuentes, Ching, and Lara-Martínez, *Remembering a Massacre in El Salvador*, 4.

13. Lindo-Fuentes, Ching, and Lara-Martínez, *Remembering a Massacre in El Salvador*, 145–48.

14. Bukharin and Preobrazhensky, *The ABC of Communism*.

15. The "Socorro Rojo" was intended to aid imprisoned Communists. It had branches in many countries. It also seemed to act as a front organization for the CP. For its intervention in many of the Salvadorian struggles, see Gould and Lauría-Santiago, *To Rise in Darkness*, 88–101.

16. Gould and Lauría-Santiago, *To Rise in Darkness*, 137.

17. Lindo Fuentes et al., *Remembering a Massacre in El Salvador*, 45.

18. Gould and Lauría-Santiago, *To Rise in Darkness*, 50.

19. On the discussions, see Lindo Fuentes et al., *Remembering a Massacre in El Salvador*, 192–93. See also Gould and Lauria-Santiago, *1932: Rebelión en la oscuridad*, 217–226, and *To Rise in Darkness*, 164–66.

20. Huyssen, *Twilight Memories*, 3.

21. Harlow, "Testimonio and Survival: Roque Dalton's *Miguel Mármol*," discusses the relationship between the intellectual and the worker. She does not, however, explore the major omission of the indigenous from the account.

22. Harlow points this out in her essay "Testimonio and Survival" in *The Real Thing*, 70–83.

23. Ciguanaba is a mythic shape-changing being who takes the form of a girl to lure men to their deaths.

24. Gould and Lauria-Santiago, *To Rise in Darkness*, chap. 7.

25. Gould and Lauria-Santiago, *To Rise in Darkness*, 221–22.

26. Although at first ladinos and the indigenous were killed, Gould and Lauria-Santiago argue that it developed into a massacre of the indigenous sometimes spurred on by local elites. See Gould and Lauria-Santiago, *To Rise in Darkness*, 223. See also the Spanish account by Gould and Lauria-Santiago, *1932: Rebelión en la oscuridad*.

27. *Cicatriz de la memoria: 1932*, dir. Consalvi and Gould.

28. Dalton, "El Salvador en el banquillo de los acusados por la masacre de El Mozote," in *El País* (Spain), International ed., 24 April 2012.

29. Danner, *Massacre in El Mozote*, 8–9.

30. El Salvador, Tutela Legal del Arzobispado, *El Mozote: Lucha por la verdad y la justicia*, 72–84.

31. Amaya et al., *Luciérnagas en El Mozote*, 17.

32. El Salvador, Comisión de la Verdad, "Caso Ilustrativo: El Mozote," in *Informe: De la locura a la esperanza*, C.1, 171–81.

33. Bonner, *Weakness and Deceit*, 113.

34. Bonner, *Weakness and Deceit*, 342–43.

35. El Salvador, Comisión de la Verdad, *Informe: De la locura a la esperanza*, 180.

36. Danner, *Massacre at El Mozote*, 50.

37. Bonner, *Weakness and Deceit*, 339.

38. Bonner, *Weakness and Deceit*, 339.

39. She is not mentioned by name in the Truth Commission Report, *De la locura a la esperanza*. For her testimony in Spanish, see Amaya et al., *Luciérnagas in El Mozote*, 60–79.

40. Danner, *The Massacre at El Mozote*, 74–75.

41. Danner, *The Massacre at El Mozote*, 77.

42. This legend is ingrained in Mexican and Central American folklore. In one version, she drowns her own children before being condemned to lament them in perpetuity.

43. El Salvador, Comisión de la Verdad, *Informe: De la locura a la esperanza*, 197.

44. El Salvador, Comisión de la Verdad, *Informe: De la locura a la esperanza*, 272.

45. Eltit, prologue to Zalaquett, *Sobrevivir a un fusilamiento*.

46. These insults imply homosexuality: *culiados* from *culo* (backside) and *huevón* (heavy balls), i.e., lazy.

Notes to Chapter Seven

1. Lazzara, *Luz Arce: Después del infierno*. This includes a summary of her declaration before the National Truth and Reconciliation Commission in October 1990 and further information on her detention.

2. The interview was first published in Spanish as *Luz Arce: Después del infierno*.

3. Eltit has published three essays on Arce: "Perder sentido" ("To lose sense"), "Vivir, dónde" ("To Live. Where?"), and "Cuerpos nómadas" ("Nomad Bodies"), which are included in *Emergencias: Escritos sobre literatura, arte y política*. See also Richard, *Crítica de la memoria*, 106–15.

4. Summary of her evidence is included in Lazzara, *Luz Arce: Después del infierno*, 32–132.

5. Merino Vega (La Flaca Alejandra), *Mi verdad: "Más allá del horror, Yo acuso."*

6. Lazzara, "Names, Dates, Places," in *Luz Arce and Pinochet's Chile*, includes

a summary of her Declaration before the Truth and Reconciliation Commission on 9 October 1999.

7. Scarry, *The Body in Pain*, 49.

8. Menninghaus, *Disgust*, 1.

9. Vidal, *Chile: Poética de la tortura política*, 127–28.

10. Vidal, *Chile: Poética de la tortura política*, 128.

11. Vidal, *Chile: Poética de la tortura política*, 129–30.

12. Lazzara, *Luz Arce and Pinochet's Chile*, 30.

13. Guzmán, *Romo: Confesiones de un torturador*, 84.

14. Eltit, "Perder el sentido," in *Emergencias*, 49.

15. Lazzara, *Luz Arce and Pinochet's Chile*, 53.

16. Vidal, *Política cultural de la memoria histórica*, 59–60.

17. Vidal, *Política cultural de la memoria histórica*, 73.

18. Vidal, *Política cultural de la memoria histórica*, 75.

19. Lazzara, "Entrevista a Luz Arce (Mexico-Chile 2002–7)," in *Luz Arce: Despúes del infierno*, 133–260.

20. Lazzara, *Luz Arce: Después del infierno*, 159.

21. Lazzara, *Luz Arce and Pinochet's Chile*, 37–38.

22. Vidal, *Política cultural de la memoria histórica*, 110–11.

23. Richard, *Crítica de la memoria*, 105–15.

24. Eltit, "Cuerpos Nómadas," in *Emergencias*, 63–64.

25. Chile, *The Rettig Report: The National Commission for Truth and Reconciliation Report* (1991), and *The Valech Report: The National Commission on Political Imprisonment and Torture Report* (2005).

26. Eltit, "Perder el sentido," in *Emergencias*, 49.

27. Eltit, "Perder el sentido," in *Emergencias*, 51.

28. Lazzara, *Luz Arce and Pinochet's Chile*, 83.

29. Rozitchner, *That Inferno*, xx–xxiv.

30. Rozitchner, *That Inferno*, xxii.

31. Torres Rivas, "Epilogue: Notes on Terror, Violence, Fear and Democracy," in Koonings and Kruijt, *Societies of Fear*, 286.

32. Richard, *Crítica de la memoria*, 5.

Notes to Chapter Eight

1. Torres Rivas, "Epilogue: Notes on Terror, Violence, Fear and Democracy," in Koonings and Kruit, *Societies of Fear*, 291.

2. Two generals, Arturo Acosta Chaparro and Humberto Quiros Hermosillo, who were arrested for drug trafficking were accused by Eureka of human

rights violations, including torture during interrogation. There were four hundred cases of disappeared in Mexico. See Martin Espinoza, "Mexico's Cold War Wounds: The Disappeared That Won't Go Away," in *La Prensa San Diego*, 13 October 2000.

3. In Argentina, after the public depositions and the publication of *Nunca Más*, the government declared a full stop (*punto final*) to the trials and cited the *obediencia debida* (duty of obedience), according to which subordinates were bound to carry out the demands of their superiors. In Chile, Pinochet had an amnesty law passed before resigning and making way for the coalition government (the Concertación) in 1990–2010. The amnesty law made it impossible to name military officers in the Rettig and Valech reports. In Brazil, amnesty laws have protected the military to the present, and the Supreme Court recently validated the 1979 amnesty law. In Uruguay, the amnesty law approved by a referendum was finally ruled unconstitutional.

4. Vidal, *Dar la vida por la vida*, 5–6.

5. Almeida Teles, "Entre o luto e a melancolia: A luta dos familiares de mortos e desaparecidos políticos no Brasil," in Macdowell et al., *Desarquivando a ditadura*, 1:151–76.

6. Fried Amilivia, "Collective Traumatic Memories of Political Forced Disappearance in the Aftermath of Uruguay's State Terror (1973–1985)," available online at www.irmgard-coninx-stiftung.de/fileadmin/user_upload/pdf /Memory_Politics/Workshop_3/Fried_Essay.pdf (accessed 5 December 2012).

7. See Kaplan, *Taking Back the Streets*; Taylor, *Disappearing Acts*; Mellibovsky, *Circle of Love over Death*; Simpson and Bennet, *The Disappeared*.

8. Kaplan, *Taking Back the Streets*, 5–6.

9. Nosiglia, *Botín de guerra*, documented the scandal of the adoption of children of the disappeared and the efforts of the Abuelas de Plaza de Mayo to restore them to their families.

10. See Gelman and La Madrid, *Ni el flaco perdón de Dios*.

11. Feitlowitz, *A Lexicon of Terror*, 16.

12. For a reflection on photographs of Jewish children victims of the Holocaust see Hirsch, "Projected Memory: Holocaust Photographs in Personal and Public Fantasy," 3–23.

13. See the cover of the Informe de Memoria Histórica de la Comisión Nacional de Reparación y Reconciliación, *Trujillo: Una tragedia que no cesa*.

14. Peru, Comisión de la Verdad y Reconciliación, *Yuyanapaq: Para recordar*.

15. Barthes, *Camera Lucida*, 32.

16. Richard, *Crítica de la memoria*, 50.

17. Richard, *Crítica de la memoria*, 51.

18. Sontag, *Regarding the Pain of Others*, 115.

19. Benjamin, "On Some Motifs in Baudelaire," in *Illuminations*, 204.

20. Huyssen, *Twilight Memories*, 7.

21. *Obstinate Memory* (1997), directed by Patricio Guzmán, was filmed in Santiago after the return to democracy.

22. Linfield, *Cruel Radiance*, 19.

23. Linfield, *Cruel Radiance*, 46.

24. Feitowitz, *Lexicon of Terror*, 24–25.

25. Feitlowitz, *Lexicon of Terror*, 28.

26. Argentina, Comisión Nacional sobre la Desaparición de Personas, *Nunca más*, 7. In English, *Nunca más: Report of the Argentine Commission on the Disappeared*.

27. Longoni, *Traiciones*, 25.

28. Vidal, *Dar la vida por la vida*, 9.

29. Hand, *The Levinas Reader*, 83.

30. Richard, *Crítica de la memoria*, 67.

31. Vidal, *Dar la vida por la vida*, 113–14.

32. Vidal, *Dar la vida por la vida*, 115.

33. Brodsky, *Nexo*, 58.

34. Brodsky, *Nexo*, 75.

35. Brodsky, *Buena memoria / Good Memory*. In this book Brodsky incorporates a family history.

36. Brodsky, "El bosque de la memoria" ("The Memory Forest"), in *Nexo*, 67–69.

37. A plan of the building is included in Brodsky, *Memory under Construction*, 49.

38. Brodsky, *Memory under Construction*, 32–33.

39. Huyssen, "The Mnemonic Art of Marcelo Brodsky," in Brodsky, *Nexo*, 7–10.

40. See *The Disappeared*, directed by Peter Sanders.

41. The exhibition *Imbunches* was shown in the Galería Época, Santiago de Chile. See Parra, Catalina, *Catalina Parra: El fantasma político del arte*.

42. Linfield, *Cruel Radiance*, 24.

43. Lerner Febres, introduction to *Yuyanapaq: Para recordar*, 17–19.

44. Sontag, *Regarding the Pain of Others*, 84.

45. Quoted by Lucy Lippard, "Susan Meiselas: An Artist Called Meiselas," in *In History*, 210.

46. Meiselas, *In History*, 179.

47. Taylor, "Past Performing Future: Susan Meiselas's Reframing History," in *In History*, 232–34.

Notes to Chapter Nine

1. Ehrenreich, "A Lucrative War: Review of *The Last Narco*," *London Review of Books*, 21 October 2010, 42–43.

2. As documented in the 2007 Annual Report of the Office of the Special Rapporteur for Freedom of Expression of the Inter-American Commission on Human Rights (IACHR).

3. Lauría et al., "Silence or Death in Mexico's Press," in *Special Report of the Committee to Protect Journalists*, September 2010, available at http://cpj.org/reports/2010/09/silence-or-death-in-mexicos-press.php.

4. For the impact of the army, see González Rodríguez, *The Femicide Machine*, 40–42.

5. Longmire, "Legalization Won't Kill the Cartels," *New York Times*, 19 June 2011.

6. Bowden, *Murder City*, 60.

7. Bowden, *Murder City*, 105.

8. Pavón, "México: Cuando ya no alcanza con morir," *Clarín*, 21 March 2012.

9. Global Fund for Women, "Statement on the Murder of Marisela Escobedo Ortiz," available at www.globalfundforwomen.org/who-we-are/where-we-stand/1844-statement-on-the-murder-of-marisela-escobedo-ortiz (accessed 5 December 2012).

10. The terms "feminicide" and "femicide" are both used, and different definitions are given. Johanna Ikonen of the Human Rights Unit of the European Parliament defines "feminicide" as the killing of women and girls with brutality. In a discussion of the terms, Rosa Linda Fregoso and Cynthia Bejarano write that "femicide" has been defined as "the murder of women and girls because they are female," whereas they define "feminicide" as "the murders of women and girls founded on the gender power structure." It is both public and private, both systematic and a crime against humanity. See their introduction to *Terrorizing Women*, 9–11.

11. Kenneth Roth, "Letter to President Calderón," Human Rights Watch, 7 May 2008, available at www.hrw.org/news/2008/05/06/letter-president-felipe-calder-n.

12. González Rodríguez, *Huesos en el desierto*, 27. His more recent book, *The Femicide Machine*, published in English, links the killing of women to the globalized order.

13. *Traspatio* (2010), screenplay by Sabina Berman.

14. González Rodríguez, *Huesos en el desierto*, 27.

15. González Rodríguez, *Huesos en el desierto*, 37–38.

16. Agamben, *Homo Sacer*, 119–35; González Rodríguez, *The Femicide Machine*, 31.

17. González Rodríguez, *Huesos en el desierto*, 59.

18. González Rodríguez, *Huesos en el desierto*, 60.

19. Washington Valdez, *The Killing Fields*, 14.

20. Rodríguez, *Liberalism at Its Limits*, 191–94.

21. *Señorita Extraviada* (2001), directed by Portillo.

22. *Bajo Juárez* (2008), directed by Sánchez Orozco, screenplay by Alejandra Sánchez and José Antonio Cordero.

23. On their webpage, a "women of Juárez" organization, Nuestras Hijas de Regreso a Casa, lists films, documentaries, theater, books, poems, songs, and blogs. See mujeresdejuarez.org.

24. The webpage of the organization Nuestras Hijas de Regreso a Casa, www.mujeresdejuarez.org, is updated regularly; I read this on 2 June 2012.

25. The International Court of Justice is a UN institution that hears cases that national institutions do not cover.

26. González Rodríguez, *The Femicide Machine*, 40.

27. Segato, "Territory, Sovereignty, and Crimes of the Second State," 88.

28. Segato, "La escritura en el cuerpo de las mujeres asesinadas en Ciudad Juárez," 79.

29. Segato, "La escritura en el cuerpo de las mujeres asesinadas en Ciudad Juárez," 81.

30. Segato, "Territory, Sovereignty, and Crimes of the Second State," 84.

31. Rodríguez, *Liberalism at Its Limits*, 167.

32. Lagarde y de los Rios, "Preface: Feminist Keys for Understanding Feminicide," xix.

33. Lorite, "Un pandemia de violencia machista desgarra Latinoamérica," *El País*, 18 February 2011.

34. Cházaro, Casey, and Ruhl, "Getting Away with Murder: Guatemala's Failure to Protect Women and Rodi Alvarado's Quest for Safety," in Fregoso and Bejarano, *Terrorizing Women*, 93–115, esp. 100.

35. Quoted in Cházaro et al., "Getting Away with Murder," 101.

36. Fregoso and Bejarano, "Introduction: Cartography of Feminicide in the Américas," in Fregoso and Bejarano, *Terrorizing Women*, 7. They do not mention gay men who are persecuted because they transgress the code of masculinity.

37. See Eldredge, *Wild at Heart.*

38. González Rodríguez, *El hombre sin cabeza,* 54.

39. *El Sicario, Room 164* (2011), directed by Gianfranco Rosi.

40. González Rodríguez, *El hombre sin cabeza,* 90.

41. Prisoners were told to run as if escaping from the execution squad and then shot.

42. See Vanderwood, *Juan Soldado.*

43. Arana, "How the Street Gangs Took Central América," 98–110.

44. See Wald, *Narcocorrido.*

45. Bolaño, *The Last Interview.*

46. Valdes, "Alone among the Ghosts," *Nation,* 8 December 2008.

47. Bolaño, "Caracas Address," in *Between Parentheses,* 35.

48. Bolaño, "Los pasos de Parra," in *Los Perros Románticos: Poemas 1980–1998,* 83–85.

49. In a note at the end of the novel, Ignacio Echevarría, Bolaño's literary executor, affirms his belief that Bolaño completed it before he died. I remain unconvinced.

50. Bolaño, *Amuleto,* 77.

51. Bolaño, "Literatura + Enfermedad = Enfermedad," available at www.letras
.s5.com/bolano290903.htm (accessed 5 December 2012).

52. Judicial police are a federal institution with a branch formed to combat drug trafficking.

53. Dussel, "Beyond Eurocentrism: The World-System and the Limits of Modernity," in Jameson and Miyoshi, *The Cultures of Globalization,* 20.

Notes to Conclusion

1. González, "The Shadows of the Building: Construction and Anti-construction," translated by David William Foster in Brodsky, *Memory under Construction,* 246.

2. CVR, "Conclusions," in *Informe,* vol. 9, esp. 43–48.

3. Meister, *After Evil,* 1.

BIBLIOGRAPHY

Actis, Manú, Cristina Aldini, Liliana Gardella, and Miriam Lewin. *That Inferno: Conversations of Five Women Survivors of an Argentine Torture Camp.* Translated by Gretta Siebentritt. Nashville, TN: Vanderbilt University Press, 2006.

Agamben, Giorgio. *Homo Sacer: Sovereign Power and Bare Life.* Translated by Daniel Heller-Roazen. Stanford, CA: Stanford University Press, 1988.

Almeida Teles, Janaína de. "Entre o luto e a melancolia: A luta dos familiares de mortos e desaparecidos políticos no Brasil." In *Desarquivando a ditadura: Memória e justiça no Brasil,* edited by Cecília MacDowell Santos, Edson Teles, and Janaína de Almeida Teles, 151–76. Vol. 1. São Paulo: Hucitec, 2009.

Alphen, Ernst van. "Symptoms of Discursivity: Experience, Memory, Trauma." In *Acts of Memory: Cultural Recall in the Present,* edited by Mieke Bal, Jonathan Crewe, and Leo Spitzer, 24–38. Hanover, NH: University Press of New England, 1999.

Alvarez, Julia. *In the Time of the Butterflies.* London: Plume, 1995.

Amaya, Rufina. "Sólo me embrocaba a llorar." In *Luciérnagas en El Mozote,* edited by Rufina Amaya, Mark Danner, and Carlos Henríquez Consalvi, 15–20. 2nd ed. San Salvador: Museo de la Palabra, 1996.

Anderson, Jon Lee. *Che Guevara: A Revolutionary Life.* New York: Grove, 1997.

Arana, Ana. "How the Street Gangs Took Central America." *Foreign Affairs* 84, no. 3 (May–June 2005): 98–110.

Arce, Luz. *El infierno.* Santiago: Planeta, 1993. Translated by Stacey Alba Skar as *The Inferno: A Story of Terror and Survival in Chile.* Madison: University of Wisconsin Press, 2004.

Arendt, Hannah. *The Origins of Totalitarianism.* 1951. Repr., New York: Harcourt Brace Jovanovich, 1979.

Argentina, Comisión Nacional sobre la Desaparición de Personas (CONADEP). *Nunca más: Informe de la Comisión Nacional sobre la Desaparición de Personas.* Buenos Aires: Editorial Universitaria de Buenos Aires, 1984.

Translated as *Nunca Más: The Report of the Argentine National Commission on the Disappeared*. New York: Farrar, Straus and Giroux, 1986.

Arguedas, José María. *Amor mundo y todos los cuentos*. Lima: Francisco Moncloa, 1967.

Avelar, Idelber. *The Untimely Present: Postdictatorial Latin American Fiction and the Task of Mourning*. Durham, NC: Duke University Press, 1999.

Bajo Juárez: La ciudad devorando a sus hijas [*Bajo Juárez: The City Devouring Its Daughters*]. DVD. Directed by Alejandra Sánchez. Mexico City: FOPROCINE / IMCINE / Pepa Films / Universidad Nacional Autónoma de México, 2006.

Barco, Óscar del. "Carta enviada a *La intemperie*; No matar: Sobre la responsabilidad." In *No matar: Sobre la responsabilidad*, edited by Pablo René Belzagui, 31–35. Vol. 1. Córdoba, Argentina: El Cíclope / Editorial de la Universidad Nacional de Córdoba, 2007. Translated as "No Matarás: Thou Shall Not Kill." *Journal of Latin American Cultural Studies* 16, no. 2 (2007): 115–17.

Barthes, Roland. *Camera Lucida: Reflections on Photography*. Translated by Richard Howard. New York: Hill and Wang, 1981.

Bataille, Georges. *Erotism: Death and Sensuality*. Translated by Mary Dalwood. San Francisco: City Lights Books, 1986.

Bauman, Zygmunt. *Wasted Lives: Modernity and Its Outcasts*. Cambridge: Polity, 2004.

Benjamin, Walter. *Illuminations*. Translated by Harry Zohn. Edited by Hannah Arendt. London: Jonathan Cape, 1970.

Betancourt, Ingrid. *Even Silence Has an End: My Six Years of Captivity in the Colombian Jungle*. Translated by Alison Anderson, with collaboration of Sarah Llewellyn. New York: Penguin, 2010.

Beverley, John. "The Margin at the Center: On Testimonio." In *The Real Thing: Testimonial Discourse and Latin America*, edited by Georg M. Gugelberger, 23–41. Durham, NC: Duke University Press, 1996.

Bolaño, Roberto. *Amuleto*. Barcelona: Anagrama, 1999. Translated by Chris Andrews as *Amulet*. New York: New Directions, 2007.

———. *Between Parentheses: Essays, Articles, and Speeches, 1998–2003*. Edited by Ignacio Echevarría, and translated by Natasha Wimmer. New York: New Directions, 2011.

———. *By Night in Chile*. Translated by Chris Andrews. New York: New Directions, 2003.

———. *Los detectives salvajes*. Barcelona: Anagrama, 2007. Translated by

Natasha Wimmer as *The Savage Detectives*. New York: Farrar, Straus and Giroux, 2007.

———. *Distant Star*. Translated by Chris Andrews. New York: New Directions, 2004.

———. *The Last Interview and Other Conversations*. Translated by Sybil Perez, with an introduction by Marcela Valdes. New York: Melville House, 2009.

———. *Nazi Literature in the Americas*. Translated by Chris Andrews. New York: New Directions, 2008.

———. *Los perros románticos: Poemas 1980–1998*. Barcelona: Lumen, 2000.

Bonner, Raymond. *Weakness and Deceit: U.S. Policy and El Salvador*. New York: Times Books, 1984.

Boullosa, Carmen. *Llanto: Novelas imposibles*. Mexico City: Era, 1992.

Bowden, Charles. *Juárez: The Laboratory of Our Future*. New York: Aperture, 1998.

———. *Murder City: Ciudad Juárez and the Global Economy's New Killing Fields*. New York: Nation Books, 2010.

Brodsky, Marcelo. *Buena memoria: Un ensayo fotográfico*. Buenos Aires: La Marca, 1997.

———. *Memory under Construction / Memoria en construcción: El debate sobre la ESMA*. Buenos Aires: La Marca, 2005.

———. *Nexo: Un ensayo fotográfico*. Buenos Aires: Centro Cultural Recoleta, 2001.

Bukharin, Nikolaï Ivanovich, and Yevgeni Preobrazhensky. *The ABC of Communism: A Popular Explanation of the Program of the Communist Party of Russia*. 1922. Translated by Eden Paul and Cedar Paul. Ann Arbor: University of Michigan Press, 1966.

Butler, Judith. *Precarious Life: The Power of Mourning and Violence*. New York: Verso, 2004.

Cabezas, Omar. *Fire from the Mountains: The Making of a Sandinista*. Translated by Kathleen Weaver. New York: Crown, 1985.

Calveiro, Pilar. *Poder y desaparición: Los campos de concentración en Argentina*. Buenos Aires: Colihue, 1998.

Canetti, Elias. *Crowds and Power*. 1962. Translated by Carol Stewart. New York: Farrar, Straus and Giroux, 1984.

Carpentier, Alejo. *The Kingdom of This World*. 1957. Translated by Harriet de Onís. New York: Noonday, 1989.

———. *Reasons of State*. Translated by Frances Partridge. New York: Knopf, 1976.

Castellanos Moya, Horacio. *El arma en el hombre*. Mexico City: Tusquets, 2001.

Castillo, Carmen. *Un día de octubre en Santiago*. Mexico City: Era, 1982.

Cházaro, Angélica, Jennifer Casey, and Katherine Ruhl. "Getting Away with Murder: Guatemala's Failure to Protect Women and Rodi Alvarado's Quest for Safety." In *Terrorizing Women: Feminicide in the Americas*, edited by Rosa Linda Fregoso and Cynthia Bejarano, 93–115. Durham, NC: Duke University Press, 2010.

Chile, Comisión Nacional de Verdad y Reconciliación (CNVR). *Report of the Chilean National Commission on Truth and Reconciliation*. Also known as the Rettig Report. 1991. Translated by Phillip E. Berryman, with an introduction by José Zalaquett. 2 vols. Notre Dame, IN: University of Notre Dame Press, 1993.

Chile, Comisión Nacional Sobre Prisión Política y Tortura. *The National Commission on Political Imprisonment and Torture Report*. Also known as the Valech Report. June 2005. www.comisionvalech.gov.cl/InformeValech .html.

Chile: La memoria obstinada [*Chile: The Obstinate Memory*]. VHS. Directed by Patricio Guzmán. New York: First Run / Icarus Films, 1997.

Cicatriz de la memoria, 1932 [*1932: Scars of Memory*]. VHS. Directed by Carlos Henríquez Consalvi and Jeffrey L. Gould. New York: First Run / Icarus Films, 2002.

Cidade de Deus [*City of God*]. DVD. Directed by Fernando Meirelles. Burbank, CA: Buena Vista Home Entertainment, 2002.

Colombia, Grupo de Memoria Histórica de la Comisión Nacional de Reparación y Reconciliación. *La masacre de El Salado: Esa guerra no era nuestra*. Bogotá: Planeta, 2009.

———. *Trujillo: Una tragedia que no cesa*. Bogotá: Planeta, 2008.

Cornejo Polar, Antonio. *Escribir en el aire: Ensayo sobre la heterogeneidad socio-cultural en las literaturas andinas*. Lima: Horizonte, 1994.

Cortázar, Julio. *Final del juego*. Buenos Aires: Sudamericana, 1965.

Cuello H., José Israel, ed. *Documentos del conflicto domínico-haitiano de 1937*. Santo Domingo, DR: Taller, 1985.

Dalton, Juan José. "El Salvador, en el banquillo de los acusados por la masacre de El Mozote." *El País* (Spain), International ed., 24 April 2012.

Dalton, Roque. *Las historias prohibidas de pulgarcito*. Mexico City: Siglo Veintiuno, 1974.

———. *Miguel Mármol*. Translated by Kathleen Ross and Richard Schaaf. Willimantic, CT: Curbstone, 1987.

——. *Pobrecito poeta que era yo*. San José, Costa Rica: Editorial Universidad Centroamericana, 1976.

The Dancer Upstairs. DVD. Directed by John Malkovich. Los Angeles: 20th Century Fox Home Entertainment, 2001.

Danner, Mark. *The Massacre at El Mozote: A Parable of the Cold War*. New York: Vintage, 1994.

Danticat, Edwidge. *The Farming of Bones*. New York: Penguin, 1999.

——. Preface to *Massacre River*, by René Philoctète, translated by Linda Coverdale, 7–9. New York: New Directions, 2005.

Debray, Régis. *La guérilla du Che*. Paris: Seuil, 1974.

Degregori, Carlos Iván. *Qué difícil es ser Dios: Ideología y violencia política en Sendero Luminoso*. Lima: Zorro de Abajo, 1989.

——. *El surgimiento de Sendero Luminoso: Ayacucho, 1969–1979*. Lima: Instituto de Estudios Peruanos, 1990.

De las Casas, Bartolomé. *A Short Account of the Destruction of the Indies*. 1542. Translated by Nigel Griffin. New York: Penguin, 1999.

Derby, Lauren. *The Dictator's Seduction: Politics and the Popular Imagination in the Era of Trujillo*. Durham, NC: Duke University Press, 2009.

Derrida, Jacques. *The Beast and the Sovereign*. Translated by Geoffrey Bennington. Edited by Michel Lisse, Marie-Louise Mallet, and Ginette Michaud. Vol. 1. Chicago: University of Chicago Press, 2009.

——. *Without Alibi*. Translated and edited by Peggy Kamuf. Stanford, CA: Stanford University Press, 2002.

Desai, Kiran. *The Inheritance of Loss*. New York: Atlantic Monthly Press, 2006.

Díaz, Junot. *The Brief Wondrous Life of Oscar Wao*. New York: Riverhead Books, 2007.

Díaz Polanco, Héctor. *Elogio de la diversidad: Globalización, multiculturalismo y etnofagia*. Caracas: Monte Ávila, 2009.

——. *Indigenous Peoples in Latin America: The Quest for Self-Determination*. Boulder, CO: Westview, 1997.

Diken, Bülent, and Carsten Bagge Laustsen. "Becoming Abject: Rape as a Weapon of War." *Body and Society* 11, no. 1 (March 2005): 111–28.

The Disappeared. DVD. Directed by Peter Sanders. New York: Eight Twelve Productions, 2007.

Dove, Patrick. "Memory between Politics and Ethics: Del Barco's Letter." *Journal of Latin American Cultural Studies* 17, no. 3 (2008): 279–97.

——. "The Night of the Senses: Literary (Dis)Orders in *Nocturno de Chile*." *Journal of Latin American Cultural Studies* 18, nos. 2–3 (2009): 141–54.

DuBois, Page. *Torture and Truth*. New York: Routledge, 1991.

Dussel, Enrique. *1492: El encubrimiento del otro: Hacia el origen del "mito de la modernidad."* Bogotá: Antropos, 1992. Translated by Michael D. Barber as *The Invention of the Americas: Eclipse of "the Other" and the Myth of Modernity*. New York: Continuum, 1995.

Echeverría, Bolívar. *Modernidad y blanquitud*. Mexico City: Era, 2010.

Ehrenreich, Ben. "Diary: Who Killed Roque Dalton?" *London Review of Books* 32, no. 12 (24 June 2010): 42–43.

———. "A Lucrative War." Review of *The Last Narco: Inside the Hunt for El Chapo, the World's Most Wanted Drug Lord* by Malcom Beith. *London Review of Books* 32, no. 20 (21 October 2010): 15–18.

Eldredge, John. *The Way of the Wild Heart*. Nashville, TN: Nelson Books, 2006.

———. *Wild at Heart: Discovering the Secret of a Man's Soul*. Nashville, TN: Nelson Books, 2001.

Eltit, Diamela. *Emergencias: Escritos sobre literatura, arte y política*. Edited and with a prologue by Leonidas Morales. Santiago: Planeta / Ariel, 2000.

———. Prologue to *Sobrevivir a un fusilamiento: Ocho historias reales*, by Cherie Zalaquett, 11–24. Santiago: El Mercurio / Aguilar, 2005.

Eng, David L., and David Kazanjian. "Mourning Remains." Introduction to *Loss: The Politics of Mourning*, edited by David L. Eng and David Kazanjian, with an afterword by Judith Butler, 1–25. Berkeley: University of California Press, 2003.

Escobar, Arturo. *Encountering Development: The Making and Unmaking of the Third World*. Princeton, NJ: Princeton University Press, 1995.

Espinoza, Martin. "Mexico's Cold War Wounds: The Disappeared That Won't Go Away." *La Prensa San Diego*, 13 October 2000.

Falla, Ricardo. *Massacres in the Jungle: Ixcán, Guatemala, 1975–1982*. Translated by Julia Howland. Boulder, CO: Westview, 1994.

Feitlowitz, Marguerite. *A Lexicon of Terror: Argentina and the Legacies of Torture*. New York: Oxford University Press, 1998.

Fischer, Sibylle. *Modernity Disavowed: Haiti and the Cultures of Slavery in the Age of Revolution*. Durham, NC: Duke University Press, 2004.

Flores Galindo, Alberto. *Buscando un Inca: Identidad y utopía en los Andes*. 4th ed. Lima: Horizontes, 1994.

Foucault, Michel. *"Society Must Be Defended": Lectures at the Collège de France, 1975–1976*. Translated by David Macey. New York: Picador, 2003.

France. *Le code noir, ou, Recueil des règlements rendus jusqu'à présent*. 1685. Fort-de-France: Société d'Histoire de la Martinique, 1980.

Franco, Jean. *Plotting Women: Gender and Representation in Mexico*. New York: Columbia University Press, 1989.

Fregoso, Rosa Linda. "The Complexities of 'Feminicide' on the Border." In *Color of Violence: The Incite! Anthology*, edited by Incite! Women of Color against Violence, 130–34. Cambridge, MA: South End, 2006.

Fregoso, Rosa Linda, and Cynthia Bejarano. "A Cartography of Feminicide in the Americas." Introduction to *Terrorizing Women: Feminicide in the Américas*, edited by Rosa Linda Fregoso and Cynthia Bejarano, 1–42. Durham, NC: Duke University Press, 2010.

Freud, Sigmund. *Civilization and Its Discontents*. Translated and edited by James Strachey. New York: W. W. Norton, 1961.

———. *On Murder, Mourning and Melancholia*. Translated by Shaun Whiteside, with an introduction by Maud Ellmann. London: Penguin, 2005.

Fried Amilivia, Gabriela. "Collective Traumatic Memories of Political Forced Disappearance in the Aftermath of Uruguay's State Terror (1973–1985)." Presentation at the Eleventh Irmgard Coninx Stiftung Berlin Roundtable on Memory Politics: Education, Memorial, and Mass Media. Berlin, Germany, 21–26 October 2009. www.irmgard-coninxstiftung.de /fileadmin/user_upload/pdf/Memory_Politics/Workshop_3/Fried _Essay.pdf.

Fuentes, Carlos. *Cuentos sobrenaturales*. Mexico City: Alfaguara, 2007.

García Hernández, Arturo, and Emir Olivares Alonso. "Posible, anular a criminales 'sin hacer un solo disparo.'" *La Jornada* (Mexico), 3 May 2012, 14.

García Márquez, Gabriel. *News of a Kidnapping*. Translated by Edith Grossman. New York: Knopf, 1997.

García Rivas, Hugo. *Memorias de un Ex-Torturador*. Buenos Aires: El Cid, 1984.

Gelman, Juan, and Mara la Madrid. *Ni el flaco perdón de Dios: Hijos de desaparecidos*. Buenos Aires: Planeta, 1997.

Gill, Lesley. *The School of the Americas: Military Training and Political Violence in the Americas*. Durham, NC: Duke University Press, 2004.

Global Fund for Women. "Statement on the Murder of Marisela Escobedo Ortiz." www.globalfundforwomen.org/who-we-are/where-we-stand /1844-statement-on-the-murder-of-marisela-escobedo-ortiz (accessed 5 December 2012).

Goldman, Francisco. *Art of Political Murder: Who Killed the Bishop?* New York: Grove, 2007.

Goldstein, Joshua. *War and Gender: How Gender Shapes the War System and Vice Versa*. Cambridge: Cambridge University Press, 2001.

Gonsalves, Marc, Tom Howes, Keith Stansell, and Gary Brozek. *Out of Captivity: Surviving 1,967 Days in the Colombian Jungle*. New York: William Morrow, 2009.

González Izás, Matilde. "Arbitrary Power and Sexual Violence." In *The Guatemala Reader: History, Culture, Politics*, edited by Greg Grandin, Deborah T. Levenson, and Elizabeth Oglesby, 405–10. Durham, NC: Duke University Press, 2011.

González Rodríguez, Sergio. *The Femicide Machine*. Translated by Michael Parker-Stainback. Boston: MIT Press, 2012.

——. *El hombre sin cabeza*. Barcelona: Anagrama, 2009.

——. *Huesos en el desierto*. Barcelona: Anagrama, 2002.

Gorriti Ellenbogen, Gustavo. *Sendero: Historia de la guerra milenaria en el Perú*. Lima: Apoyo, 1990. Translated by Robin Kirk Chapel as *The Shining Path: A History of the Millenarian War in Peru*. Chapel Hill: University of North Carolina Press, 1999.

——. "The Quota." In *The Peru Reader*, edited by Orin Starn, Carlos Iván Degregori, and Robin Kirk, 316–27. Durham, NC: Duke University Press, 1995.

Gould, Jeffrey L., and Aldo A. Lauria-Santiago. *1932: Rebelión en la oscuridad: Revolución, represión y memoria en El Salvador*. San Salvador: Museo de la Palabra y la Imagen, 2008.

——. *To Rise in Darkness: Revolution, Repression, and Memory in El Salvador, 1920–1932*. Durham, NC: Duke University Press, 2008.

Grandin, Greg. *The Blood of Guatemala: A History of Race and Nation*. Durham, NC: Duke University Press, 2000.

——. "The Instruction of Great Catastrophe: Truth Commissions, National History, and State Formation in Argentina, Chile, and Guatemala." *American Historical Review* 110, no. 1 (February 2005): 46–67.

——. *The Last Colonial Massacre: Latin America in the Cold War*. Chicago: University of Chicago Press, 2004.

Granito: How to Nail a Dictator. DVD. Directed by Pamela Yates. New York: Skylight Pictures, 2011.

Guatemala, Oficina de Derechos Humanos del Arzobispado de Guatemala. *Guatemala, Nunca más: Informe del Proyecto Interdiocesano de Recuperación de la Memoria Histórica* (REMHI). 4 vols. Guatemala: ODHAG, 1998. Translated by G. Tovar Siebentritt as *Guatemala: Never Again! The Official Report of the Recovery of Historical Memory Project*. London: Catholic Institute for International Relations and Latin America Bureau, 1999.

Guatemala, Comisión para el Esclarecimiento Histórico (CEH). *Guatemala: Memoria del Silencio; Informe de la Comisión para el Esclarecimiento Histórico.* 12 vols. Guatemala City: Comisión para el Esclarecimiento Histórico, 1999.

———. "Acts of Genocide." In *The Guatemala Reader: History, Culture, Politics,* edited by Greg Grandin, Deborah T. Levenson, and Elizabeth Oglesby, 386–94. Durham, NC: Duke University Press, 2011.

Guevara, Ernesto "Che." *Episodes of the Cuban Revolutionary War, 1956–58.* Translated by Victoria Ortíz. New York: Pathfinder, 1996.

Guzmán, Abimael. "Desarrollar la guerra popular sirviendo a la revolución mundial." In *Guerra popular en el Perú: El pensamiento gonzalo,* edited by Luis Arce Borja, 220–32. Brussels: L. A. Borja, 1989.

———. "We Are the Initiators." In *The Peru Reader,* edited by Orin Starn et al., 310–15. Durham, NC: Duke University Press, 1995.

Guzmán, Nancy. *Romo: Confesiones de un torturador.* Santiago, Chile: Planeta, 2000.

Haiti. *The 1805 Constitution of Haiti: Second Constitution of Haiti.* 20 May 1805. www.webster.edu/~corbetre/haiti/history/earlyhaiti/1805-const. htm (accessed 5 December 2012).

Hand, Seán, ed. *The Levinas Reader.* Oxford: Blackwell, 1989.

Harlow, Barbara. "Testimonio and Survival: Roque Dalton's *Miguel Mármol.*" In *The Real Thing: Testimonial Discourse and Latin America,* edited by Georg M. Gugelberger, 70–83. Durham, NC: Duke University Press, 1996.

Hassan, Riaz. "What Motivates Suicide Bombers?" *Daily Times* (Pakistan), 5 September 2009. www.dailytimes.com.pk/default.asp?page=2009/09/05 /story_5-9-2009_pg3_6.

Hirsch, Marianne. "Projected Memory: Holocaust Photographs in Personal and Public Fantasy." In *Acts of Memory: Cultural Recall in the Present,* edited by Mieke Bal, Jonathan Crewe, and Leo Spitzer, 3–23. Hanover, NH: University Press of New England, 1999.

Hunefeldt, Christine, and Milos Kokotovic, eds. *Power, Culture, and Violence in the Andes.* Brighton, UK: Sussex Academic Press, 2009.

Huyssen, Andreas. "The Mnemonic Art of Marcelo Brodsky." In *Nexo,* by Marcelo Brodsky, 7–10. Buenos Aires: Cultural Recoleta, 2001.

———. *Twilight Memories: Marking Time in a Culture of Amnesia.* New York: Routledge, 1995.

Hylton, Forrest. *Evil Hour in Colombia.* London: Verso, 2006.

Iffland, James. *Ensayos sobre la poesía revolucionaria de Centroamérica.* San José, CR: Editorial Universitaria Centroamericana, 1994.

James, C. L. R. *The Black Jacobins: Toussaint L'Ouverture and the San Domingo Revolution.* 2nd ed. New York: Vintage, 1963.

Jáuregui, Carlos. *Canibalia: Canibalismo, calibanismo, antropofagia cultural y consumo en América Latina.* Madrid: Iberoamericana, 2008.

Jonas, Susanne. *De centauros y palomas: El proceso de paz guatemalteco.* Guatemala: FLACSO, 2000.

Jouvé, Héctor. "La guerrilla del Che en Salta, 40 años después." In *No matar: Sobre la responsabilidad,* vol. 1, edited by Pablo René Belzagui, 11–30. Córdoba, Argentina: El Cíclope / Editorial de la Universidad Nacional de Córdoba, 2007.

Kaplan, Temma. *Taking Back the Streets: Women, Youth, and Direct Democracy.* Berkeley: University of California Press, 2003.

Kirk, Robin. *Grabado en piedra: Las mujeres de Sendero Luminoso.* Lima: Instituto de Estudios Peruanos, 1993.

Kokotovic, Misha. *The Colonial Divide in Peruvian Narrative: Social Conflict and Transculturation.* Brighton, UK: Sussex Academic Press, 2007.

Koonings, Kees, and Dirk Kruijt. "Violence and Fear in Latin America." Introduction to *Societies of Fear: The Legacy of Civil War, Violence and Terror in Latin America,* edited by Kees Koonings and Dirk Kruijt, 1–30. London: Zed Books, 1997.

Kristal, Efraín. *Temptation of the Word: The Novels of Mario Vargas Llosa.* Nashville, TN: Vanderbilt University Press, 1998.

Lagarde y de los Ríos, Marcela. "Feminist Keys for Understanding Feminicide: Theoretical, Political and Legal Construction." Preface to *Terrorizing Women: Feminicide in the Americas,* edited by Rosa Linda Fregoso and Cynthia Bejarano, xi–xxvi. Durham, NC: Duke University Press, 2010.

Lanata, Jorge. *Muertos de amor.* Buenos Aires: Alfaguara, 2007.

Lauría, Carlos, Mike O'Connor, Monica Campbell, and José Barbeito. "Silence or Death in Mexico's Press: Crime, Violence and Corruption Are Destroying the Country's Journalism." A Special Report of the Committee to Protect Journalists, September 2010. www.cpj.org/reports/cpj_mexico _english.pdf.

Lauria-Santiago, Aldo A. "The Culture and Politics of State Terror and Repression in El Salvador." In *When States Kill: Latin America, the U.S., and Technologies of Terror,* edited by Cecilia Menjívar and Néstor Rodríguez, 85–114. Austin: University of Texas Press, 2005.

Lazzara, Michael J. *Luz Arce: Después del infierno*. Chile: Cuarto Propio, 2008.

———, ed. *Luz Arce and Pinochet's Chile: Testimony in the Aftermath of State Violence*. Translated by Michael J. Lazzara with Carl Fischer. Foreword by Jean Franco. New York: Palgrave Macmillan, 2011.

Lemebel, Pedro. *De perlas y cicatrices: Crónicas radiales*. Santiago, Chile: Lom, 1998.

Levi, Primo. *The Drowned and the Saved*. Translated by Raymond Rosenthal. New York: Vintage, 1989.

Lida, Raimundo. *Letras hispánicas: Estudios, esquemas*. 1958. Mexico City: Fondo de Cultura Económica, 1981.

Lindo-Fuentes, Héctor, Erik Ching, and Rafael Lara-Martínez. *Remembering a Massacre in El Salvador: The Insurrection of 1932, Roque Dalton, and the Politics of Historical Memory*. Albuquerque: University of New Mexico Press, 2007.

Linfield, Susie. *Cruel Radiance: Photography and Political Violence*. Chicago: University of Chicago Press, 2010.

Lins, Paulo. *City of God*. Translated by Alison Entrekin. London: Bloomsbury, 2006.

Lipstadt, Deborah. *The Eichmann Trial*. New York: Nextbook / Schocken, 2011.

Littell, Jonathan. *The Kindly Ones: A Novel*. Translated by Charlotte Mandell. New York: Harper, 2009.

Longmire, Sylvia. "Legalization Won't Kill the Cartels." *New York Times*, 19 June 2001.

Longoni, Ana. *Traiciones: La figura del traidor en los relatos acerca de los sobrevivientes de la represión*. Buenos Aires: Norma, 2007.

Lorite, Ana. "Una pandemia de violencia machista desgarra Latinoamérica." *El País* (España), 18 February 2011.

MacKinnon, Catharine A. *Are Women Human? And Other International Dialogues*. Cambridge, MA: Harvard University Press, 2006.

Manrique, Nelson. *El tiempo del miedo: La violencia política en el Perú, 1980–1996*. Lima: Fondo Editorial del Congreso del Perú, 2002.

Mayer, Enrique. "Peru in Deep Trouble: Mario Vargas Llosa's 'Inquest in the Andes' Reexamined." *Cultural Anthropology* 6, no. 4 (November 1991): 466–504.

Mbembe, Achille. "Necropolitics." Translated by Libby Meintjes. *Public Culture* 15, no. 1 (winter 2003): 11–40.

Meiselas, Susan. *In History*. New York: Steidl / International Center of Photography, 2008.

Meister, Robert. *After Evil: A Politics of Human Rights*. New York: Columbia University Press, 2011.

Mellibovsky, Matilde. *Circle of Love over Death: Testimonies of the Mothers of the Plaza de Mayo*. Translated by Maria Proser and Matthew Proser. Willimantic, CT: Curbstone, 1997.

Méndez Gastelumendi, Cecilia. "The Power of Naming, or the Construction of Ethnic and National Identities in Peru: Myth, History and the Iquichanos." *Past and Present* 171 (May 2001): 127–60.

Menjívar, Cecilia, and Néstor Rodríguez. "State Terror in the U.S.–Latin American Interstate Regime." Introduction to *When States Kill: Latin America, the U.S., and Technologies of Terror*, edited by Cecilia Menjívar and Néstor Rodríguez, 3–27. Austin: University of Texas Press, 2005.

Menninghaus, Winfried. *Disgust: The Theory and History of a Strong Sensation*. Translated by Howard Eiland and Joel Golb. Albany: State University of New York Press, 2003.

Merino Vega, Marcia Alejandra. *Mi verdad: "Más allá del horror, yo acuso ..."* Santiago, Chile: ATGSA, 1993.

Meyer, Mary Kay. "Negotiating International Norms: The Inter-American Commission of Women and the Convention on Violence against Women." In *Gender Politics in Global Governance*, edited by Mary Kay Meyer and Elisabeth Prügl, 58–71. Lanham, MD: Rowman and Littlefield, 1999.

Milgram, Stanley. *Obedience to Authority: An Experimental View*. New York: Harper and Row, 1974.

Montejo, Victor. *Testimony: Death of a Guatemalan Village*. Translated by Victor Perera. Willimantic, CT: Curbstone, 1987.

Montoya Rojas, Rodrigo. *Elogio de la antropología*. Lima: Instituto Nacional de Cultura and Universidad Nacional Mayor de San Marcos, 2005.

———. "Power, Culture, and Violence in the Andes." In *Power, Culture, and Violence in the Andes*, edited by Christine Hunefeldt and Misha Kokotovic, 9–28. Brighton, UK: Sussex Academic Press, 2009.

Monsiváis, Carlos. *Apocalipstick*. Mexico City: Random House Mondadori, 2009.

Nicario. "Memories of a Cadre" in *The Peru Reader*, edited by Starn et al., 328–35. Durham, NC: Duke University Press, 1995.

Nosiglia, Julio. *Botín de guerra*. Buenos Aires: Cooperativa Tierra Fértil, 1985.

Notícias de una guerra particular [*News from a Personal War*]. DVD. Directed by Kátia Lund and João Moreira Salles. 1999; Burbank, CA: Miramax Home Entertainment, 2004.

Ong, Walter. *The Presence of the Word: Some Prolegomena for Cultural and Religious History.* New York: Simon and Schuster, 1967.

Parra, Catalina. *El fantasma político del arte: Catalina Parra.* Edited by Paulina Varas. Santiago, Chile: Metales Pesados, 2011.

Parra, Guillermo. "Poor Poets: Roque Dalton and Roberto Bolaño." *Venepoetics,* 22 March 2007. venepoetics.blogspot.com/2007/03/poor-poets-roque-dalton-and-roberto.html.

Paz, Octavio. *The Other Mexico: Critique of the Pyramid.* Translated by Lysander Kemp. New York: Grove, 1972.

Perú, Comisión de la Verdad y Reconciliación (CVR). *Abusaruwanku: Violación de mujeres, silencio e impunidad; La violencia contra las mujeres en el informe de la Comisión de la Verdad y Reconciliación.* Lima: Comisión de Derechos Humanos / Movimiento Manuela Ramos, 2003.

———. *Informe final de la Comisión de la Verdad y Reconciliación.* August 2003. www.cverdad.org.pe/ifinal/index.php.

———. *Yuyanapaq: Para recordar; Relato visual del conflicto armado interno en el Perú, 1980–2000.* Lima: Comisión de la Verdad y Reconciliación, 2003.

Philoctète, René. *Massacre River.* Translated by Linda Coverdale. Preface by Edwidge Danticat, with an introduction by Lyonell Trouillot. New York: New Directions, 2005.

Piglia, Ricardo. "Ernesto Guevara: The Last Reader." *Journal of Latin American Cultural Studies* 17, no. 3 (2008): 261–77.

———. *El último lector.* Barcelona: Anagrama, 2005.

Pino, Ponciano del. "Uchuraccay: Memoria y representación de la violencia política en los Andes." In *Jamás tan cerca arremetió lo lejos: Memoria y violencia política en el Perú,* edited by Carlos Iván Degregori and Elizabeth Jelin, 49–93. Lima: Instituto de Estudios Peruanos, 2003.

Poole, Deborah, and Gerardo Rénique. *Peru: Time of Fear.* London: Latin American Bureau, 1992.

Popol Vuh: The Definitive Edition of the Mayan Book of the Dawn of Life and the Glories of Gods and Kings. 1558. Translated by Dennis Tedlock. New York: Simon and Schuster, 1985.

Popper, Karl Raimund. *The Open Society and Its Enemies.* 2 vols. 4th ed. London: Routledge, 1962.

Prestol Castillo, Freddy. *El masacre se pasa a pie.* 1973. Repr., Santo Domingo, DR: Taller, 1998.

Rejali, Darius. *Torture and Democracy*. Princeton, NJ: Princeton University Press, 2007.

Richard, Nelly. *Crítica de la memoria: 1990–2010*. Santiago, Chile: Universidad Diego Portales, 2010.

Rodríguez, Ileana. *Liberalism at Its Limits: Crime and Terror in the Latin American Cultural Text*. Pittsburgh: University of Pittsburgh Press, 2009.

———. *Women, Guerrillas and Love: Understanding War in Central America*. Translated by Ileana Rodríguez with Robert Carr. Minneapolis: University of Minnesota Press, 1996.

Roncagliolo, Santiago. *Abril rojo*. Madrid: Alfaguara, 2006. Translated by Edith Grossman as *Red April: A Novel*. New York: Pantheon, 2009.

———. *La cuarta espada: La historia de Abimael Guzmán y Sendero Luminoso*. Barcelona: Debate, 2007.

Roth, Kenneth. "Letter to President Felipe Calderón." *Human Rights Watch*, 6 May 2008. www.hrw.org/news/2008/05/06/letter-president-felipe -calder-n.

Rozitchner, León. "Artículo en el *Ojo Mocho*, no. 20 (Agosto 2006): Primero hay que saber vivir: Del vivirás materno al no matarás patriarcal." In *No matar: Sobre la responsabilidad*, edited by Pablo René Belzagui, 367–406. Vol. 1. Córdoba, Argentina: El Cíclope / Editorial de la Universidad Nacional de Córdoba, 2007.

———. Prologue to *That Inferno: Conversations of Five Women Survivors of an Argentine Torture Camp*, edited by Actis, Manú, Cristina Aldini, Liliana Gardella, and Miriam Lewin, xix–xiv. Nashville, TN: Vanderbilt University Press, 2006.

Rychen, Jailee. "Catalina Parra: Stitching Together Reality." *Catalogue MINI / Goethe-Institut Curatorial Residencies;* Solo exhibition of art by Catalina Parra. Ludlow 38, New York. 22 May–26 June 2011.

Sáinz, Gustavo. *Fantasmas aztecas: Un pre-texto*. Mexico City: Grijalbo, 1982.

Salazar, Alonso. *Born to Die in Medellín*. Translated by Nick Caistor, with an introduction by Colin Harding. London: Latin America Bureau, 1990.

Saldaña Portillo, María Josefina. *The Revolutionary Imagination in the Americas and the Age of Development*. Durham, NC: Duke University Press, 2003.

El Salvador, Comisión de la Verdad para El Salvador (CVES). *De la locura a la esperanza: La guerra de 12 años en El Salvador*. San José, Costa Rica: Editorial Departamento Ecuménico de Investigación, 1993. Translated as *From Madness to Hope: The 12-Year War in El Salvador;* Report on the Commis-

sion on the Truth for El Salvador. www.usip.org/files/file/ElSalvador
-Report.pdf.

El Salvador, Tutela Legal del Arzobispado de San Salvador. *El Mozote: Lucha
por la verdad y la justicia; Masacre a la inocencia*. San Salvador: Oficinas
del Arzobispado de San Salvador, 2008.

Sanford, Victoria. *Buried Secrets: Truth and Human Rights in Guatemala*.
New York: Palgrave Macmillan, 2003.

Sarmiento, Domingo Faustino. *Facundo, o, Civilización y barbarie*. Caracas:
Biblioteca Ayacucho, 1977. Translated by Kathleen Ross as *Facundo:
Civilization and Barbarism*, with an introduction by Roberto González
Echevarría. Berkeley: University of California Press, 2003.

Scarry, Elaine. *The Body in Pain: The Making and Unmaking of the World*.
New York: Oxford University Press, 1985.

Schirmer, Jennifer. *The Guatemalan Military Project: A Violence Called Democracy*. Philadelphia: University of Pennsylvania Press, 1998.

Segato, Rita Laura. "La escritura en el cuerpo de las mujeres asesinadas en
Ciudad Juárez: Territorio, soberanía y crímenes de Segundo Estado."
Debate Feminista 37 (April 2008): 78–102.

———."Territory, Sovereignty, and Crimes of the Second State: The Writing
on the Body of Murdered Women." In *Terrorizing Women: Feminicide in
the Americas*, edited by Rosa Linda Fregoso and Cynthia Bejarano, 70–92.
Durham, NC: Duke University Press, 2010.

Señorita extraviada [*Missing Young Woman*]. VHS. Directed by Lourdes
Portillo. New York: Women Make Movies, 2001.

Sepúlveda, Juan Ginés de. *Tratado sobre las justas causas de la guerra contra
los indios*. 1547. Mexico City: Fondo de Cultura Económica, 1941.

El sicario, Room 164. DVD. Directed by Gianfranco Rosi. New York: Icarus
Films, 2011.

Silva Santisteban, Rocío. *El factor asco: Basurización simbólica y discursos
autoritarios en el Perú contemporáneo*. Lima: Fondo Editorial Pontificia
Universidad Católica del Perú, 2008.

Simpson, John, and Jana Bennett. *The Disappeared: Voices from a Secret War*.
London: Robson Books, 1985.

Soares, Luiz Eduardo, André Batista, and Rodrigo Pimentel. *Elite da Tropa*.
Rio de Janeiro: Objetiva, 2006. Translated by Clifford E. Landers as *Elite
Squad*. New York: Weinstein Books, 2008.

Sofsky, Wolfgang. *Violence: Terrorism, Genocide, War*. Translated by Anthea
Bell. London: Granta, 2003.

Sontag, Susan. *Regarding the Pain of Others*. New York: Farrar, Straus and Giroux, 2003.

Soto, Hernando de. *The Other Path: The Invisible Revolution in the Third World*. Translated by June Abbott, with a foreword by Mario Vargas Llosa. New York: Harper and Row, 1990.

Souza, Percival de. *Narcoditadura: O caso Tim Lopes, crime organizado e jornalismo investigativo no Brasil*. São Paulo: Labortexto, 2002.

Starn, Orin. "Maoism in the Andes: The Communist Party of Peru; Shining Path and the Refusal of History." *Journal of Latin American Studies* 27, no. 2 (May 1995): 399–421.

Starn, Orin, Carlos Ivan Degregori, and Robin Kirk, eds. *The Peru Reader: History, Culture, Politics*. Durham, NC: Duke University Press, 1995.

Strong, Simon. *Shining Path: The World's Deadliest Revolutionary Force*. New York: HarperCollins, 1992.

Taussig, Michael. *Shamanism, Colonialism, and the Wild Man: A Study in Terror and Healing*. Chicago: University of Chicago Press, 1986.

Taylor, Diana. *Disappearing Acts: Spectacles of Gender and Nationalism in Argentina's "Dirty War."* Durham, NC: Duke University Press, 1997.

———. "Past Performing Future: Susan Meiselas' *Reframing History*." In *In History*, by Susan Meiselas, 232–36. New York: Steidl / International Center of Photography, 2008.

La teta asustada [*The Milk of Sorrow*]. DVD. Directed by Claudia Llosa. Saint Charles, IL: Olive Films, 2010.

Theidon, Kimberly. *Entre prójimos: El conflicto armado interno y la política de la reconciliación en el Perú*. Lima: Instituto de Estudios Peruanos, 2004.

———. "How We Learned to Kill Our Brother?: Memory, Morality and Reconciliation in Peru." *Bulletin de l'Institut Français d'Études Andines* 29, no. 3 (2000): 539–54.

Theidon, Kimberly, and Enver Quinteros Peralta. "Uchuraccay: La Política de la Muerte en el Perú." *Ideele: Revista del Instituto de Defensa Legal* 152 (February 2003): 27–31.

Theweleit, Klaus. *Male Fantasies*. Translated by Stephan Conway, with Erica Carter and Chris Turner. 2 vols. Minneapolis: University of Minnesota Press, 1987.

Timerman, Jacobo. *Prisoner without a Name, Cell without a Number*. Translated by Toby Talbot, with an introduction by Ilan Stavans. Madison: University of Wisconsin Press, 2002.

Torok, Maria, and Nicolas Abraham. *The Shell and the Kernel: Renewals of*

Psychoanalysis. Translated and edited by Nicholas T. Rand. Vol. 1. Chicago: University of Chicago Press, 1994.

Torres Rivas, Edelberto. "Notes on Terror, Violence, Fear, and Democracy." Epilogue to *Societies of Fear: The Legacy of Civil War, Violence and Terror in Latin America*, edited by Kees Koonings and Dirk Kruijt, 285–300. New York: Zed Books, 1999.

El traspatio [*Backyard*]. Directed by Carlos Carrera González. Screenplay by Sabina Berman. Los Angeles: Maya Entertainment, 2010.

Tropa de Elite [*Elite Squad*]. Directed by José Padilha. New York: IFC Films, 2008.

Turits, Richard Lee. *Foundations of Despotism: Peasants, the Trujillo Regime, and Modernity in Dominican History*. Stanford, CA: Stanford University Press, 2003.

Ubilluz, Juan Carlos. "El fantasma de la nación cercada." In *Contra el sueño de los justos: La literatura peruana ante la violencia política*, edited by Juan Carlos Ubilluz, Alexandra Hibbett, and Víctor Vich, 19–85. Lima: Instituto de Estudios Peruanos, 2009.

Ubilluz, Juan Carlos, Alexandra Hibbett, and Víctor Vich, eds. *Contra el sueño de los justos: La literatura peruana ante la violencia política*. Lima: Instituto de Estudios Peruanos, 2009.

Uceda, Ricardo. *Muerte en el pentagonito: Los cementerios secretos del ejército peruano*. Bogotá: Planeta, 2004.

United Nations Economic and Social Council, Commission on Human Rights. *Preliminary Report Submitted by the Special Rapporteur on Violence against Women: Its Causes and Consequences; Ms. Radhika Coomaraswamy, in Accordance to Commission on Human Rights Resolution 1994/45*. 22 Nov. 1994. UN doc. E/CN.4/1995/42.

Vaissière, Pierre de. *Saint-Domingue: La société et la vie créoles sous l'ancien régime (1629–1789)*. Paris: Perrin, 1909.

Valdes, Marcela. "Alone among the Ghosts: Roberto Bolano's '2666.'" *Nation*, 8 December 2008.

Vanderwood, Paul J. *Juan Soldado: Rapist, Murderer, Martyr, Saint*. Durham, NC: Duke University Press, 2004.

Varas, Paulina, ed. *Catalina Parra: El fantasma político del arte*. Santiago, Chile: Metales Pesados, 2011.

Vargas Llosa, Mario. *Contra viento y marea*. Vol. 3. Barcelona: Seix Barral, 1986.

——. "Inquest in the Andes." *New York Times Magazine*, 31 July 1983.

————. *La fiesta del chivo*. Madrid: Alfaguara, 2000. Translated by Edith Grossman as *The Feast of the Goat*. New York: Farrar, Straus and Giroux, 2001.

————. *Lituma en los Andes*. Barcelona: Planeta, 1993. Translated by Edith Grossman as *Death in the Andes*. New York: Farrar, Straus and Giroux, 1996.

————. "Questions of Conquest: What Columbus Wrought, and What He Did Not." *Harper's Magazine*, December 1990, 45–53.

————. *La utopía arcaica: José María Arguedas y las ficciones del indigenismo*. Mexico City: Fondo de Cultura Económica, 1996.

Vasconcelos, José. *Ulises criollo*. Mexico City: Promexa, 1979.

Verbitsky, Horacio. *El vuelo*. Buenos Aires: Planeta, 1995. Translated by Esther Allen as *The Flight: Confessions of an Argentine Dirty Warrior*. New York: New Press, 1996.

Vich, Víctor. *El caníbal es el otro: Violencia y cultura en el Perú contemporáneo*. Lima: Instituto de Estudios Peruanos, 2002.

Vidal, Hernán. *Chile: Poética de la tortura política*. Santiago: Mosquito Comunicaciones, 2000.

————. *Dar la vida por la vida: La agrupación chilena de familiares de detenidos desaparecidos; Ensayo de antropología simbólica*. Minneapolis: Institute for the Study of Ideologies and Literature, 1982.

————. *Política cultural de la memoria histórica: Derechos humanos y discursos culturales en Chile*. Santiago, Chile: Mosquito Comunicaciones, 1997.

Wald, Elijah. *Narcocorrido: A Journey into the Music of Drugs, Guns, and Guerrillas*. New York: HarperCollins, 2002.

Washington Valdez, Diana. *The Killing Fields: Harvest of Women; The Truth about Mexico's Bloody Border Legacy*. Burbank, CA: Peace at the Border, 2006.

Weismantel, Mary. *Cholas and Pishtacos: Stories of Race and Sex in the Andes*. Chicago: University of Chicago Press, 2001.

Williams, Gareth. "Sovereignty and Melancholic Paralysis in Roberto Bolaño." *Journal of Latin American Cultural Studies* 18, no. 2–3 (2009): 125–40.

Zaid, Gabriel. *De los libros al poder*. Mexico City: Grijalbo, 1988.

Žižek, Slavoj. *The Plague of Fantasies*. London: Verso, 1997.

Zurita, Raúl. *Anteparadise*. Translated by Jack Schmitt. Berkeley: University of California Press, 1986.

DATE DUE

JUN 1 1 2014	
	WIDENER
WIDENER	FEB 1 0 2015
SEP 1 0 2015	
AUG 0 7 2015	WIDENER
	FEB 1 0 2016
AUG 1 0 2015	

BRODART, CO.   Cat. No. 23-221